301.41   LSCA - 1992

D1414328

BACKSTREETS

Backstreets

Prostitution, Money, and Love

Cecilie Høigård and Liv Finstad

Translated by Katherine Hanson,
Nancy Sipe, and Barbara Wilson

The Pennsylvania State University Press
University Park, Pennsylvania

First published in Norway as *Bakgater*
Copyright © 1986 Pax Forlag

This English translation and revisions, copyright © 1992 Polity Press

First published in the United States of America in 1992 by The Pennsylvania State University Press, Suite C, 820 North University Drive, University Park, PA 16802

ISBN 0–271–00877–6 (cloth)
ISBN 0–271–00878–4 (paper)

Library of Congress Cataloging in Publication Data
A CIP catalogue record for this book is available from the Library of Congress.

Typeset in 10 on 12 pt Palatino by Graphicraft Typesetters Ltd., Hong Kong
Printed in Great Britain by T.J. Press Ltd., Padstow

This book is printed on acid-free paper.

It is the policy of The Pennsylvania State University Press to use acid-free paper for the first printing of all clothbound books. Publications on uncoated stock satisfy minimum requirements of American National Standard for Information Sciences— Permanence of Paper for Printed Library Materials, ANSI Z239.48–1984.

Contents

Preface   vii

1 The Prostitution Scene   1
An ordinary day   1
Tricks   6
The prostitution market in Oslo   9

2 The Main Participants   15
"If things had been okay I never would have started:"
    Becoming a prostitute   15
A life under the influence . . .   23
The customer – faceless and nameless   25

3 Inside Prostitution   40
In it for the money: The economics of prostitution from
    the women's point of view   40
Fast fuck: The women's view of what the customer buys   50
Customer violence   57
"It's not me he's fucking:" The women's defense
    mechanisms   63
Is there anything good about it? What ties the women to
    prostitution   75
The buyer's trick – an entire project   84
What is he paying for? How customers experience the
    trick   90

4 After Prostitution   106
"I've left my body on the street:" Delayed damage to the
    women   106
Modest dreams: The women's hopes for the future   117

5 **Indoor and Outdoor Prostitution**   124
   A shifting market: Different types of prostitution   124

6 **What Ever Happened to the Pimp?**   133
   Prostitutes' views of pimps   133
   Who are the pimps? Pimps reported to the police   140
   Non-violent boyfriend-pimps   143
   Violent boyfriend-pimps   146
   "Stable" pimps   150
   A familiar face: The pimps that get caught   156
   The pimp's functions   160

7 **The Fight against Prostitution**   173
   Opposition to prostitution   173
   Prostitution projects: About Scandinavian assistance
      programs   188
   Two suggestions for criminal law reforms   199
   Convenient images – harmful images   205

Appendix: Sources of Information   209

Bibliography   216

Index   220

Preface

This book is the result of many years of research on prostitution. We are especially grateful for the invaluable assistance and support we have received from two very different environments. First of all, we are deeply indebted to the women, the customers, and the pimps who have patiently met with us and tried to express their experiences in the world of prostitution. Some of the women, in particular, have been extremely generous with their time. It's a pity not to be able to thank them by name.

The other environment is our workplace, the Institute of Criminology and Criminal Law in Oslo. A number of our colleagues have put considerable work into this book. But we also wish to express our appreciation for the general atmosphere at the Institute. It is both a secure and an exciting place to work, where it's always possible to propose unfinished, often off-the-wall ideas, and get a worthwhile response.

This book is a joint effort on the part of the authors. We have discussed the material with each other over a period of many years. For practical reasons Cecilie Høigård has done the actual writing of most of the book. On occasion it has seemed most natural to write "I" and not "we," and in those cases "I" is Cecilie Høigård.

We have provided the participants in the book with names. These names are, of course, not their real names. Information about the individuals' backgrounds has been altered to protect their anonymity.

Liv Finstad and Cecilie Høigård
Oslo, September 1991

Backstreets is a revised version of the Norwegian *Bakgater* (Pax Forlag, Oslo, 1986). New research material has since been added.

1

The Prostitution Scene

An ordinary day

One Thursday Elisabeth and I drive up to Lambertseter, an older suburb on Oslo's east side. It's ten o'clock in the morning. I'm going to try to interview Inga. The chances of finding her at home are best in the morning. Inga lives with her lover Elin in an apartment-building near the mall.

We ring the buzzer at the main entrance.

Nobody answers.

We take a walk to the mall and then try again. Elisabeth leans on the buzzer this time. Still no answer. The door is locked. I'm ready to give up, but Elisabeth says she's sure Inga is home. She rings the manager's buzzer, and he lets us in. Standing outside their apartment on the fifth floor, we try the doorbell. No use.

We plant ourselves on the floor in the hall, drink Coke, smoke, and read the newspaper. Half an hour later Inga cautiously sticks her head out the door. She explodes when she sees Elisabeth. She and Elin were sure that the cops had been ringing their doorbell. It scared the shit out of them. Me she ignores.

Elisabeth tries to calm Inga down, after a while with some success. Inga explains why she is on edge. She couldn't get their morning fix the night before. So now she and Elin are sick, she says. Elin comes out. No way are we getting into the apartment. After a little negotiating I am at least allowed to drive them downtown. They have to get heroin. On the way to the car Elin runs in to the bank to change a Swedish 1,000 crown bill. She returns crestfallen and cursing. The bank refused to change it. They said that bringing such big bills into the country was against currency regulations.

In the car Inga utters her first friendly words to me: "Nice music you're playing." The car radio is tuned to "light morning music." I offer to try and change the 1,000 crown bill at my bank. The mood is somewhat better after that. We joke around a bit that I'll get caught for violating currency regulations.

My bank won't change the bill either. The teller suggests I try another bank at Egertorvet where they're willing to change large bills. It costs 100 crowns.[1] That suits us fine. Egertorvet is a small square marketplace in the center of Oslo. Here, the city's outsiders gather. Here, there is large-scale drug trade. Prostitution's backstreets are nearby.

I exchange the money for Inga and Elin because they are too well-known at Egertorvet. Inga insists on giving me 40 crowns for the transaction. I refuse but end up accepting the money.

The hunt for smack begins. This is Elin's job. She walks right over to a young boy and enquires. She's told to wait a little, the smack is on its way. We sit down on the steps outside the bank with Coke and rolls. We sit and wait. Gradually, Egertorvet fills up with people on the same errand as Inga and Elin. Three or four groups form, all of them waiting for smack. I offer a cigarette: Winston. Wrong brand. Later they take Prince cigarettes from Elisabeth. People come and go, asking each other if the smack isn't coming soon. All told there are probably 15 to 20 people, slightly more women than men.

There's a rumor circulating that there are a lot of plainclothes cops on the square. Tension and restlessness pervade the atmosphere. On the surface the square is calm. Unsuspecting tourists and locals are strolling around, eating ice cream under the broiling sun and listening to the violinist. He's a virtuoso, playing flashy music like Fiocco's "Allegro" and Fritz Kreisler. He reaps enthusiastic applause between numbers, but not much money in his violin-case. It's hot. There is a growing uneasiness in the groups that are waiting. Inga and Elin start arguing. Others have managed to get hold of smack; not Elin. Inga chews Elin out; she's feeling pretty rotten. Elin takes a walk up to the Palace Park, but comes back empty-handed. There are plainclothes cops everywhere today.

A bank employee comes storming out and tries to chase us off the steps. We move over about six feet. Elin shouts obscenities at the bank employee. Soon the empty space on the steps is filled by a new couple who have come to wait. Elisabeth points Benny out to me. Benny has been on drugs for 12 years. He has a body as skinny as a

---

[1] Currency values as of January, 1991: 100 crowns = $16.98 or £8.74. Or, $1 = 5.89 crowns; £1 = 11.44 crowns.

boy's and the face of an old man. Benny has smack. But Inga and Elin don't want to buy from him, even though they're getting desperate. They tell me he has a reputation for ripping people off. His stuff isn't always pure. Mette, a 20-year-old who is sitting with us, is willing to chance it.

Benny contemptuously refuses her, "You're just a whore." Inga asks him, "How 'bout me? Aren't I a whore?" Benny: "No, 'cause you're an okay chick."

After Benny has left, Mette shows us the marks on her throat. Benny wanted to sleep with her last night. When she wouldn't, he tried to strangle her. That's why he's pissed off.

The violinist packs up and turns the pavement over to the Rex Ramon Streetband. It's a one-man orchestra – Ramon has a guitar and mandolin on his lap, a harmonica attached to his guitar, tambourines on both feet, and a bass drum on his back. He plays old Bob Dylan tunes, from before Dylan's fall from grace. Mr Tambourine Man. He gets lots of applause and more money than the violinist.

Vilhelm and Frida arrive. They go straight to the group perched on the window-sill of Samson's bakery, without saying hello to us. Not so strange that they don't say hello, even though Elisabeth and I know them. Vilhelm and Frida were featured in a series of articles this summer in *Dagbladet*, Norway's second largest newspaper. First they were interviewed as a typical junkie couple in the big city. Then a nice man from the country contacts the newspaper and offers to let them live on his farm. Fresh country air is supposed to be good for drug addicts. Front-page story. Under the newspaper's spotlight Vilhelm and Frida are transported to detox, sixteenth ward, Ulleval Hospital. Readers follow the agonies they suffer from withdrawal. The psychiatrists in the ward are interviewed. Vilhelm and Frida have brave and cheerful words for the press: "Now or never. We're going to make it." The newspaper readers bid them farewell as they depart for the country and a new life. A heartwarming story. Now they are back in Oslo, back on the square, only a week later. I think to myself that the newspaper will undoubtedly not carry any more stories about Vilhelm and Frida.[2]

The tone between Inga and Elin is becoming increasingly bitter. Elin isn't doing her job. Other people have bought, but Elin hasn't scored anything. Several others in the square are in the same fix

---

[2] Vilhelm appeared one last time in *Dagbladet* – a year later when he was killed in a car accident. He was high at the time.

as Elin. Too many plain-clothes men around. "This is fucked. It's a fucked way to spend the whole day, just to get what we've gotta have to feel okay. We don't get high. We take it just so we can function normally," Inga says.

We're chased away from the steps of the bank again. There's a steady flow of street musicians. Now a young girl has started up on her Hardanger fiddle. In contrast to her predecessors, her performance is a total fiasco. "Stop that godawful screeching" and "Please, spare us," they call out from Samson's bakery.

Ellen sits down beside us. She is in her early twenties, and has long, attractive, blond hair. She can scarcely hold her head upright and her speech is slurred. She has taken Valium because the smack hasn't come. She gives me half of her roll. She is with Olav. He's between 50 and 60, has thin, slicked-back hair, a leather jacket, and blue gabardine pants. He's sober.

Olav talks about himself like he's a male version of Florence Nightingale. He asks if I use smack too. Ellen interjects "You can trust Olav. He's really wonderful. He's so nice, you can't imagine. He's helped me many times. Now he's gotten me into a detox house. I should have gone today, but I'm putting it off 'til tomorrow." Elin explains to me that this detox clinic is Norway's best: "They give you Aporex and Valium. You can really calm down there. I hope that Inga and I can go there too. This fucked-up life is just for now. It's going to be different for us too, someday." Olav gives me his Florry recipe: "Every time I walk across Egertorvet there's a flock of girls trailing behind me. I give them what they need. Do you know what that is? I'll tell you, it's tenderness and care, that's what. That's what it's all about. Two days at home with me and the amount of smack they use is cut in half. After four days it's down to a quarter. The whole secret is tenderness and care." While we're talking he puts his arm protectively around Ellen, who leans her heavy Valium head on his shoulder. Towards me he acts like a gentleman, ceremoniously standing up to light my unfashionable Winstons. I am smoking too many. I, too, am caught up in the tense atmosphere.

Inga bitches at Elin. Elin isn't aggressive enough. Of the two of them, Inga is in worse shape. They still haven't had their morning fix and it's going on 3:00. Nonetheless Inga shows concern for me, thinks it's really stupid for me to be "wasting my time." In the course of the afternoon it's more or less been agreed that I'll interview her when she's had a fix and calmed down a little.

Around 3:30 the deal is made. Elin has managed to buy four bags of heroin for 1,200 crowns.

They shoot up while we're still in town. Today they just can't wait until they get home. Neither of them gets high: they just feel "well", as they put it. They're dissatisfied with the quality of the heroin. Elin goes up to the park and buys a bag of Thai with the last 300 crowns.

Around 4:30 we're back at their apartment in Lambertseter.

Inga and Elin live in a modern, one-room apartment with a sleeping alcove, tea-kitchen, and balcony. They apologize with the usual hostess phrases – excusing the mess. There is no mess. Everything is neat and tidy. A lace tablecloth on the coffee table, magazines sorted and meticulously stacked on the bookshelf, many small decorative objects on the shelves.

Elin is going to do the grocery shopping while I interview Inga. They make a list. All they have is 100 crowns. They sit calculating, crossing out some things, adding others.

The interview goes well until Elin gets back. She doesn't like it that I'm interviewing Inga. Besides, she's exhausted from all the tension at the square. She constantly interrupts: "Why are you asking about that? I don't like it." And "our personal life is our own." I'm sweating, aware that most of the textbook rules on how to conduct an interview are now being broken. Finally I say: "Maybe it would be easier if you went somewhere else for the time being." Terrible blunder! I forgot that it's a one-room apartment.

Elin explodes: "That's the limit! How rude can people be! I won't be thrown out of my own place. Where'd you think I should go? To the bathroom maybe? If anyone's leaving, it'll be you, not me."

What can I say? I stammer something awkward about not meaning it that way.

Inga tries to smooth things out: "There there, Elin. I know you're exhausted, but you don't need to take it out on Cecilie. Take it easy now."

The atmosphere is strained. We continue the interview, after a fashion.

Towards the end of the interview Inga becomes restless. She has to go out on the street to get money for tonight's and tomorrow morning's fixes.

Elin is unhappy: "The whole day's been ruined. Inga and I almost never have an evening together. Today we had money too. We'd planned to get some smack and come right home. Goddamned cops. Inga was going to take a nap in the afternoon and then we could spend the evening together. This was supposed to be such a nice day. And then everything got screwed up. It all went to hell."

When we leave, Elin says: "You'll have to excuse my behavior a little while ago. I just got kind of mad at you, you see." I mumble something. I feel guilty that I've played a part in screwing up their day.

I drive Inga downtown around 7:30 p.m. She gets out by Egertorvet, thanks me for the ride and waves goodbye. She's going to sell herself until she has 1,200 crowns. That's four tricks, or eight hand jobs.

Tricks

I sit talking with Marianne one Friday morning. She tells me that her prostitution week looked like this: Sunday, one or three tricks, she can't quite remember. Monday, three tricks. Tuesday, no tricks. Wednesday, three tricks. Thursday, two tricks. I ask her to tell about her last two tricks, the Thursday tricks.

Marianne: "It was yesterday afternoon. It rained. I stood down there someplace, I think it was Queen's Street. He stopped his car. I look in, he's a skinny little runt. I open the car door and ask if he wants a trick.

"'Yeah, get in,' he answers. So I get into the car.

"'Well, do you want a trick?' I ask him again.

"'Yeah, what'll it be if we go to my place? I live in Kolbotn.'

"'Well, then I take 350, and you have to drive me back.' That's okay with him. I get the money.

"'On the way I ask, 'Hey, what do you do?'

"'I work for the government,' he says sort of proud, 'in the Postal Service.'

"'Is it nice?' I ask, but don't bother to listen to the answer.

"When we come up on the ridge out at Ekeberg, I start chatting again, 'God, what a beautiful view.' I also ask him if he comes down to the district a lot.

"'No, but I've been there a few times. I wish it wasn't like this.'

"He rented a room in a big house in Kolbotn. It was down in the cellar, through the furnace room, and into a a little room. I took off my boots. He put those warmer-things in them. It was totally clean in his room. He didn't even take the spread off of the sofa. I started to undress, but kept my blouse and socks on. He was really slow. So

I rolled a rubber on him. I laid under him. He started really carefully and slowly.

"God, this is going to take an hour, I thought. So I started to breathe heavily to get him excited. He didn't say a single word. He didn't even breathe heavily. The whole thing took five minutes. He didn't try to kiss me or anything like that.

"I went and washed myself. I looked around the room a little. He only had one record. 'You've gotta start buying records,' I said. That was all that was said in the room.

"On the way back to town he told me that he not was married. Otherwise we didn't say a word on the way back. Oh yeah, he did talk about something or other. That he was going to try and take the university entrance exam. I just answered 'yeah' and 'really.' He dropped me off at Egertorvet. I walked down toward Metropol.[3] I met Doris there. It was still raining, so we leaned against the building. Doris told me that she'd just come out of detox. She said she just wanted to do hand jobs. She had finally started her period again; yesterday was the first day. It's because she's been off drugs for two months. First one guy came up. But then another guy was waving at me. He wanted two girls. 'We'll do it in my apartment,' Doris said.

"We took a cab. He sat in front, and Doris and I got in the back. We got the money in the cab. He didn't say a word on the way. Once we were in the apartment Doris wanders around chattering away. She apologized for the mess, but it was as neat and clean as it always is. I'm totally quiet, my head feels totally empty. He hasn't said one goddamn word yet. Better get it over with.

"'What position did you have in mind, since you want two of us?' I ask.

"'I can go for most anything, as long as it's not too perverse.'

"So I went into the bathroom and took off all my clothes. He sat on the sofa.

"'Can't you warm him up first?' Doris said.

"I unbuckled his belt and took his clothes off. Asked him to lie down on his back and then I sat on top of him. The whole thing took three minutes before he came.

"I went and washed myself in the bathroom. When I came back into the living room, Doris was under him. She grinned at me over

[3] Metropol is a gay restaurant in Oslo, also frequented by prostitutes as a "resting spot."

his shoulder and waved. She had to give him a hand job before he could come again. He was in her once or twice, I think. Doris was pretty smart: 'I'm so tight. Can't I give you a hand job then you'll get a little variety tonight?' she said to him. He was embarrassed that his performance hadn't been more impressive.

"'I'm not exactly 15 any more,' he said. My God. Doris asked if he was married. He was. He had two kids, seven and four. He was supposedly out at 7–11 buying Donald Duck comic books for them. Doris gave him hers so he'd have his alibi intact when he came home.

"The whole thing in the apartment took about 15 minutes."

Questions posed in the book

Our study attempts to get within Marianne's narrative and understand the content of prostitution.[4] As a starting point we have a simple definition of prostitution: buying and selling sexual services for cash payment. Much could be said about the problem of definition (see, for example, Borg et al., 1981, pp. 42–53). We have resisted the temptation. This book is not about the difficult borderline cases which make the question of definition important. We have instead chosen to allow a definition of prostitution to evolve in the course of the book. The main subject of this book is prostitution's content. We are interested in what happens in the actual exchange of sex for money, and what happens with the parties involved in this exchange. What is exchanged? What ties are there between sex and money? What happens to women over time when they prostitute themselves? What are men looking for in prostitution? Who is the pimp, really? What is the relationship between the pimp and the prostitute? Should prostitution be fought? Can it be fought? The questions stand in line, waiting to be answered.

Some readers will have met women like Marianne. They have perhaps hurried past them on their way home to dinner and a quiet evening with their spouse. Some people react with irritation – at the decline of morality or the depravity of today's youth. Others react with pity. Reactions like these can easily be brushed aside.

There are probably fewer who will search for connections between the lives they live and Marianne's.

How is prostitution possible? What are the similarities and differ-

---

[4] See the appendix for a discussion of sources and terms.

ences in the encounter that takes place between participants in prostitution and other encounters between men and women? What images of women and of men make prostitution possible? What do the contents of prostitution tell us about the conditions for sexuality in our society? In prostitution certain aspects of the relationship between the sexes are dramatized, exaggerated, typified. An analysis of the contents of prostitution can serve as a magnifying glass on our own lives. "Deviance" can illuminate "normality." This is another of the book's themes.

We begin by placing Marianne's two tricks within an overview of Oslo's prostitution market.

The prostitution market in Oslo

We will start with a broad picture of the prostitution market in Oslo. Our point of departure is the location where the contact between the prostitute and the customer is established. In some types of prostitution, such as sex clubs, the contact and the trick occur at the same location. In street prostitution and advertised prostitution the trick is turned at some place other than where contact is established.

Backstreets

Street prostitution in Oslo is carried out over an area extending from the Central Railroad Station, up Prinsensgate, down to City Hall and along the road below Akershus Fortress: Four main traffic arteries going north–south with ten smaller cross-streets. The quarter is made up of back streets leading into Oslo's main street, Karl Johan. The backstreets are also located close to the city's night spots, but the fact that these streets border on the harbor discourages through-traffic. Some of the streets in this area are actually closed to through-traffic. This is primarily a business district composed of office buildings, empty of life after the close of the workday. As a marketplace for sex trade the location is ideal. It is central, while at the same time there aren't many reasons other than prostitution for coming to this part of town during evening and night-time hours.

There is a certain amount of drifting between the streets. However, most of the women have their own relatively stable territory. The youngest women work at the far end of the quarter, down around Skipper Street, the Central Railroad Station, and the end of

Prinsens Street. At the Central Railroad Station there is also a certain amount of male prostitution. The older women keep to the upper end of the quarter.

Tuesday and Thursday are the easiest days on the street. Saturdays are hopeless. The weekend is family time, at least until the fathers get home from an outing to the family cabin or start to get restless towards the end of the weekend. The majority of Oslo's street prostitution takes place in the middle of the week between 6 p.m. and midnight.

Street prostitution and advertised prostitution are the most common forms of prostitution in Oslo.

Advertising

Advertised prostitution usually takes place privately – either in the woman's apartment, or in an apartment at her disposal. Occasionally hotel rooms are also used, or the woman goes to the customer's home. The vast majority of the contacts are arranged through the magazine *Contact*. The magazine makes no attempt to conceal its role as procurer. Some of the letters printed in the magazine are "thank you's" to the magazine for acting as intermediary for prostitutes. The most common code-word in *Contact* is "generous." An examination of a typical number of *Contact* revealed that of the 26 ads under the heading "Woman seeking friend," 20 used the code-words "well-situated" or "generous." The ad from Liz and Lotte was typical: "Liz and Lotte, 24 and 26 years old, seek well-situated men for delightful morning get-togethers in the cozy surroundings at our place! Bring your desires, and we'll fill them! Only clean and sober men are welcome!" *Contact*'s activities are clearly illegal in relation to Norwegian penal codes regarding procuring. The magazine has been reported to the police several times, most recently in 1989 by Norway's largest women's organization, the Women's Front. The police, however, have made no attempt to stop its activity.

In *Contact* for March 1985, there is an advertisement, placed by a firm, for clean, discreet hostesses and private secretaries. In the same magazine there is also an ad for an escort service – the name of the firm and the telephone number are identical to those listed under the ad for hostesses and private secretaries. An interview with the proprietor reveals a modest operation. It is difficult always to have someone answering the phone since the business has no formal offices. The proprietor knows some women who are engaged in other forms of prostitution. She contacts them when she receives requests from clients. She has worked at a massage parlor which dealt extensively in prostitution. In addition she has been involved in advertised and street prostitution. She confirmed our impression that Oslo's call-girl activity is small scale, private, and well-concealed. It is her belief, after six years in the prostitution market, that she is the first to try to establish a more organized escort and call-girl network.

Dagbladet, one of Oslo's larger daily newspapers, is the other major publication which prints ads for prostitutes and clients. In 1984, *Dagbladet* was reported to the police for its procurement activities. The case was dismissed for lack of evidence. Since then the newspaper has changed the policy of its column "Meeting Place." Today, the newspaper does not accept overt ads for prostitution, and the previous code-word, "well-situated," is now banned from the newspaper. Prostitutes and customers try instead to formulate their messages in other ways. We have been told that this has led to several misunderstandings.

Today's *Dagbladet* can hardly be called a "clean" newspaper. Its double standard continues to flourish. One can still see articles which adopt a stand against prostitution right next to ads whose intent, one can reasonably assume, is to procure. Instead of personal ads there are now ads for a more organized sex trade, such as trips to Thailand or marriage tours to the Philippines. These operations have clear racist undertones.

In our in-depth interviews, several of the woman mentioned *Dagbladet* as a place to advertise. This newspaper has also come up in a number of the cases filed against pimps.

Fredrik, a former pimp Cecilie has been in contact with for several years, was probably the first in this country to use *Dagbladet*. He relates: "We began by advertising in the Saturday paper. I noticed the system in *Ekstrabladet* [daily newspaper in Denmark]. I figured it must be possible to get something like that going in Norway. I wrote the copy for the ads and Eva took them to the newspaper. The first advertisement we submitted was much too direct and was rejected, but by moderating certain words and expressions, we got them published.

"We had to argue with the people who took the ad copy. They actually censored the wording of the copy we wanted printed. You were allowed to say two half things instead of one whole. I wanted to write precise copy stating what this was all about. I asked for a list of words that were permitted and a list of those that weren't, but I never got it."

Hotel and restaurant prostitution

Prostitution occurs at a handful of hotels in Oslo. The SAS Hotel is mentioned much more frequently in the interview data than any other. At the SAS Hotel, as at a number of other hotels, the contact is made in the bar or in the nightclub. The customer is usually staying at the hotel and the trick takes place in his room.

Though there was prostitution at several other Oslo restaurants during the period under investigation, the activity at The Rainbow restaurant and nightclub was uniquely systematic. This is how Katrine described what prostitution was like at the restaurant before it was sold to new owners in 1982:

"There are about ten regulars who go there every night. On top of that there are ten or fifteen others who drop in sometimes. The customers are usually staying at one of the downtown hotels, for example the SAS or the Viking. Hotel rules say they can have ladies in their rooms before eleven p.m. When I'm working I go into the bar with a newspaper, sit down at a table, and read my paper. If a man comes over to me, I get right to the point. I might say, for example, "Well, well, out having a good time tonight? Because I assume you know why I'm here." If he takes me up on my offer, we discuss the price right away. It's 700 crowns, 1,000 if he wants to eat dinner first. After dinner we go to his hotel room. If it's after eleven the night clerk has to be bribed, that costs between 50 and 100. I don't go to the nightclub at The Rainbow because then I get johns who are too drunk. And I quit a little before twelve; if it hasn't happened by then I'll just have to do without."

Cecilie asks: "Does The Rainbow try to stop you?"

"No, of course not. It's in their interest, the employees get a lot of tips this way. For example, the customers tip the bartender extravagantly in order to impress the ladies. We tip a lot too, I give the doorman ten crowns every time I go through the door and I tip the bartender. I try hard to get along with the employees, I'm really dependent on that. And, well, it's discreet at The Rainbow – a lot of people go there just to enjoy themselves and they have the right to be left alone."

In 1982 The Rainbow changed hands and the new owners changed the name to Casablanca. The clientele became different and younger. Prostitution disappeared from the restaurant. No new restaurants have the dubious honor of taking over The Rainbow's role. This is not to say that restaurant prostitution has disappeared. The manner in which prostitution is carried out is the same as Katrine described it at The Rainbow, with one important exception: the systematic cooperation between prostitutes and restaurant employees does not exist. The extent of restaurant prostitution is probably considerably less than it was just a few years ago. This fact has also been confirmed in conversations with prostitutes.

Organized prostitution

In the middle of the 1970s four sex clubs were closed in Oslo as a result of court proceedings. In the spring of 1985, Studio 40, a sauna on Oslo's east side, was closed after a raid. Prostitution in clubs and massage parlors operates on a much smaller scale in Oslo than, for example, in Denmark. Due to police prosecution it is clear to everyone, both inside and outside the sex clubs, that this is a business in direct conflict with Norwegian criminal law. As long as it is illegal to promote professional sex an operator of a sex club is faced with an irresolvable dilemma. On the one hand, he cannot set out on a course which is openly in opposition to the law, because he then risks having the police at his door. On the other hand, he is dependent on publicity in order to attract members and clients. The operator of a sex club has to find a balance between two important considerations: the need for publicity and the need for anonymity. Sex-club operators maneuver in dangerous waters.

In 1989 two different enterprises were uncovered in Oslo which exploited women from the Third World. One of the enterprises imported women from the Dominican Republic. The women were placed in private apartments or massage parlors. The customers were recruited through *Contact* magazine. Two Dominican men were charged in the case, one of whom had legal residence in Norway through his marriage with a Norwegian citizen. It is the opinion of the police that the enterprise was based in the Dominican Republic, thus making the case difficult to investigate.

The second case involved the exploitation of four women from Thailand and one woman from Brazil. A total of six people were indicted in the case, five men and one woman. The accused were between 23 and 28 years of age, with no previous police record. The accused had picked up women in their homeland, taken them to Norway on tourist visas, and established them in a private apartment. Once again, the magazine *Contact* was used to recruit customers.

Contact can be made and tricks turned in many, many ways – the diversity and imagination of human beings have their place in prostitution. There are most certainly activities in prostitution's periphery which fall outside the descriptions in this chapter. However, we are relatively certain that the forms of prostitution which are carried out in Oslo in a systematic manner have been covered in our discussion.

2

The Main Participants

"If things had been okay I never would have started:" Becoming a prostitute

Among those we interviewed, the average age for the woman's first trick was 15½. The oldest was 23; the youngest 13.

Fifteen-year-olds. We know several 15-year-olds. They struggle with their German lessons, have crushes on David Bowie and on boys in the class above; they've just started experimenting with mascara and they read teen magazines. Not children, and not adults. Some have begun to have sex, even though according to Norwegian law they're under the age of consent.

How can 15-year-olds be so different? Or more accurately, how can 15-year-olds live such dissimilar lives?

Social background of the women

Prostitution researchers have attached a great deal of importance to describing the social background of prostitutes.[1] The picture is relatively unambiguous. It is women from the working class and the lumpenproletariat[2] who are recruited into prostitution. Their backgrounds are also marked by irregular home lives and adjustment difficulties in school and in their working lives. This is established knowledge in prostitution research. We have not placed a particular emphasis on rechecking this, and our own data are not particularly

---

[1] See for example Bracey (1979) and Bowker (1978). In Scandinavia Stig Larsson (1983) has impressive statistics. See also Martinussen (1967) and Finstad et al. (1982).

[2] Literally the "ragged proletariat", people on the fringes of the working class who do not sell their labour.

illuminating on this point.[3] The social background of the 664 women registered by the police is not systematically documented. The women from the Oslo Project have the same background patterns as international literature describes (Finstad et al., 1982). The 26 prostitutes we interviewed also fit this pattern.[4]

The most startling aspect of the social background of those we interviewed is their extensive experience of institutionalization. Of the 26 women only three had not been institutionalized at all. Orphanages, women's homes, reform schools, child and adolescent psychiatric institutions, alcohol and drug rehabilitation clinics, prisons – the whole of institutional Norway is richly represented. And most have a history of *many* institutional stays. Anita, for instance, had the following institutional career: raised in a children's home in western Norway until the age of 14. Then placed in a foster home. Ran away after two months. Placed in a group home in Oslo. Left on her own for a group home in the country near the Swedish border. Ended up at a psychiatric clinic in Oslo. Afterwards at a mental hospital in Oslo, then another mental hospital, and then back to the psychiatric clinic again. Now she is in a mental hospital just outside of Oslo, and says she's been in five times in the last nine months. Anita is 20. She has been institutionalized 12 times. There are few months in her life when she has not been in an institution. There are several other women who have institutional careers like Anita's. The women's narratives contain few praises of these institutions; the stories of neglect and unhappiness are many.

They are young when they turn their first trick. Nonetheless, 15 of the 26 had been institutionalized before that first trick.

This is an important discovery – not only because these figures tell of young women who are already rejected by normal society *before* they become prostitutes, but also because institutions are revealed to be important training grounds for prostitutes (see Bondesson, 1968, Davis, 1978). In institutions many young people in trouble are stowed together like surplus wreckage. They often run away together, without money. What could be more natural than that they exchange knowledge about ways to survive?

[3] A thorough check of this demands a great deal of statistical data (see for example Larsson, 1983). In-depth interviews are definitely not the method for obtaining this type of information. To learn a little about many people or a lot about a few people – we have to choose. As usual, approaches to the problem determine the method.
[4] The Norwegian edition of *Backstreets* gives a detailed description of the backgrounds of these 26 women (Høigård and Finstad, 1986).

The first trick

Kari: "It started at the Salvation Army school. That's where I got to know Aina. I got to be good friends with her. She'd learned to smoke hash in Copenhagen, it was in Christiania. She'd been on the street there too. So she knew what it was all about. The first time we knocked back a few beers and then did a trick together."

Knowing what it is all about. The women don't learn much in the way of concrete details before their first trick. Where you should go is important. All of the 26 woman interviewed turned their first trick at well-known prostitution sites. One had her debut at The Rainbow restaurant. The others began on the street.[5] This emphasizes the significance of a known, visible prostitution market.

The other thing you have to know is how much to ask for different tricks. Anita: "Birgit and I became friends at the group home. We really hit it off. We used to get dressed up. I had a devil's cape and looked like Alice Cooper. But we didn't start then. It was later in 1977 when we both didn't have any money. Birgit was together with Georg then, I was on Psiloybin.[6] Georg said he could show us where we should go and how to act. He said we should walk calmly back and forth until a car came. Then we should take 300 crowns. I got a john who was 70 years old. I went with him to his office. It was totally disgusting. But I didn't think about it too much. I'd done so many weird things, I'd been doing group sex since I was a little kid. My sex life was already screwed up. I didn't tell the old man it was my first trick. After that Birgit and I worked every day."

Inga didn't know much beforehand either. "I didn't know anything except where they were, that they were at the Bank Square. I'd asked around a little before. I'd heard a little about what to do from hanging out at Egertorvet too. They said you should go up to a car and ask if he wanted a trick."

Most tricks are performed by just one woman. It is only on occasion that they work in pairs: it is harder to get work for two. But the first trick is different. Half of the women worked together with a girlfriend their first time.[7] Often the girlfriend has worked before

---

[5] Stig Larsson's data from Malmø also show that the great majority of women start on the street.

[6] A chemical substance which induces a reaction similar to that of LSD.

[7] Larsson has comparable results. In his data a second prostitute is influential at the start in three-fifths of the cases. In comparison, a pimp is the instigator in one-fifth of the cases (1983, p. 93).

and knows what it is all about. In this way an important part of the training is a form of participatory observation.

A gradual process

Not much concrete knowledge is demanded for starting in prostitution. That does not mean that "just anyone" can come out of nowhere and start tricking. It is a marked characteristic that most of the girls associate with other street kids for quite a while before they turn their first trick. (This is also emphasized in the American studies of Bracey, 1979 and James, 1978.) Here is where self-image is molded, norms for behavior are learned: what counts and does not count, what it is to be a woman or a man.

The *social* learning is extensive. The seeds are often planted early, long before the girls become a part of the group of street kids.

In *Hard Asphalt*, Ida summarizes it like this: "As the years went on prostitution got closer and closer. It was still unthinkable, but not so unthinkable. My best friends were on the street. The alchy friends of my dad always talked about how he could earn good money off me and Berit. Later on, in the crowd I hung out with, it was drummed into us over and over that a woman's body was her most important asset. I saw it every day" (Halvorsen, *Hard Asphalt*, 1987, p. 180).[8]

Ida's description shows how the image of women prevalent in her environment ate away at her and how she eventually to some extent incorporated that image into her view of herself. This process represents an essential and necessary self-transformation a woman undergoes before she begins to prostitute herself. Women who can rest secure in their own worth as individual people and who have a view of their body and sexuality as sources of personal pleasure will have a solid defense against prostitution. But how many woman have solid defenses of this type? Different images of women exist side-by-side in our society. We believe that all women in our society have at some time, most likely many times, come up against the notion that our greatest asset is our body. It is one of the more common images of women which makes prostitution possible.

Not all women become prostitutes. The presence in society of this image of the body as an asset is obviously not the only factor responsible for some women prostituting themselves. But in addi-

---

[8] In 1982 Liv Finstad and Cecilie Høigård wrote *Hard Asphalt* with Ida Halvorsen (pseudonym). This was an account of Ida's own life as a prostitute.

tion to the well-known factors of social class, economics, and the degree of involvement in traditional society, the degree to which a woman adopts this female image as an image of herself is crucial.

Ida travelled in circles where this image of women was almost absolute. The lack of competing female images enabled the image of a woman's body as potential capital to assume enormous proportions; it was readily available as a model for Ida's behavior.

Learned self-image and a learned attitude to one's own sexuality are central elements in the process towards prostitution. At times learning can take place under very dramatic and painful circumstances, as in the sexual abuse of children. Neither we nor Swedish prostitution researchers have systematically asked about the incidence of incest among women. In retrospect it is easy to see that we should have. A number of foreign studies seem to indicate a close correlation between being an incest survivor and being a prostitute, though the results are not definitive (see for example James, 1978; Silbert and Pines, 1981; Fields, 1981; Benward and Denssen-Gerber, 1975). The quality of these studies varies, and they also give very different answers as to how strong the connection is. Several of the Norwegian aid projects for prostitutes emphasize the connection between incest and prostitution (see also chapter 7).

Male images are not necessarily defined in relation to female images; but female images will often also define male images – as to what men can and cannot do with women. After her interview was finished, Jane said to me, "Make sure to say that lots of women are prostitutes because they've lost respect for men. Like me with my dad. I saw how he treated women. He played around with other women behind Mama's back the whole time. And all the whippings he gave me. If things had been OK I never would have started. Lots of women feel like me. They don't respect men."

The road to prostitution is a process in which the women's experiences cause a breakdown in their respect for themselves, for other women, and also for men. Such individual experiences are seldom sufficient reason for prostitution. It is only when the experiences are translated and incorporated into the collective experience which the girls share with other youths that prostitution becomes a viable alternative.

Peer-group significance is effectively summarized by Anna's account of her first trick. "I was part of the Stener Street gang then. It started with us hanging out at the amusement park in town. Old guys asked if we'd go behind the fence with them or if we would jerk them off. They gave us money to see our underwear – it was insane. It was really fun too – we were really disgusting towards them. Like we'd run away after we'd gotten the money. One time a girl had sandpaper in her hand when she went to jerk some guy off. The whole thing was just a game. But I felt pressured by the others. In the beginning I used to ride along with the other girls when they did tricks. That was before I started. It was too gross. The old geezers were often really stingy with the paint thinner or with the money. The creeps started nagging at me; they wanted to have me 'cause I was younger. Totally disgusting."

After a while her girlfriends also started to nag at Anna. Anna felt it was leeching not to turn tricks. She did have less money than the others then. Often they shared their paint thinner with her. But sometimes they wouldn't share. "You can turn tricks too, you know – go behind the fence and get some cash," they'd reply. She remembers her first trick as if it were yesterday. "I was 14 years old. It was totally disgusting. I thought the devil was gonna come and get me. I'd been living it up on the thinner then suddenly the can was empty. God, what do I do now? I asked myself. I went with an old goat who was 190 years old. His dick was *so* little. [Indicates a couple of centimeters between her thumb and index finger.] I was completely high. I thought he'd been sent by the cops to make a fool out of me with that little dick. I thought that cops were fucked when they'd do something like that. But that I was even more fucked to be going along with it. Afterwards I felt like everything was shit, and I was a goddamned whore. That's just what you are."

Your gang and your girlfriends. These are the important socialization factors before the first trick is turned. Several others besides Anna describe a subculture of sharing, in which prostitution is an act of solidarity, and abstention is sponging. One should share both the good and the bad, contribute a share to the household accounts. This picture differs from the one that occasionally appears in newspapers and in fiction. Here the image of the sleazy pimp who lures or threatens unwitting young women into service predominates. This is wrong. Of the 26 women interviewed, 24 mention other girlfriends or the crowd they hung out with in answering how they found out about prostitution and who told them how they should behave. In 13 of these cases it was, as we've already mentioned, a girlfriend who went along on the first trick.[9]

There are two responses that deviate from this pattern. One has a number of similarities with the notion of men as villains of the

[9] In a study from New York, Armstrong (1983) finds the same pattern.

drama. Lisa: "It was the summer I turned 17. I had moved away from home. I got to know three boys and they seemed all right. One evening all four of us went out drinking as usual. I got pretty drunk. 'Now you do this and that,' the boys said. They forced me to go through with it. They stood, one in each corner, and made sure I didn't take off. Afterwards we went right down to a nightclub and drank up the money there. It went on that way. They took everything I earned. They hung out with a psychopath who got a share of the money. He bought a Corvette, a two-seater, real American."

Cecilie: "Could you get rid of them?"

Lisa: "It wasn't that I was in love. But I was completely car-crazy. And I got a few black eyes when I didn't feel like working. But the most important thing was that I was car-crazy."

In the second instance it was also a man who was the instigator. Fredrik and Eva had a child when they were both 18 years old. They had a very meager income. Fredrik and Eva's story is atypical. They had no contact with fringe groups or street kids beforehand. Fredrik: "We were in a desperate situation. My pay just didn't do it. We had almost no money. Then I read in the newspaper about a prostitution trial. It made big headlines. It was about a woman who claimed she made 300 crowns per trick for performing sexual services for men in cars. It was right there in print. We discussed it a little, talked about how much you could earn if you had so-and-so many tricks. We couldn't really understand how you could earn so much. We didn't know a single person who did that kind of thing and in terms of background we had no connection to this at all, apart from my experiences at sea. Eva was hesitant to start; she was afraid it would have consequences for our relationship. I reassured her that my love for her would grow when she also earned money for our mutual benefit. There were so many things we needed money for. After a lot of talk back and forth over several weeks, we decided that she'd try it. We agreed that she would only accept 300 crowns, because that was the price we'd read in the paper. The first evening she tried the street, she talked with a lot of people and asked for 300 crowns. But she didn't get any tricks. The price was much too high. The usual price at that time was 100 crowns for a quick one in a car. It was just some damned nonsense in the newspaper about 300 crowns a shot. But OK, 100 crowns was a lot of money too, and as soon as you started doing tricks the money piled up pretty quickly."

For her part Eva believes that they needed money, but that money isn't the only explanation. "At that time we really needed money, but that doesn't actually explain why, because there were thousands in the same position as we were. I can't understand why we started. We were total novices; we didn't have any idea about it. If I'd known what I know today, I'd never have started. It was definitely a gamble."[10]

The whole panorama is represented. At the one extreme, several boys getting together to threaten and pressure a girl into prostitution; at the other end, women who eventually come to see prostitution as a gradual consequence of belonging to a fringe group and of the example set by girlfriends. Numerically, the second group predominates. Their situation is typical. It is also the situation we recognize from the women we got to know in the Oslo Project. The man as "villian" exists only as the exception which proves the rule. The fact that he exists at all allows the stereotype to survive.

Reactions to the first trick

A few of the women describe their first trick with words like "disgusting," "totally fucked," and similar expressions. The customers suffer under the names "creeps," "dirty old geezers," and other choice insults.

Almost all the women describe their subsequent tricks and their customers in this way. But in terms of the first prostitution experience there are many who were surprised that the whole thing went as painlessly as it did. Ida: "God, is it so easy to fuck your way to money? Here I'd been going around worrying for the longest time and it was just . . . just child's play . . . I was 23 years when I actually crossed the line. A grandmother's age to be starting. It was simple and undramatic. I didn't become another person, like I'd thought. It was easy-earned money" (Halvorsen, *Hard Asphalt*, 1987, pp. 185–6).

Many women think like Ida. Jane, for example: "God yes, I remember my first trick all right. It was four years ago. I was out partying a fair amount then. I got drunk and hung out at low-life restaurants. I was never an easy lay. I wasn't the kind to trade myself for a glass of beer. My girlfriend and I were out. We were pretty pissed and didn't have any more money. My girlfriend had a

---

[10] What separated Fredrik and Eva out from thousands of others in the same position, I don't know. In spite of the fact that we have spoken with each other endless times over many years, I don't thoroughly understand their story.

regular customer. But then she was sick. We looked him up. I wasn't nervous, but, like, excited-nervous. I thought it was kinda fun and exciting. He said I should touch him. I had to turn my face away when I did it. Then he said I should get undressed. Of course when I'd done it I had to go out and pee. He barely stuck it in, then he came. I got 250 crowns for it. He was happy, because it was my virgin trick. When I came back to my friend I said I wanted to do another trick right away. It was easy money, I thought. My head was totally empty."

The majority of customers probably react like Jane's. It's an extra refinement when a girl has her virgin trick. Many women tell of how they later pretended it was their virgin trick. Then they could get a little extra money. "New women getting tricks fastest" is an expression of the same. The women tell of how some customers preach morality to them and warn them against starting with prostitution *after* they have gotten their paid-for ejaculation. This type of moralizing isn't popular.

However, there are honorable exceptions. Inga: "I remember my first trick very well. It was because the john was so great. I'll tell you, there are lot of nice johns too. Like this guy. He figured out that it was my first time. It was because I didn't know the places you're supposed to go to. I said to him, 'Well, you already know where we can go.' Then he understood. He talked with me instead. He asked if I really knew what I was getting into. He said it was a hard life and that I had to be careful of drugs. He said that I seemed honest and nice and that I shouldn't start. Afterwards he wanted to pay me. I didn't want to take the money since I hadn't done anything for it. But he said I'd deserved it. So I took it."

A few women dreaded their first trick for a long time, like Ida did. Then they find out it's not so bad after all and that there is lots of money in prostitution. It is easy to continue then. The real shit comes later.

A life under the influence . . .

Drugs are a good peg to hang sorrows on. The authorities and a unanimous press have made the peg overly conspicuous and prominent in the landscape. Difficult problems receive simple explanations. Frayed relationships between people, institutional life, school setbacks, unemployment, anxiety for the future, the threat of war and atomic bombs, hopelessness and resignation – it seems almost too intense to come to grips with. Pegs come in handy then.

When all this is said, it is still important to emphasize that drug use *is* clearly a large and additional burden for adolescents who are already on the fringe. It is the combination of a difficult living situation, and a means of escape which costs considerably more than legal substances like the alcohol and pills that adults use, that causes problems to multiply.

Drug use is a central element in many prostitutes' everyday life. Getting high and intoxicated are central elements in the street culture where the women often hang out. Drugs are readily discussed: The effect of this or that substance, the quality of what's available, the drought in the city. Drugs provide a platform common experience, they are something to share, something to talk about. To an outsider the pharmacological knowledge of these women appears formidable.

In the interview material only three women say they have never used drugs or alcohol. The remaining 23 all tell of abuse that at times has made them hard-pressed to function "normally." Five describe themselves as combined misusers – of both drugs and alcohol. Seventeen have used a great deal of both drugs and alcohol but rely considerably more on drugs than on alcohol.

Important differences between the women are concealed behind these figures. Common to all is that their abuse has been extensive and is experienced as extremely troublesome by the women themselves. But otherwise the material ought to be divided in two. In one group we find women who, for periods of time, use a lot of hard drugs, alcohol, and pills. But this use is to some degree tied to social situations, parties, and the hunt for a high; in many ways it is similar to the rest of society's use of alcohol. In the other group we find those who call themselves "hooked." Their drug use is bound up in regular routines, like Inga's and Elin's. Nine of the 26 women have this type of relationship to drugs. When this is the case, drugs and the hunt for drugs become the primary focus of their lives. It is striking how virtually their entire day is organized around this one objective. It is a stressful life, as the day at Egertorvet was. Wake-up fix, midday fix, and evening fix. They shoot up not to get high but to get "well." Frida says, "I take morphine to get normal. And morphine has a moral effect too. It makes me conservative, middle-class. Morphine makes me like my mother." Their relationship to their drug use has much in common with a diabetic's relationship to insulin injections. It's important to shoot up at regular, established intervals or they get ill. "To be a slave to drugs" is an image that is frequently used in the narcotics debate. The image of being a slave lends to drug abuse associations to a determinate fate, loss of control, and thereby can become simply a convenient peg. The slave image is convenient but it is not appropriate. However, the fact that the *notion* of being a slave can itself become enslaving is something several of the interviews confirm.

The customer – faceless and nameless

While international research has investigated the prostitute, put her into charts and analyzed her, research on customers is rare. For researchers, as well as for the population in general, prostitution has until recently been synonymous with prostitutes. Customers are well-hidden in the hazy outskirts of prostitution, faceless and nameless.

The small quantity of Anglo-saxon research on customers that exists is generally of strikingly poor quality.[11] In many cases, the very manner in which data were collected and processed was inadequate. Discussions regarding the sample chosen, sources of error, and methodological problems are often insufficient or non-existent (see for example Gibbens and Silberman, 1960; Gibbens, 1963; Janus, Bess, and Saltus, 1977; Stein, 1974). The question of research ethics is seldom mentioned (this is particularly troublesome in Stein's study). Occasionally, sensational journalism would be a more appropriate label than research (this is particularly true for Janus, Bess, and Saltus). A notable exception is Eileen McLeod's original and serious study (1982).

Measured in terms of the normal standards for quantitative research, a review of this material is discouraging. No one has managed to produce data that can be generalized. A number of the researchers operate with sizeable samples (for example Stein, 1974; Janus, Bess, and Saltus, 1977) – indeed, so sizeable that they are on the boundary of the believable. Despite their size, these samplings cannot be generalized, since the samples are not randomly drawn. Measured in terms of standards for qualitative studies, the results are equally discouraging. Apart from McLeod's, the studies do not

---

[11] Prieur and Taksdal (1986) present a more detailed overview of international customer research.

probe very deeply into the individual customer's experiences. Several of the studies referred to above use a technique whereby they take quite a large sample of unrepresentative men and ask them a few simple questions. The end result is sloppy, middle-of-the-road research. Their results cannot be generalized, nor does this form of research provide the same type of opportunity as in-depth interviews for penetrating deeply into the content and meaning of the phenomenon.

In our opinion, the Norwegian study with which we have been involved is better. When the material for *Backstreets* had been collected, we started a project that dealt solely with customers. Cecilie Høigård was the project director; however the burden fell primarily on two research assistants, Annick Prieur and Arnhild Taksdal. The results are now published in book form (Prieur and Taksdal, 1989). This section and "What is he paying for?" in chapter 3 (pp. 90–97) are, to large extent, based on Prieur and Taksdal's book.[12]

This study consisted of two parts. The first part was a simple questionnaire filled out by 1,001 Norwegian men who were randomly chosen. The second part involved in-depth individual interviews with a varied sample of customers, totalling 74. The unique aspect of this study is that it provides the possibility of dealing both with the question of breadth and generalizability, and with the question of depth and understanding.

Customers in numbers

The questionnaire was administered by Norway's leading survey institution. In studies of this nature there is always a conflict between the probability that the answers are reliable, on the one hand, and the desire for a high response rate, on the other.[13]

In this study the emphasis was placed on increasing the prob-

[12] In the Norwegian edition of *Backstreets* (1986) the knowledge about customers is primarily tied to the information that the prostitutes gave, though in addition I had conducted five in-depth interviews with customers. Prieur and Taksdal's work provides an entirely different, and more solid foundation of knowledge about customers; these two sections have therefore been rewritten. Prieur and Taksdal's book provides, of course, a much more thorough presentation – both empirically and analytically – than we can give. One can only hope that the book will be made available in English.

[13] Prieur and Taksdal discuss this more extensively. They also clarify the concrete decisions and choices that have been made (Prieur and Taksdal, 1989).

ability that those who responded would give truthful answers. It doesn't help to have a lot of answers if they are untrue. With a low response rate but reliable answers, we will have obtained some conclusive information about those who answered. This also provided a starting point for calculating maximum and minimum figures for the entire sample. Moreover, this type of interview design has enabled us to make some statements about those who did not answer, in relation to normal background variables.

A group of 1,001 randomly chosen Norwegian men over 15 years of age was asked to participate in the study. Of these, 564 returned the questionnaire; a response rate of 56.4 percent. The response rate was lowest for those who were oldest. The response rate was lowest also for those with the least education and among social security recipients and pensioners – factors that vary with age. Place of residence and marital status had little effect on non-response rates.

In the study, 13 percent of those questioned answered that they had, one or more times, "paid for sexual contact/intercourse with a prostitute." If we assume that all non-respondents did *not* have this type of experience, this produces a minimum figure of 7 percent. However, this is an unlikely assumption. Because customer activity is a breach of established norms, it is more likely that the study provides figures which are under-reported. If the figure of 13 percent is representative, then every sixth or seventh Norwegian over the age of 15 has bought sex.

Number of prostitution experiences	Percentage
1	25
2–3	26
4–10	29
11–20	4
21–50	3
50+	2
Unknown	10
Total	99

These customers have, on the whole, few prostitution experiences; the data show that one-fourth have bought sex once. An additional one-fourth have been customers two or three times. The median is three times. The arithmetic mean is considerably higher – seven tricks. A number of sailors with a multitude of prostitution experiences have raised the average. The vast majority of the customers – 80 percent – had only bought sex abroad.

When the researchers compared the men with and without prostitution experiences, the most striking factor was the *similarity* between the two groups. Customers can be found in all age groups,
parts of the country, occupations, and social strata. Among the
customers there were slightly more single men, and there was
slightly more dissatisfaction with cohabitation and sex life among
those who were married. Also, customers were somewhat more
frequently men who travel a lot and men with more money. But the
tendencies are not very pronounced.

Customers interviewed

Large, representative, quantitative studies can give us the answer to
questions about proportions. But this method is totally unsuited to
illuminating the question of the *meaning* of a social phenomenon for
the participants.

The in-depth interviews conducted in the Norwegian study of
customers provided an excellent opportunity for delving more deeply into this type of question. In order to recruit participants for the
personal in-depth interviews, Prieur and Taksdal approached the
press in May of 1985, requesting coverage. They wanted customers
to telephone them. The researchers received good coverage in many
newspapers and radio programs over the entire country. A focus
was placed on customers having the opportunity to speak out and
be heard. Accordingly, customers in this portion of the study were
self-recruited. A total of 74 interviews were conducted; 46 of these
were telephone interviews and 28 were face-to-face interviews. The
researchers have kept in touch with some of the customers and followed their progress over an extended period of time.

The customers interviewed had much more extensive experience
of prostitution than the customers in the mass survey. The vast
majority also had experience of Norwegian prostitution. Only 10
percent had had three or fewer tricks. Over one-half had bought sex
between 20 and 50 times, and over one-third had bought sex more
than 50 times. Accordingly, this is, on the whole, a "weightier"
group of customers. This type of customer represents a far greater
proportion of the volume of Norwegian prostitution than the customers reached through the mass survey. It is these *habitual buyers*
who sustain the buyer side of Norwegian sex trade.

As with customers in the mass survey, these customers were
characterized by their great diversity in terms of age, civil status,

and social background. One group of customers was married; they told the researchers that they went to prostitutes because of something they didn't get from the women they live with. Another group was single; they said they went because they didn't have a woman to live with. For a few of the men who were interviewed, buying sex appeared independent of whether they were living with women or not. It was more a question of a special social situation – like being at sea.

Sailor customers

One of the most striking things about the sailor customers was how "natural" prostitution was in their opinion. It just turned out that way. That's how it was. A guy is horny after he's been out a long time, the women are forward, and they are all over in the districts the sailors frequent. Everybody else used prostitutes. All of the interviewed sailors were teenagers the first time they went to prostitutes; the youngest were 15. They see what the older men do, and they want to do the same. Or they're dragged along by their older buddies, at times in such a brutal manner that some felt raped. Peter said: "I resisted the best I could, but what's a 16-year-old out on his first voyage got compared to a couple of real sailors, a husky officer and a few other guys who'd decided. They followed me to the door, and they told the woman to make sure that I wasn't a virgin when I came out again. I would call it rape, well, to the extent that you can call it that when it's a boy. When I came out afterwards the guys were standing there clapping, what I really wanted to do was to throw up." Prostitution is a manhood ceremony the older men hold for the boys on their first trip. It is the ticket into the community of men. And for many it is obvious that prostitution really has more to do with being together with the guys than being with a woman. Stein says: "It's an experience, something that you've done in this or that city, and it's always the most fun when you experience something with other people. You've got to go someplace, you've got to do *something*. You've been working a lot and you've got a few hours to cram in all you can of free time." A leisure activity with the guys, not with a woman.

But it is not only that. Sailor prostitution isn't only a quick two-minute fuck, it can also be a reserve marriage. A woman in every port often means *one* woman in every port. The same woman every time he comes back there, not several. Often they live together while he's there. She makes food and irons his shirts in addition to providing sexual services. And even when the relationships didn't go that far, it was, as Per says, "often the only way to come in contact with people. The only way to get the human contact that you don't get when you only work with guys." Men at sea live closely together, but nevertheless they maintain a certain distance from each other. Women aren't just sex for the man. Women also represent security, closeness and home – no matter where in the world they may be. Peter says that the reason he went to prostitutes was a "lonely feeling, wanting to be close even if it was just for a little while. I guess it's that you start feeling a little sorry for yourself, need close contact with the opposite sex." It isn't necessarily sex that is Peter's primary desire, it is something else he is longing for, but he resolves it through a desire for sex. The men lack words for this longing that do not include sexuality as an excuse. Their needs are sexualized. The sailors not only find a girl in every port: "Women restore order out of chaos, and give a man a feeling of normality and security. There's safe harbor in every girl" (Prieur and Taksdal, 1989, p. 85).

It is rare for people who take advantage of power differences between themselves and others to themselves understand the extent of that power – what it entails for others and how it characterizes their interactions. The sailor customers are no exception. Several realize that prostitution is a question of poverty. However, none of them mentions his own position in relation to these women. Many describe the prostitutes abroad as friendlier, more willing to serve, more interested in pleasing the man. None of them sees this in terms of the power difference between a white man from a rich country and a woman in a poor country.

Per says, "Norwegian sailors have a good reputation, that's 'cause they're too nice, and they have a lot of money. They can use an average year's pay in that country on one night. Yeah, and they're less violent." On this phenomenon Prieur and Taksdal comment: "To be too nice means to be nicer that you *need to be*. The expression itself reflects in this context that also niceness is something that is included in the exchange, something that is weighed and measured in terms of its return. If one is *too nice* it's because one really has the power to give less. The basic premise for the scale that Norwegians score highly on, is differences in power and wealth. This is a condition necessary for prostitution's existence. We could perhaps, with a certain degree of correctness, say that Norwegian male culture is more respectable than many others, or that women in other cultures are more subservient and occupied with pleasing the man. However, when cultural differences are used as an explanation, the power perspective often melts into the background. We think that a more accurate perspective would be that Norwegian women have a stronger position than women in many other countries. Women in most places in the world are more powerless. If one doesn't question the power difference, then one has an excellent starting point for chivalrousness" (1989, pp. 76–7).

Single customers

A large majority of the men in this group use Norwegian street prostitutes. And they use them often. They constitute a large proportion of the buyer side in the Norwegian sex trade. It is not a mere coincidence that the single customers were single at the time of the interviews. They have problems establishing lasting ties to women. They are characterized by distance, anxiety, and helplessness toward women. Buying sex can be a flight from performance expectations and from confrontations with their own inadequacies or failures. Cato relates: "When everything gets screwed up at the disco, when your pants are too short or your hair doesn't look nice enough, then you jump in a cab and you say you're going home and then you say 'no, hell, drive down the strip.' Then you drive down and look for one that maybe looks like somebody you were in love with in 1958. You want company, the sexual is just secondary. It isn't unusual that I wake up with a woman and I don't know who she is, but I get real happy 'cause there's a woman there."

We cannot elaborate on where the difficulties with women began for each individual customer. Some brought up experiences from early childhood. Hans: "I have a little anxiety and some communication problems, that's why I don't have any other choice. My self-respect is at rock bottom, it's about zero. I had a bad childhood, a cold orphanage. I feel a little helpless as a person, life just isn't swinging. It's only in prostitution that it swings more." Others point out their appearance or small flaws. Kjetil answered in this way as to why he went to prostitutes:

"Yeah, you understand that when you look at me."

"Oh????"

"If I'm going to have any sexual contact, then it's got to be with prostitutes. Somebody laughed in my face one time, and that really hurt. I was checking out this girl, and she came over to my house a lot. Then all of the sudden one day she said "don't go imagining that I'm interested in you, you're so fat.' Since then I haven't even tried."[14]

Married customers

The in-depth interviews in the customer study revealed two different types of married customers. One is relatively young, and hasn't been married long. He is content and pleased with himself, and more or less satisfied with his wife and his sex life. But he thinks it could be a bit more varied and exciting. Variety is the spice of life, and he gets variety from the prostitutes. He's pleased with that. Why not?

Bjørn, for example, expresses a non-problematic relation to himself, to his wife, to sex life at home – and to his prostitution experiences. Over the last three or four years he's gone to the same prostitute approximately once a month: "I felt like having a real woman." Bjørn is 31 years old, has been married for five years, has one child, and makes a reasonably good income driving a truck. Taksdal asks him about his sex life with his wife – is he satisfied?

"Yes, I am, can't complain, apart from the fact that I've always fancied a slightly different type of female body. Otherwise, it's always been excellent."

"How often do you have intercourse with your wife?"

"It varies, but a few times a week at least. Two or three times."

"Does your wife comply each time you ask?"

"Yes, generally no problem."

"What about those things you mentioned – sucking you off, licking . . .

"Not to the same *extent* as a prostitute. She won't go the whole hog, to put it bluntly."

Håkon also makes love to his wife as often as he wants, about three times a week. Both partners take the sexual initiative, and his wife generally complies with his wishes. He classifies their relationship as "good." He lives out of town, but visits Oslo occasionally.

"I don't know anybody in Oslo, so it happens the easy way. That's what does it. When you go down the street, and see them

---

[14] A while after the interviews were finished the researchers received a radiant telephone call from Kjetil: he'd found a girlfriend. Though the relationship didn't last very long, he'd gotten proof that he had a chance. He hasn't been a customer since then.

standing there, you feel you want a piece of the action, at least I do."

"But you're married . . .," blurts out the interviewer.

"Yeah, but I'm spending the week in Oslo, and I'm on my own. So when I see them there, I just get aroused."

When asked how his wife would react if she had known that he went to a prostitute, Tom answers:

"She'd have been pretty pissed, I think. Yeah."

"Only that?"

"No, she'd be pretty jealous, there'd have been a horrible fight."

Magne answered the same question in this way:

"I wouldn't get anything the first two weeks at least."

A wife who's pissed off or no sex for two weeks – answers that are concerned with how it will effect *him*.

The younger husbands live in good sexual relationships, but they want some additional experiences. On this, they express few scruples. What they often want is particular sexual acts that can be bought for money. They are primarily satisfied with their prostitution experiences. They present both their marriage and their prostitution as fairly problem-free. There is nothing much to understand or explain. That's how it is.

The other group of married customers paints a totally different picture. The man is older. He may even have celebrated his Silver Wedding anniversary: at any rate, he's been married for a long time. He had little or no sexual experience prior to marriage, and was reasonably satisfied with his conjugal sex life for the first few years. However, it began to decline, and for a long period has been virtually non-existent. He brings to the prostitute all his pent-up longing for intimacy, bodily contact, and sex. He is not as satisfied with prostitution as his younger brothers. Not everything can be purchased for money. Martin says "It's a nervous strain to have sex with a prostitute. Sometimes when I'm with a prostitute, I have to think about my wife if I'm going to come at all. That's what hurts. I think about how wonderful it was with my wife. It happens quite often, if I'm with someone new. With the ones I've known for some time, and I care about, then I have no problem. But it never happens the other way around. It's so corny, like a cheap novel you'd read, something like 'but this was the woman he truly loved' . . ."

When married men go to prostitutes, it has often been interpreted as an expression of a whore–madonna concept (see for example Janus, Bess, and Saltus, 1977; Gibbens and Silberman, 1960; Winick, 1962). The man wants a madonna as a spouse and a mother for his children, and a whore for letting out his sexual needs. As sexuality is experienced as dirty, he cannot soil those he loves with this type of desire. The Norwegian customer study saw few traces of married customers who wanted to keep their wives "pure." "The vast, vast majority want a playful, horny wife. If they don't get it, they want a warm and loving prostitute" (Prieur and Taksdal, 1989,p. 139).

The women's images of customers

Acts of prostitution are often silent acts. Strangers meeting fleetingly can always talk about their jobs. That is also one of the few topics of conversation between prostitutes and customers. The possibility that the other will investigate is minimal. So they can always exaggerate a little and make themselves sound better. The women often say that they are students with little or no money. Preferably students of philosophy, art history, or sociology. The women believe that some customers like to hear these stories; it makes the whole thing a little French and piquant. The customers can, for their part, make themselves appear more important than they otherwise are. There have obviously been many customers who have operated using various celebrities' names.

As research material for *Backstreets* – before the customer study was conducted – we systematically asked the women about who their customers are. The answers fit well with the customer study, with one exception. There was thorough agreement that customers are different kinds of men in terms of age, income, and appearance. But while the customer study showed that street prostitution in Oslo is mainly kept afloat by single customers, the women insisted that the majority of the customers are married men.[15]

Eva: "The typical john is someone who's married, lives in an Oslo suburb, has three children – well, let's say two children – nothing at all wrong with these men. It's mainly the normal guy, the normal Ola Nordman who's a customer. All that stupid stuff people say about social work, about being some kind of service for the handicapped, that we're performing acts of mercy, it's just bullshit."

Some women described the customers as everything between two extremes to emphasize that the customer can be anyone.

---

[15] We can only speculate as to the foundation for this discrepancy. It is possible that because the public stereotype of a customer is a single man who can't get sex other than through prostitution, it was particularly important for the women to stress how many married men were customers.

Laila: "The johns, they're all kinds. From the worst social snobs to the decent working guys. For the most part customers are all alike. The only difference is whether they do it with or without a rubber."

Lisa: "Customers are anything from psychopaths to angels."

Pia: "Lots of them were married and had a Volvo or BMW. Then you had construction workers living at building sites, and lonely old men."

Kari: "Johns are all sorts of men, from working guys to company directors. The second group is the worst, they're so stingy. The more you have, the more you want, as they say. They're used to getting something for their money. The ones with little money and junk cars pay the most; I can get 100 or 200 crowns extra off them."

Randi: "All kinds of strange men. I've had one from the Justice Department. I get managers of shops, yeah and lots of guys who are hard up."

Randi shares Kari's view that rich men are the worst. "The worst is that sort of well-established gentleman with a nice car who wants to discuss things with you. They're the worst when it comes to haggling over the price. Otherwise there's no big difference between them."

Inga: "Most of them are working guys. Then you have those damned company directors."

Anna doesn't agree with Inga that they are mostly workers. "Mostly they're guys with suits and office jobs."

Mona also believes Inga is wrong. "For the most part they're what you'd call uppercrust types – directors, shipowners, cabinet ministers. They're well-off. Poor people can't afford it. But there are lots of students and ordinary people too."

The women give a similar impression of range in term of marital status and age. Old, young, married, single, divorced; they're all represented.

One rotten apple in every basket

The women are particularly eager to talk about one type of customer: customers with jobs that should indicate more sense. This applies particularly to doctors and policemen. These stories have the feel of wandering tales – something they've all heard about. However, some of the stories originate from personal experience.

Randi: "I've had a lot of doctors. Once I had a doctor who did heart stuff, he was in Oslo for some seminar. He was a real creep. He had three kids at home. He gave me money and a whole bottle full of Valium. Even though I'd told him I was an ex-addict. He asked if I was sure it wouldn't set me back, getting a whole bottle. Nah! I answered, I couldn't bring myself to say no to such great drugs. Luckily I managed to quit. He was fucking irresponsible, a doctor and everything. I've had two or three like that who've given me drugs in addition to money."

Mona: "I've had a cop. He even drove back and forth in his police car. He refused to drive me all the way back, because he was so afraid that some of his buddies would see him."

It's not hard to imagine customers boasting of having jobs they don't have in order to make an impression on the women. However it is a fact that both doctors and policemen are customers. In the Oslo Project, the Oslo doctor previously mentioned surfaced repeatedly as a man the women slept with to get drugs. Several times, independently of each other, two of the woman we've become close friends with told us that they had just been to the doctor's in order to trade sex for drugs. One of them has two regular doctors' offices she goes to when she plans a binge.

However, we have run across no other data that substantiate the claim that these two professions are over-represented as customers, even though the women mention them frequently. Policemen and doctors are of central importance to the women. These two professions are supposed both to protect and to control them. Yet, they turn out to be no better! It is likely that doctors and policemen are named so often because it is a way of showing us that customers *are* anybody, and that there is no reason to have illusions about the "authorities."

Images of customers

In defense of prostitution it has been argued in the Norwegian debate that prostitution provides an opportunity for sex for men who otherwise are without a chance in the "normal" sex market. The needs of distinctively ugly or disabled men have been particularly emphasized. (We refrain from commenting on the views of the sexuality of disabled or ugly people on which this argument rests.) In our material we have found little support for this argument. For the most part, the women laugh or make fun of us when we bring the subject up. Of the many customers described to us, we've only encountered one man with a wooden leg. A further four or five of the customers described are somewhat physically unusual.

The message from the women is this: the customer is an ordinary man. This contrasts sharply with the image of the customer as a deviant. Other international qualitative studies give the same results as ours (for example, Jaget, 1980; McLeod, 1982).

The Norwegian survey and quantitative studies from other countries concur in puncturing the image of the customer as deviant and atypical. Judged in relation to such usual background variables as education, work, income, and social status, the customers are as diverse as the rest of the population (see for example Månsson and Linders, 1984; Persson, 1981; and especially Prieur and Taksdal, 1989).

As a result of the quantitative studies, the original image of the customer as a deviant man has been replaced with a second image of the customer as the average man. In-depth interviews with a large number of customers have provided the opportunity to develop a third level of knowledge about customers. We believe it is of value to compare this change in the images of the customer with developments in the image of the criminal.

In early criminology the criminal was put forth as a rather deviant male. Then came large, self-reported criminal studies (see for example Christie et al., 1965) which concluded that we all commit crimes – there is no qualitative difference between lawbreakers and non-lawbreakers. Criminality was common behavior. A third level of knowledge came when the methods behind self-reported criminal investigations were improved. Though it was correct that the majority broke the law, most people seldom committed crimes. Large amounts of society's total volume of criminal acts could be traced back to a small and distinctive group that committed crimes of a completely different dimension than the average citizen. One specific characteristic that separated this group from the general public was its low social status (see Balvig, 1982). Social phenomena often follow this distribution. Many people own a little bit. But it is a small, distinctive group that controls large portions of society's total wealth. Most people drink a little. But it's a small, distinctive group that is responsible for large portions of society's alcohol consumption.

This distribution pattern appears to fit Norwegian prostitution customers. The survey revealed that a relatively high proportion of Norwegian men had been customers once or just a handful of times during their lifetime. However, the tricks aren't evenly distributed among the customers. A small group of *habitual buyers* is responsible for a considerable proportion of the total volume of prostitution.[16] Because this group is so small, it cannot be identified by traditional survey methods.

Are the habitual buyers different? Prieur and Taksdal have, as described in the previous section, divided the habitual buyers into categories: sailors, single men, and younger and other married men. The sailors do not differ from other Norwegian men. Having been out to sea isn't distinctive either, in an old seafaring nation like Norway. Buying women in the Third World is less of a break with established norms than buying women in Norway. For this group it is primarily the social situation that provides reasons for prostitution. As unemployment makes a thief, life at sea makes a prostitution customer.

We can't argue that the married men differ either, though we shy away from the thought that most marriages are as dim and grey as the older husbands described them, or that most young husbands are as lacking in insight and reflection as the young married customers seem to be.

As for the last group – the single customers – the situation is different. Among the habitual buyers it is the single men who form the "hard core." They have even *more* customer experience than the others interviewed. The single customers are different in two ways. First, they aren't particularly physically deviant or ugly – but *they feel ugly*. Prieur and Taksdal comment, "It is not the cosmetic or fashion industries alone that influence people's appearances. When you meet someone full of life, energy or curiosity, you notice it from afar. Defeat, insecurity and self-contempt also leave scars. Appearance combines with other characteristics, with one's personal history, with situations and coincidences. Too much excess weight, a skin disease, or legs of different lengths can undoubtedly be disadvantages when it comes to meeting people. But they cannot provide a satisfactory explanation as to why a man remains single. We could find married men any day who resemble in appearance the single men we interviewed" (1989, p. 88). But the *feeling* of lacking attractiveness without a doubt means something for one's courage and ability to approach the opposite sex.

Secondly, *remaining* an unmarried man can, in itself, be seen as a kind of deviance from the norm. We live in a culture with strong expectations that men and women should combine to form pairs,

---

[16] In Prieur and Taksdal, 1989, pp. 32–5, a number of calculations have been conducted to document this.

and where the definition of success for a man is also dependent upon this. Deviation from this can influence self-image. Remaining single also entails losing the learning experience that lies in the daily company of a woman. All the single men express distance towards women. And time works against these men. Many are in a cycle where the distance perpetually increases. Faltering self-confidence and anxiety toward women can be the start of an vicious circle, with a string of new defeats, and constantly sinking self-esteem. So buying sex can give a moment's relief. In a longer perspective, it is damaging – the distance from other women merely increases. Arne says: "I think you become emotionally screwed up if you keep that stuff up for a long period of time, I think so. For me to have a long-term relationship would be really, really tough."

The farther we look into this hard core of single habitual customers – those with the most prostitution experiences – the clearer the picture becomes of people who are "on the outside." They characteristically have difficulties holding down a job or managing their own finances, and they have a limited social network. Put bluntly: the more customer experiences a man has, the more different he is.

The picture of a customer as "anybody" isn't destroyed by the Norwegian interview study. It's important to retain the fact that many "normal" Norwegian men have bought sex. But the picture has gained depth and complexity – as so often occurs when we learn more about a social phenomenon. It isn't just *anybody* who has many prostitution experiences and who makes up the bulk of the buyer side in Norwegian prostitution.

3

Inside Prostitution

In it for the money: The economics of prostitution from the women's point of view

Some years back one of us wrote that there are four main reasons for prostitution: money, the sense of belonging, drug use, and an image of women that promotes prostitution (Finstad et al., 1982). A few years older and a little wiser, we are no longer particularly pleased with this way of phrasing it. Money is *the* reason for prostitution. We know of no woman who prostitutes herself for any reason other than money. We concur with Larsson's insistence on this: "Prostitution is a question of money. In spite of the banality of this claim it deserves to be repeated. Far too many researchers who work with the sex trade overlook the sex trade's money transactions. For prostituted women prostitution is a way of getting money. It is – as we've seen – only after many misgivings that they take the step into prostitution. Their reason for needing money varies" (Larsson, 1983).

In describing four main reasons for prostitution many factors are blended together. The reason for it – money. Why one needs money – drug use. That there might be something OK about this way to make money – milieu. And the possibility of earning money this way – an image of women that promotes prostitution.

But the money is fundamental. Without the money prostitution would cease to exist.

Inga describes prostitution prices like this: "It was 150 crowns for a full screw when I started. Now it's 250 for the full job and 300 if you have to take a taxi back. After midnight it's also 300. Then there's hardly any women out, so the johns are lucky if they can get a trick. At a hotel it's 500. For the whole night it varies from

1,200–1,500 up to 2,000. The usual price for a hand job is 150. But sometimes I can get 200–300 for it."

Fixed minimum prices

On the question of price, the majority answer like Inga: with a rather long and detailed price list. These prices have varied over time. But at any given point in time the various services have their fixed minimum prices. There was nearly total uniformity of the minimum prices quoted by the women. The system of minimum prices is an exact parallel to the internal solidarity employees exhibit when it comes to the question of pay. Personal interests coincide with common interest. If someone sells herself cheap, it affects all the others. Prices fall.

The women are preoccupied with this. "Not to go under the price" is one of the strongest norms on the street. Taking tricks without a condom falls in the same category. Both of these transgressions are punished.

Katrine: "Those who go below the price get frozen out."

Cecilie: "But how do you know about it?"

Katrine: "That's easy enough. Like, for example at The Rainbow. A john who's tried a lot of women for 500 crowns and who's been turned down. The price is 700 minimum. Heaven help the woman who goes with him."

This is the usual way to get caught – going off with a john the other have rejected because of the price. There are also other ways to get caught.

Mona is full of disgust for those who force the price down, and wreck things both for themselves and others. She says that those who commit this sin are often totally new or so old and used up that they have a hard time getting tricks. Mona turns a trick now and then on the street and pretends she's new in front of women she doesn't already know. She asks them what she can take for the tricks. Mona says that those who operate by undercutting prices are literally chased away.

The vast majority adhere to the norms regarding minimum prices and condoms. But the system of control isn't watertight.

Pia. "When I'm a little sick, I cut my price, and once in a while I don't bother with a rubber."

Cecilie: "What do the others say about that?"

Pia: "I haven't gotten any reactions. I don't exactly talk about it."

The punishment if they're discovered is verbal harassment, being

physically chased away, and, primarily, a far-reaching disgust from
the other women. Sometimes in conversation it was said to us about
a particular woman: "She goes below the price." With that the
woman was characterized.

One fuck = one fix

Though the prices vary over time, they are remarkably stable from
act to act and from woman to woman at any given point in time. It is
as if the market's wise invisible hand rolls the dice and they come
up the same every time. What determines the price?

Vilhelm, pusher and small-time pimp, has this explanation: "The
prices are set by the price of smack. A trick for a bag. Now it's 300
crowns a fix. In 1977 a fix cost 200 crowns, so did a trick. Then a lot
of pushers got ratted on and arrested. The city dried up, a few
months later the price stabilized to 300 a bag. Then a trick went up
to 300 too, right away. You see it in the routines too. Most of them
that are hooked need three shots a day. They've got a steady
routine. After their wake-up fix they turn a trick to finance the
midday fix. After that fix they do two night tricks, one to finance
their evening fix and one for the wake-up fix the next day."

It is true enough; the women who see themselves as hooked have
their daily routines, shifting between shots and tricks, as Vilhelm
describes. We have attempted to check the correlation between
tricks and prices over time, and it is largely true that one trick equals
one shot of heroin or morphine. The correlation is, to be sure, not as
automatic or immediate as Vilhelm describes. However, over time
the two amounts adjust to each other. This can be interpreted as a
sign of the close connection between drug problems and prostitution, and as an indicator that the proportion of prostitutes who have
drug/alcohol problems is so massive that they also determine price
levels for women who go out for other reasons.

The system of fixed minimum prices clearly applies throughout
the western world (see, for example, Borg et al., 1981; Jaget, 1980;
McLeod, 1982). But these minimum prices vary wildly from country
to country. As far as we know, there is no place in the world where
the price per trick is as high as in Scandinavia. Kari, who has
international experience, shares our assessment. "Norway is the
best place to go. Here they've got the highest prices and the cops
leave you alone. Last summer I was in Stockholm. I was nabbed by
an undercover cop after two or three weeks. London is hopeless.
When I was there I tried to work the hotels. I charged £100. The

Table 1   The price for a street trick and for a fix[a]

Place	Trick	Fix
Oslo (Nkr)	300	300
Malmø (Skr)	200	150
Stockholm (Skr)	200–300	200
Copenhagen (Dkr)	200–300	200
Hamburg (DM)	50	40
Amsterdam (Nkr)	130	30
London (£)	5	3
New York ($)	10–12	12 (speed 6)

[a] The drug prices have come from inspector Kobbhaug at the Oslo police department and from de Fine, head of Criminal Intelligence at Interpol. Trick prices are more uncertain. They stem in part from a study of the international literature, in part from interviews with customers. Because the material was collected from several different sources, an exact synchronization in time was impossible.

guys just backed off; they were used to paying £20 at a hotel. And in New York it's practically free."

What is the correlation between tricks and the price of a fix elsewhere in the western world? By assembling many different sources we've constructed table 1.

We must emphasize that the figures are inexact. However, as the illustration of a tendency, the table suffices. With the exception of Amsterdam, the similarity between the two amounts is striking. Tricks pay more than or, more often, the same as a fix costs. If the price of drugs is lower in one place than another place, the price of a trick is also lower. This doesn't necessarily have to mean that the price of drugs mechanically determines the price of tricks (or vice versa). Perhaps the table reflects a reciprocal-value relation in an illegal economy that is in turn decided by other factors like the supply of women, the supply of drugs, and the country's general price level.

The varying price of tricks in different countries might also be linked to the price of female labor in these countries and the size of the female labor market. The price of sex thus becomes a reflection of women's general economic position in the society. We haven't yet had occasion to follow up this lead. This could be another promising theme for future research.

High incomes

The pimp data (see appendix) contains information on the monthly income of 31 prostituted women:[1]

  5 earn up to 5,000 Nkr a month
  10 earn between 5,000 and 10,000 Nkr a month
  10 earn between 10,000 and 20,000 Nkr a month
  6 earn more than 20,000 Nkr a month

There is a clear tendency for those who have been prostitutes the longest to quote the highest monthly income. This is presumably due to the fact that those who haven't been prostitutes very long work more erratically and more often have other sources of income.

The incomes look exorbitant on paper. In all, 16 women say that they earn 10,000 crowns or more a month. Tax free.

Before we comment further on the pimp data's picture of the women's earnings, we will listen to what the women we interviewed say about it.

Anita: "Obviously it varies. It's a question of how many tricks you do. If I only feel like doing one trick, then it's only 300. It was easier to earn good money before. I got 2,000–3,000 crowns for the whole night. Now it's too dirty; there are too many drug whores. Then it's harder to hold to the prices. And it's harder to get a trick. When I was a pro I earned a hell of a lot. On a normal day I was out on the street from 10 to 3. Then I ate a nice dinner, often a steak and some wine. Then I went out again from around 4 or 5 to 6:30.Then I had a drink and then I was out again from 9 o'clock onwards. I kept it up for two years. I earned about 360,000 crowns in each of those two years."

Jane: "2,000 crowns is a good night. Sophie got over 3,000 here one night, even though she looks like a rat. A bad night is one or two tricks."

The prostituted women who say they are "really hooked" say that they use 1,000–3,000 crowns a day on drugs. What they *say* is one thing. Perhaps they're talking about that one day when everything worked out and they used that much. Or perhaps they're talking about what they *should have* to manage reasonably well. What they *really* make and use may well be another matter. We have witnessed

---

[1] Again: $1 = 5.89 crowns. £1 = 11.44 crowns. Or, 100 crowns = $16.98 or £8.74.

this, close up, over several years. It's an alarming fact that a small number of women use such quantities. Maybe it is 50 women, maybe it is 100. We don't know. In any case, they are far fewer than the mass figures that the Norwegian authorities operate with. But they do exist.

This image needs clarification. They don't use these quantities every day, year after year. The women's lives are punctuated by, among other things, frequent stays in institutions. It is during those periods when they're on the skids that these quantities apply: Periods that can extend for weeks and occasionally for months.

When they're on the skids, life easily becomes the hand-to-mouth economy that Ida describes. "Money, smack, money, smack, money, smack. Mostly that means fuck, smack, fuck, smack, fuck, smack." (Halvorsen, *Hard Asphalt*, 1987, p. 232). This is also Inga's daily life. Elin sounds like the wife of an overworked businessman when she complains that she and Inga have so little time to be together. In terms of some considerations it may be good that drugs are so expensive. But for those who feel they're addicted, the situation is desperate when drugs cost so much in relation to what the rest of us can intoxicate ourselves with. I smoke about two packs of cigarettes a day now. It quite certainly will have some dismal health-related costs for me in the future. But the social costs are small – among other reasons, because 40 cigarettes cost me an affordable 60 crowns a day. For those who use drugs to the large extent we are now speaking of, the alternatives are prostitution, pushing, or other criminality. Often, it becomes a mixture. Pickpocketing customers takes place along with tricks. No normal paycheck can finance this kind of drug use.

In other words, narcotic users can, at times, earn large amounts through prostitution. But this also varies greatly. What about the others, those who aren't addicted? Is there that much money to earn?

Fredrik has thought a lot about this. He and Eva started on the street because of a newspaper article about prostitution earnings. He writes to me:

"Asmervik [author of a best-selling Norwegian novel about the life a prostitute] is probably the worst person to have ever written about income from prostitution. In his book he operates on 1 million a year for Suzanne. Insane. Inconceivable that it's even possible. Where does he get that gigantic amount from? It's pure fantasy, nothing else, like that novel he threw together. Can he furnish *any* proof for an amount that even comes close to that?

"The police can be totally screwed, like that policewoman A. M. Aslaksrud Gran. Several times she's gone out and said that prostitutes earn such-and-such. Always the top amounts. Those kinds of statements actually serve to recruit to the trade. At least that's how it seems. Journalists pounce on it, pull out their multiplication tables, then sit down and figure it out for 365 days a year. They don't consider days off or low-income days. Afterwards the calculations are blown up to huge headlines in the papers. It's almost like sporting feats. If, for example, soccer king Tom Lund scores two–three times in a game, everyone thinks that's exceptional. But that doesn't mean he's going to score 20 or 30 times in ten games. Even a ten-year-old soccer fan would say it was impossible. But the press?

"This doesn't mean that I'm trying to trivialize the fact that prostitutes earn big money. But we have to continue to stick to reality. The ordinary industrious full-time prostitute doesn't earn the kind of magic amounts that the press is suggesting. For a brief period, maybe – but as yearly income, no way."

It is interesting that it is Fredrik who says this. He and Eva are probably the two in our in-depth interviews who have earned the most money and who have had the most purposeful relationship to prostitution. They have kept strict accounts over the years as to what prostitution has given them in ready cash. Fredrik also believes that it is precisely the profit that makes prostitution a legitimate "profession", there's no reason for him to downplay the profit. The parallel to Tom Lund's goals is useful. We believe this is what often happens, that someone takes a good day and multiplies it by the number of days in a year. So when Anita says that she earned around 360,000 crowns a year, she's probably arrived at that after reckoning on 1,000 crowns a day. We believe that something similar also occurs with the highest earnings in our studies on pimps. In addition, in the cases where a woman is having the pimp prosecuted, declaring high income serves her interests. The more money the pimp has gotten, the more reprehensible he'll appear.

This is not particularly sly. Most likely the women are hardly conscious of it. It is easy to forget all the days you didn't trick, especially when the past feels as if it was an endless series of tricks. And it is understandable that prostituted women have greater reason than others to exaggerate a bit when they talk about their income. Eva comments: "The women lie through their teeth about what they earn. They do it to justify something that most people think is morally reprehensible. Anything can be defended if only the price is high enough."

All in all, we believe that the reasons for over estimating income are stronger than those for underestimating it. In other words, the incomes that are given in this chapter are probably well on the high side compared to reality.

But all the same, exaggerations aside, Fredrik, too, says there is big money in prostitution. It depends on what you compare it to. Women have their *own* money less often than men. If they have their own money, it is often *less* money than men. For some women, prostitution becomes an answer to women's relative poverty in our society. In relations to most other women's income, prostitutes' incomes are sky-high. In relation to men's, prostitution income is still in the upper stratum (see also Mcleod, 1982, p. 17). This impression is obviously strengthened by the fact that these incomes are not taxed.

Easy come, easy go

Kari immediately takes the offensive when I interview her: "I am a Capricorn so you know I'm really ambitious. My father stopped giving me money when I was 16. But I wanted my degree and education. If you don't have an education all you get is washing jobs. I'm going to be a hairdresser and a cosmetologist. I'll work until I've paid for my studies and until I've saved up enough money for my own beauty parlor. And I want a house and car. I know a lady who's worked for ten years. Now she's 29. She has 700,000 in her savings account. She earned it all at The Rainbow. I'm not going to waste my time working 9–4, and wearing myself out. I can't get a student loan, because my father earns too much. I have to have money for the rent and the bills. So there's no other way. But I know where I'm going. My life's okay. It's horrible for junkies who have to prostitute themselves. They've got the choice between the street and crime once they get hooked – they should have legal quotas instead. But for people like me prostitution is okay. When you control it yourself."

Kari and I talk for a long time. I feel we are getting along well. After a while she probably starts to trust me more. In any case it comes out that the road ahead isn't quite so direct and uncomplicated. School isn't going too well. Her drug use is extensive. The beauty parlor becomes steadily more distant. "If I'd saved 100 crowns for every trick I'd turned I'd be rich now. But the money goes on taxis and getting drunk. "'Easy come, easy go.' I can make

1,000 crowns tomorrow and put it in the bank. But nothing will come of it. In the beginning I kept accounts. I stopped it after the first 30,000 had disappeared."

Nor is the role model who has 700,000 in her savings account so great when it comes down to it. "The bank book is in her fiance's name. He's like a pimp. She's 29 now and pretty soon she won't be making big bucks. Then he'll take off with the bank book and she'll be left behind."

Kari has been a Christian. She had good grades at school. She sees my flute and tells me that she once played both the piano and the flute. "There's nothing like that anymore. I have an empty life. I eat, sleep, earn money, spend money. That's it."

We have ascertained that prostitutes' earnings are skyhigh in relation to what the majority of women earn. What do they spend their money on? The goals can be divided into four categories:

- saving up capital which yields a return;
- investing in permanent properties, like houses, furniture;
- daily maintenance;
- "partying".

To work for a fixed period in order to earn so-and-so much, to buy yourself a beauty parlor or a small shop, to retire and live on the profits for the rest of your life – there are many besides Kari who have this image. In discussing prostitution over the years with "the man on the street", this notion has often been presented as typical. Like many other generalizations regarding the typical life of a prostitute, this idea is also essentially wrong. None of the prostitutes or ex-prostitutes we know has lived such a life. Nor has it surfaced in our interview material. In our pimp data there is only one case that can conceivably be placed in that category: a portion of her earnings were invested by her pimp in a large drug buy.

Investing in permanent properties is not a widespread practice either. Eva and Fredrik have invested in a house that is particularly well-equipped. Fredrik: "It's worth 750,000 crowns now." Anita, who estimates that she's earned 720,000 in two years, bought an apartment with part of the money. But she didn't manage to hold onto it in the long run. She says that the rest of the money went on "living it up." No one else in our interview material has made any permanent investments. In the pimp interviews three say that the money has gone on residences. An additional 12 pimps used the money to buy cars.

Both in the pimp material and in the interview material, the vast majority use the money for daily expenses or for "partying." It is not always easy to differentiate between these. The expenses of daily life often have dimensions that, for two middle-class people like the authors, seem almost immorally exorbitant. Katrine tells us this about the women at The Rainbow: "They usually eat out every day, buy expensive clothes; they often buy a dress and a pair of shoes a week. And they put some money aside to have frequent vacations. You know, you can get a little lazy from this kind of life. There've been people who've worked 20 years and who still work and they've earned huge amounts. But they have nothing left."

Anna says she works because she needs money for rent. But then she adds thoughtfully, "I don't use the money for that, not really. I use the money to calm down afterwards. I use it for going out."

The majority are like Anna. A number of times we were struck by how some women have a form of divided economy. Welfare money, health benefits, or other legal income is used for the straight life, like rent and bills. Prostitution money is squandered on going out, on drugs and alcohol, on lots of clothes. Dirty money is worthless. It burns a hole in your pocket and has to be used quickly. Gotten rid of. Women who rake in large sums on prostitution can have a extremely stringent budget when it comes to daily expenses. They sweat over, add up, and budget the legal money though the ends will never meet, while simultaneously thousands of crowns can be spent on "going out." This is one of the paradoxes of a life in prostitution.

Jane explains it this way. "Trick money is worthless. I'm a lot more careful with the 850 I get every two weeks on my job than with the 1,500 I make on a night. I haven't bought anything special with the money I've earned on the street. That way I avoid having reminders around when I look at things. But if I had I'd at least have gotten something for it."

High daily expenditures appear to be a common trait in prostitutes' lives, independent of national boundaries. The English prostitution researcher McLeod writes:

"Visiting the homes of women who are working on the game and relatively independent of ponces, I've found that suites of furniture, carpets, clothes, wallpaper, decor, toys, hairstyles and aperitifs are forever changing. Even if the women acquire a good deal of money under their control it soon passes into the purchase of goods which in turn have to be replaced. . . . Some women working as prostitutes accumulate substantial savings, but they seem to be very few. For many, the end product of all their determination, all their hard work and the vilification they suffer is to be locked into conventional patterns of consumerism" (McLeod, 1982, p. 57; see also Barry, 1979, p. 116).

Consumption is highly prized in the straight world, of course. And prostitution also provides a special consumer spending pattern. Many live expensively in boarding houses and hotels. Many have to eat out. Nonetheless, we interpret prostitutes' spending as something more than normal high consumption. Money becomes a drug. Spending takes on an intense, feverish character. We believe this is primarily due to the fact that the woman to a considerable degree is robbed of a number of central roles in life. The career role and the self-affirmation associated with carrying out a job provide no positive identity for "the whore". The role of family member or lover or spouse is not a part of the majority of the women's lives either. So the role of consumer takes on added importance. That's when you live, that's when you are yourself, that's how you have learned to spend your free time. Prostitutes have learned to see their bodies as objects, as capital. Money doesn't smell. But it is contagious.

Other acts also become tied to money. It is as if prostituted women live through their consumption of money to a much greater extent than other women. The central actions of daily life unfold under money's power. D., a French prostitute, says this:

"It's always need, money's behind prostitution. There comes a time when you're in a fix. And for a girl, a woman, when she's in a fix, she's always got one thing left that's worth something – her body. In the end, you can see what a woman's worth – her body. ... And then, among the girls, there's maybe a kind of looseness with money that starts creeping in, and also fear. You start developing a different attitude to money. You live 'through' money and what you can buy with it, in the same way those people live through their shop or their profession. What's important for us is spending money, the moment of spending it – it's very difficult to be really economical. So there is a kind of looseness with money. And a kind of fear. You don't feel like everybody else any more" (Jaget, 1980, p. 70).

Fast fuck: The women's view of what the customer buys

Lots of strange things happen in the world. And lots of strange things happen on the street too. But for the most part it's all about fairly simple, boring things:

Eva: "You don't know how impersonally it all happens. So I'm going to tell you. They don't demand anything from you. You take a taxi down to the street. Then a car stops – you see right away that most of the cars are down there just to have a look. You get into the car and ask him if he wants a trick. It costs so-and-so much, you say. That's fine with him and you tell him where to drive. Then down with one pant leg. The whole thing probably takes about two-and-a-half minutes. Men's sexuality is totally unbelievable, and the worst part is that they come back again and again. Of course they're often sexually excited beforehand – even if you wanted to you wouldn't have time to get caught up in it. It takes ten or fifteen minutes from the time you get into the car until you're back again. I've met some people who you wouldn't have thought needed that kind of contact. Ninety per cent of the men had a wife. I don't understand it; at home, no matter what, they'd have had a better time. I was just an icicle, wanted it over as fast as possible. I think it's unbelievable every time."

Ulla uses fewer words to describe the same thing: "They do it to empty themselves. That's all."

Several of the women express astonishment at men's sexuality, which they experience as extremely basic.

I asked Pia if she usually dresses up when she is working.

Pia: "No, but I try to put on clean clothes. It's not necessary to dress up. It works anyway. These guys aren't particular. I don't understand men's sexuality. They lack feelings. They're controlled by their pricks. They have their brains between their legs, that's what controls all their behavior."

Most of the customers are married, according to the women. A bad sexual relationship with their wives can explain their behavior:

Hanna: "The customers are basically assholes. It can't be that great for them either. I'm ice cold, I don't feel anything sexually. But I guess it's not all of them that have a sexual relationship with their wives."

Vilhelm: "If they can't eat at home, they have to eat elsewhere."

Occasionally the women express disgust at married men behaving like this. Particularly if they brag about it as well, like one of Inga's customers: "Some are completely revolting. There was one bragger who thought he was really hot shit. He told everybody he had an old lady at home asleep. 'I'm going out for a little air,' he'd told her. That's not right."

"Emptying himself:" that's the most common way the women describe it. With no more ado. But some men also want to talk. This is number two on the list of customer's motives. Anita: "Some pay just to talk. They're lonely. I feel sorry for them."

Inga: "Lots of them are really all right. They help you. They've helped women get apartments. The okay customers accept you; they can talk with you and accept you. But there are sleazebags too. The kind that rip you off if they see you're a junkie. Talking ones can be a little weird too sometimes. Right now I have three regulars; one I've had for seven months. He's the kind who only wants to talk. I'm supposed to be his daughter or something. So he talks about morals to me and lectures me. I get 300 crowns for that. There's another guy like that down there, another woman's got him."

Some customers are clearly after something more than the quick sexual release. They want their relationship to the prostituted woman to be characterized by more reciprocity. Jane say, "There are men who ask if they can pay extra to satisfy me sexually. Totally crazy!"

According to Eva, there is a story that circulates among the customers. We're not sure if it has to do with normal vanity or the dream that the impossible will someday happen. "I'll tell you a story I've heard many times, it keeps circulating. The customers had a strange notion sometimes. They would tell you about a friend, or a friend of a friend, who contacted a prostitute. Then the prostitute had fallen so deeply in love with him that he'd gotten it for free. It's incredible the number of men who came up with that exact same story."

Other men want long-lasting friendships. Jane: "Several of the johns have become interested in me and asked if they could help me, if I wanted to move in with them and stuff. Not on your life!"

Boredom in the conjugal bed. Loneliness. Desire for friendship. Prostitution can be a *replacement* for more usual forms of sexuality and companionship. But there are also some customers who do it because they're searching for something special, something that gives prostitution an extra quality other types of sexuality don't have.

Lisa: "Yesterday I had a really great-looking 20-year-old, I don't understand what he wanted with me. He could score with whoever he wanted whenever he wanted. He said it was more exciting this way."

Jane: "There are guys who like excitement. And people who are a little perverse, they think it's exciting to do it up in an office building and at the Seaman's Club."

When Anna was working in Stener Street, and customers asked if she was old enough, she lied about her age. "Sometimes they still ask if I'm old enough. Now and then I meet old customers. They ask if I can fix them up with some really young chicks."

The longer you've worked the street the harder it is to turn a trick. Customers want variety.

Inga: "If you're down there day after day, it's hard to get customers. You're not new and exciting. They'd rather have a new one every time. But there are some who want the same woman too."

The concept of prostitutes as women who, through their deep insight into physiological reactions, are able to help give birth to love, has little supporting evidence in our research. Katrine's reaction is typical: "I think that samaritan stuff is a load of shit."

Mona is the only one who believes that prostitutes are especially skilled when in comes to sex. She mentions a man who has problems with his wife and is unsure how to satisfy her. Mona is able then to suggest ideas from her own expertise. "Before I started working I didn't know anything about sex. Everything I've learned, I've learned down here. We're looked upon as people who know everything about sex. And I know everything."

Piquant fantasies, things that are different: these are also motives. Katrine illustrates men's desire for a little "thrill" like this: "I know a woman who advertised. 'Younger woman seeks well-to-do woman for morning cuddle.' She got tons of answers, but all of them were from men!"

Some men become customers because they want a woman to lend some glamour to their lives. That applies particularly to indoor prostitution.

Kari: "Last summer I placed my usual ad in the paper about young woman with own apartment seeks well-off man. I got 40–50 answers.... That's how I get regular customers. Now, half a year later I have two regular customers from that ad. They pay me 500–1,000 each time. They're easy to fool; they let me convince them. I'm maybe going to get a car out of one of them. They're proud, they feel like they're supporting a mistress. But those old, wrinkled men make me nauseous."

Katrine, who operated out of The Rainbow, says: "Now and then the customer wants to go out and eat dinner first – then the whole thing costs 1,000 crowns. When we go out and eat, the customer tries to pretend he's a man of the world." Katrine giggles, disdainful of how they don't quite fit the role. "They've seen in the movies that a man is supposed to suggest something on the menu or order for the lady. So they like to do that. They try to make interesting conversation and play man of the world, but they can't manage. They're incredibly boring. My role is to cast a glow over them, so the older men look like they're out with an attractive woman, who looks expensive. After that, we go to a hotel room."

Cast a glow over them. Or cast a glow over a gray, ordinary life. Create a little party. Buy something fancy and pleasing – a fancy woman.

Eva: "People have strange ideas about prostitution. I'll tell you a story that illustrates that. I got an answer to an ad in the newspaper from a guy who was a school principal in western Norway. He was a corpulent little gentleman. I was supposed to meet him at nine-thirty in the morning. He told me he'd been to the liquor store and I didn't think anything about it. I thought, well, that's fine, it's right in the neighborhood. But then it turned out that he'd bought a half-bottle of red wine that he thought we'd sit and enjoy. My God, it was nine-thirty in the morning, what did he think? That all I did was party and get drunk at nine-thirty in the morning? I wanted to get it over with. I had the next appointment in half-an-hour. Later, after I'd put in another ad, I got a second letter from him, saying that he'd met a prostitute once before, but that it had been a big disappointment."

Pia mentioned that she didn't need to get dressed up, since the customers weren't very particular. Other women have different experiences. Some customers have fantasy images that turn them on. The whole thing goes faster if you live up to the images. Jane is one of those who dresses up to walk the streets. She has suits or dresses, make-up, huge belts, and sexy underwear. "Lots of the customers like it if you look like a whore," she tells me. Elisabeth breaks into the conversation. "It's either one or the other. Either it's supposed to be little innocent-girl style, or it's supposed be whore-style." Jane: "Yeah, that's right. I have a little-girl style too. Then I make myself up to look discreet and innocent. And I wear a wig, the kind with bangs."

Elisabeth also said something similar: "Boy, you know how terribly shy I am about anything that has to do with sexuality. But when I worked down there, I made contact in ways I never used otherwise. It has something to do with the way you walk and your eyes, with your total body language. Not so that everybody around notices it, but that those who are supposed to notice, notice. You know, since I stopped, I haven't gotten a single invitation. [Laughs]

I don't think it's because I've gotten old and ugly. It's which signals you send out."

To look whorish. If a woman looks whorish that's a sign that she is lewd and available. Her physical appearance descibes her character and her needs. Therefore the responsibility is hers. Again we see one of prostitution's many paradoxes. When a prostitute gets dressed up as a whore, it does not originate from her own fantasies and needs. She becomes the physical manifestation of men's fantasies and needs. It is men's fantasies about women and sexuality that create the whore. The prostitute creeps into a mold created by someone else. "More than once I watched their metamorphosis before going down on to the street – an unbelievable, fantastic, harrowing metamorphosis. So I really saw physically at work the oppression they're victims of – beatings, make-up, disguises, transformation of the voice, neutralization of the body. It was impossible not to understand how my eyes, like other people's eyes, were the cause of it, and that I was responsible, like all men, the clients, the males. I was one of them, no doubt about it, no getting away from it. After that, all that remains is to come to terms with it, to relearn how to live" (Jaget, 1980, p. 188).

Some normal deviations

Most of the customers are average men who want average sexual satisfaction. The women agree on this. Nonetheless, most of them have a good story to tell when we talk about customers who are a little "special." A good story: exactly that, precisely that cynical. The women often laugh when they talk about crazy customers. That people can be so screwed up! The laughter can sometimes be mixed with shades of contempt and vengefulness. Men are stupid, but not without their entertaining sides. Detailed stories of crazy guys are willingly told and exchanged for other stories about crazy johns.

We will not go into much detail here. But we include a few instances as they can shed a little light on what certain men look for in prostitution.

Among the more bizarre desires, one is very prevalent: the desire to be little and to be dominated.

Ulla: "One time I met a john on the street with a really cool car. 'Can you be dominating?' he asked. I said I'd try but he wouldn't get his money back if he wasn't satisfied. OK, that was fine with him. I had to beat him while he jerked off. He wanted me to take his sperm in my hand when he came and pour it in his mouth. When he came, I couldn't handle it. I just slapped the sperm in his face and went to the bathroom and threw up. He was satisfied anyway and asked for my phone number."

Anita: "In general they're not that perverse. But I had a slave once. He wanted to crawl on the floor and lick my toes. It almost gave me an orgasm; it was fantastic, wonderful."

For some customers it's important to be bullied along the way. Jane: "I was supposed to oppress this guy. I was supposed to say, 'You fucking piece of shit,' and stuff just before he came. Nonsense!"

Not all customers who want to be bullied are so rewarded. Randi tells of turning a trick with a girlfriend. "He wanted to do what we told him to do. So first we gave him a paperback. He read it in a couple of hours. Then we gave him the vacuum cleaner so he could help us clean up. Afterwards we handed him a bunch of nails so he could put up a shelf for us. Then it was the book again. He took out his wallet and everything and said he was just going out to make a phone call. Then he took off. I don't see why he put up with it."

The other theme that appears repeatedly is tricks involving piss and shit.

Marie: "A lot of it's really gross. There are a lot of perverse johns, but not that much violence. There was one guy who wanted me to sit on a glass plate and shit. And he'd watch from underneath."

Jane: "He was a good-looking upper-class guy. We drove to his house on the west side. He went into the bathroom. Okay, I thought, he's probably washing himself. Then he called for me to come in. When I came in he was lying in a tub full of water. 'Take your clothes off and piss on me,' he says. 'Okay, but then I have to get extra,' I said. You get cold from a life like that."

The pornography industry, which is primarily based on men as buyers, has a number of magazines that focus completely on themes such as these. So the market is there. There prostitution market for "sinful sex" probably caters to the same needs. Lewd whores dressed as nuns, preferably with a gold cross, surrounded by other religious symbols – this type of pornography also exists. Few things express more directly how puritanism makes its mark on sexuality. Sexuality is sinful and filthy. It can be most successfully aroused when we think of sin and filth. Sin and filth titillate.

C., a French prostitute, has reflected on this:

"When it comes down to it, men need to feel that sex is dirty, forbidden, in order to enjoy it. Anyway, promiscuity, dirt and sex are the same thing for them. They can't help wanting it, but at the same time they don't want to accept it. So they arrange things so that they can despise the woman instead of themselves. When a guy asks for 'specialities,' he never blames himself for asking, he blames the woman for agreeing to it. And that goes for sex in general, for the simple act itself, and for all men, whatever they may say. Basically, to men a woman's cunt is something dirty. They make out women's sexuality is dirty, but deep down it's their own they can't stand. So they blame women, but since a wife is like a mother and they have to respect her, they find scapegoats for themselves, butts, the prostitutes. We take it for all women, for all the others" (Jaget, 1980, p. 103).

We might say that C. is a bit sweeping when she maintains that all men are like this. Nevertheless, the sort of men who do have these kinds of desires might serve to shed some light on our own sexuality. There are many of us who, not always, but occasionally, use pictures that in reality we loathe, to "turn ourselves on." For some, it may be images of power and powerlessness, dominance and submission, cellars, subway stations, oil, leather, rubber, and brutality. For others feces can be more titillating than flowery meadows. There's no reason to moralize over it, but all the more reason for profound confusion about the oppressive, distorted pictures of sexuality we are handed. All the more reason to dream of and to fight for another sexuality, both our own and others.

Customer violence

There is one "specialty" none of those we interviewed would service. While they didn't mind having masochists as customers, none of them wanted sadists. It was too dangerous. Randi: "I've never been beaten but I've gotten lots of offers. Some of them cruise around a lot down there. I've had offers to be scratched lightly, but I wouldn't dare. Suddenly they'd freak, and they'd stick the knife in you."

The women's fear is well-founded. The prostitution milieu is a violent milieu. A few pimps use violence (see chapter 6). But it is without doubt customers who are responsible for most of the violence against prostitutes. The great majority of tricks take place without traditional violence. The majority of customers are peaceful men. But not all. If the woman has had *many* customers, there is a strong probability that she has experienced customer violence. Nineteen of the 26 women we interviewed have been exposed to varying forms of violence once or, more often, many times; from slaps to rape, from confinement to threats of murder. The seven who have not been exposed to violence say they've been lucky, and simultaneously talk of violent episodes friends have been victims of.

In the Swedish report on prostitution, Hanna Olsson examined ten murders of prostitutes committed within a ten-year period in Stockholm, Gothenburg, and Malmø. The most common method of murder is strangulation. The murder cases present a picture of impulsive acts, explosive outbursts of rage, often under the influence of alcohol – the customer's impotence awaking hatred and the desire for revenge (Borg et al., 1981). We also find that same pattern in our interviews, but with fewer fatal outcomes.

Anna: "It was last summer. It was a guy I knew from before, the kind who only wants to chat. He had been on a trip to Spain and hadn't managed to get any women on the trip. Maybe that was why. Anyway it got warm in the car, and we agreed to go to his house because he had some booze. Then we got the cops after us. We drove around trying to get rid of them. He refused to drive me home afterwards. He drove into the woods. 'Now I'm in for it,' I thought. He was a complete animal. He dragged me down by my hair, tore off my pants, and stretched my sweater 'til it was ten feet long. I was scared to death. He got a stranglehold on me; he had his hand on my throat the whole time. Fortunately I was lying on top of him. I managed to relax, so he couldn't manage to rape me when he was on the bottom. I cussed him out: 'Are you thinking of raping me or something?' 'I want you to suck me,' he said. I just wanted to throw up. But I managed to jerk him off. He came right away. Afterwards he was totally confused; he buried his face in his hands and moaned, 'What have I done, what have I done?' Since then I haven't seen him. He just hit the high road."

Katrine tells of the time she and her girlfriend took a customer with them to Katrine's apartment. They were supposed to get 500 each. "When we asked for the money, he got pissed. 'Don't you trust me?' 'Sure, it's just a rule we have.' It ended up with him writing a check for the amount. But he got more and more difficult as we discussed it. Suddenly it was as if a curtain came down over his brain. He swung at me and said he could kill me if he wanted. I tried to get out of the apartment, but he grabbed me by the hair – this guy was seven feet tall and four feet wide. We both tried to take off but then he took my girlfriend hostage. Finally we got him thrown out. We were broke and frustrated and scared. But I went out and turned another trick right away."

Along with more impulsive explosions of rage, there is also another pattern of violence. A pattern which appears to involve more planning. It's connected to confinement or imprisonment. Several women tell about this.

Imprisonment gives the customer complete control. He is no longer someone on the assembly line having to try to get satisfaction within the scant time alloted. The woman is there at his disposal all the time; she has no possibility of rejecting him or his sexual desires. He can act out all his disgust and fear of women – and she can't leave him. She is no longer his employee, she is his slave. The woman no longer has any power over him; she is under his subjugation. He alone has unlimited power.

Inga: "There is a lot of violence. The newspapers write too little about it. I especially remember one time with a guy up on the east side. We drove up there in a taxi around ten or ten-thirty one night. I didn't get out until eleven or twelve the next day. He raped me many times. He tied me up and threatened to kill me. 'If I kill you and put your body somewhere, no one will be able to know it was me who did it,' he said. I reminded him of the taxi driver. 'He won't recognize me again,' he said. Of course I was afraid. But almost the worst thing was the thought of Elin – she was at home waiting and she was afraid too."

Ester: "There is violence every week down there. I was locked up myself for three days one time. I was raped and beaten. I got a black eye and my eye swelled up – I looked awful afterwards."

Mona: "I was locked in a cellar for two days. The only thing I thought was reporting him when I got out. But when I got away I couldn't remember the address."

Some of the violence is connected to the money. Either to get more for the same price or to get the money back afterwards.

Katrine: "There was a Moroccan who threatened me with a knife because he wanted sex several times. You're supposed to pay for each time. But I like my life better than money, so the only thing to do was roll over on my back. He raped me several times in a row."

The women's techniques for protecting themselves

As with the issue of minimum prices, self-interest joins with the common interest when it comes to protection against violent attackers. When we ask the women if they cooperate, this is the other instance they mention. They warn each other and watch out for each other.

Inga: "We're a group of five women who usually work together. We have a good system worked out. When one of us turns a trick, she tells someone else. That woman looks at the car and at the guy. She knows which parking place the woman doing the trick uses. If it takes too long before she gets back, she tells the cops to drive there."

Cecilie: "Has that ever happened?"

Inga: "One of us went in a white Volkswagen to the pier. She never came back. We drove down there and found her unconscious. She'd been hit five or six times on the head."

Cecilie: "But what if the woman you're working with gets a trick in the meantime, isn't it difficult to keep up?"

Inga: "Then she tells a third woman. We also give each other a sign if there's a guy we shouldn't go with. If I'm in the car and one of the women gives a signal that he's not okay, then I say, 'Sorry, I can't go with you. I just found out that there's a guy waiting for me.'"

Anna: "How you should act you learn mainly from experience. But we learn from each other too. Not classes and schools and stuff. But we tell each other stories that we learn from. And we're warned by others in the gang against creepy customers. 'Don't turn a trick with him.' But we don't have anything like writing down car numbers or something – we don't have our own security system."

Writing down the license number is important for some who work together. But it can also be a protective measure for more solitary workers.

Jane: "I've been lucky. Once there was somebody who refused to pay, and that could have turned into something. I tapped my forehead and said, 'I have your license number up here.' 'Let's hear,' he said. So I said it. Then I got the money. I memorize license numbers. I learned it as a little kid. Before I started school, there was a guy in a car who tried to trick me. He waved at me and got me to stick my head in through the car door. 'Have you seen a cock before?' he said. There he sat with everything showing. He wanted me to come along with him. Of course I didn't understand anything, but luckily my girlfriend dragged me away. Right afterwards three other girls on our street were raped in a garage. They were ruined for life. 'Remember to write down the license numbers,' my mother said to me. So I've done it from the time I was small. And I do it now. I get the license number before I get into the car."

Psychology comes in handy on the street. Several of the women mention this as important if you want to avoid violence. Like Anna.

"You have to be hard as nails, slam your fist on the table and be in charge. No one has complete control, control varies for most of us. I'm no particular expert. What I do is let them talk as much as possible – then I get a feeling for what I can and can't do. *When* I get the money varies. I come to an agreement with them after a while, not right away. I won't have just anyone. I use the car trip to check them out, I talk with them. I always ask what they do. I discuss porno with them too, but that's stupid, because I make myself sound more liberal than I mean to. But then I ask, 'Do you like those kind of weird things too?' Then I can test them a little. So I talk a lot with them beforehand."

Some of the women carry weapons.

Ulla: "I've never been attacked by customers. But I've been lucky. So for safety's sake I have a little lead weight I carry in my hand. Then I can hit harder."

Randi: "The customers look at you as something inferior. I had a pervert once. He locked me in his office at one o'clock in the afternoon. He hit me with a cane and jerked off. I'd gotten 1,000 crowns off him. I got scared after a while, with the doors locked and everything. I had a spray can with tear gas that I used. I only got him in one eye. I'm going to go to Germany and get some nerve gas – that's more reliable."

But not all dare to use weapons.

Anna: "I don't dare have a knife. Pretty soon I'd have the knife at my throat. I use my arms and legs if I have to."

Helen: "The only thing I take with me are my powers of persuasion. I have gotten to them psychologically. I say that I really understand them and stuff. That's the safest way, to try to talk your way out of it. That and doing what they demand."

Police protection?

We have shown how the women use various methods to avoid customer violence: mutual protection, taking license numbers, screening beforehand, weapons. Nonetheless, sometimes things go wrong. What do they do then?

The police are of little help. Frida, Vilhelm, and I talk.

Frida: "There's no point in reporting customer violence. R. reported a rape and nothing happened."

Vilhelm doesn't think that's strange. "You have to take the rough with the smooth."

The women claim that the police see it the same way as Vihelm.

Rape and other customer violence are things that "go along with the job," the risk associated with the job. It makes no difference if the rape occurs outside prostitution.

Jane: "U. was raped on her way home from the subway. He got a stranglehold on her and stuck his prick so far down her throat that she almost suffocated. She took a taxi down to the police station to report it, but she didn't get anywhere. The police said they lacked evidence. And that she probably had encouraged him, maybe they'd danced together earlier that night or maybe she'd slept with him before."

Ulla answers this way to the question of reporting to the police: "Yuck, the horny pigs. I can't stand them. Once I was down there, I was there because I couldn't pay the taxi driver and he drove me right to the station. I was pretty high, to be honest. They found equipment, amphetamines, and hash on me. They roughed me up. And one of them forced a number on me in the john. No point in reporting him. I wouldn't have gotten anywhere. They despise us, they don't bother to hear what we tell them. Or else it's that we don't deserve anything better when we're so stupid."

Generally it seems that women are often met with offensive reactions when they attempt to report a rape. The prostituted woman's position is even weaker.

Everyday violence

I often felt that the women talked about violence in a strange way. Bluntly, without any special dramatization, they could relate kidnappings, confinement, rapes, and death threats as if these were almost normal occurrences. See, for example, how briefly Ester describes what must have been three days in hell (p. 59). This contrasts sharply with other parts of the women's narratives, parts that are pure literary pearls of intensity and empathy.

Olsson had the same experience in her in-depth interviews: "In the interviews the women often mentioned violence in passing – 'There's nothing to say about it.' And when they talked it was in a tone of voice and in a way as if it was about quite everyday events. The way they talked in no way reflected what they were talking about." Olsson interprets this as a survival strategy on the part of the women: "The abnormal becomes normal. Since it happens to all the others it's nothing significant. Banalizing becomes a method of denying the significance of what happens in one's own life. When one lives in a difficult reality and doesn't see any possibilities for change, the denial becomes a part of a survival strategy" (Borg, 1981, p. 345). The same mechanism is reported in other rape cases (see for example Kongstad, 1981).

There is also a second and simpler explanation for the women's everyday narratives. The abnormal doesn't *become* normal to them; it *is* normal. In our material the majority of women had experienced a great deal of physical violence earlier in life as well: parents who hit, institutional personnel who abused them. Like Anita. Her parents were both lumpenproletariat. Both were murdered on the street. "The orphanage I grew up in was a terrible place. One of the head teachers was dismissed because of child abuse. We were shut up in the cellar. It was full of rats." Or Jane: "I got knocked around a lot by my father. He used to lock me into a storeroom without windows. Sometimes he hit me so hard my nose bled and he threw me from wall to wall. That made me really hard. I thought, what the hell, and went out and played after all the beating."

It's possible that the women have been so exposed to violence that they have become socialized to accept violence as a part of life. Besides, it is a question of the yardstick you use to measure. When life is otherwise characterized by degradation, humiliation, and insult, then perhaps violence doesn't appear as intolerable and extraordinary. Violence is uncomfortable, but not dramatic or unexpected. Life is no bed of roses, after all.

"It's not me he's fucking:" The women's defense mechanisms

E. works as a prostitute in France. She takes the customers to her home. She is careful to have a special customer-sheet on her bed. "Never, never will he lie on *my* bed. He'll lie on a special sheet, on a blanket, but not on the bed that's my own bed. My sheets are my property, identity, that's where I bury my head, that's where I feel me, in my own smells. This might seem odd of course, since there's contact between the clients and my skin; you'd think my skin was closer to 'me' than the sheet, but I can wash my skin afterwards. My body can be cleaned, and besides, this body isn't the same body – the one the client gets isn't the real one, it's not mine. I never go to bed at night – even if I'm exhausted, worn-out – without at least having taken a shower or a bath" (Jaget, 1980, p. 151).

How do you avoid prostituting yourself when you prostitute yourself? Doesn't the statement contradict itself? On the contrary – it is the fundamental question for prostitutes around the world. Prostituting yourself is providing something of value for money; providing something that can't be translated into the language of money without being destroyed. The vagina is rented out. But nothing more. You never get my thoughts. Not my mind, not my soul, not my mouth. There's something that is mine alone and that you'll never get hold of. I'm not really there. Prostitutes have worked out an ingenious, complex system to protect "the real me," the self, the personality from being invaded and destroyed by customers.

The most important single contribution in the Swedish Report on Prostitution is Hanna Olsson's formulation of this phenomenon – how to protect yourself. Under the heading "What is not for sale," she describes prostitutes' two defense mechanisms: not allowing touching of important body parts, and non-participation. To preserve her integrity and preserve her self, a prostitute must maintain clear boundaries. She can't allow the customer anything that has a personal meaning for her. The prostitute thus creates a clearly defined split between the "private" and the "public" self. That is how the prostitute attempts to preserve what is most important – the ability to feel (Borg et al., 1980, pp. 301–4; see also McLeod, 1982, pp. 40–1).

There is scarcely any other single theme that gives so much insight into what the tenor of prostitution is for women who prostitute themselves. We have been able to elaborate on and concretize Olsson's groundbreaking observations. The protective mechanisms are much more ingenious and saturated with meaning than described in the Report on Prostitution. And they are nearly universal. In the international literature prostitutes tell of such mechanisms – relatively unnoticed by "professional researchers" before Olsson's investigation. In our own material there are only two of the women who don't tell of a variety of methods of protecting the self.

Turning off

"You wouldn't go into the jungle disguised as a lamb; it's instinctive, but after all, it's only instinct which prompts us to put a screen in front of our real personality, to shelter it" (Jaget, 1980, p. 150).

It is well known that people in jobs with great emotional stress develop their own protective mechanisms for maintaining an emotional distance from their work (McLeod, 1982, p. 38). People who perform autopsies and funeral-home operators develop their own macabre humor. It's a matter of turning off feelings. Some prostituted women describe it in exactly the same way, as an act of will, pure and simple. Like Laila: "You have to turn off. It's easy enough; it has nothing to do with feelings and sex; it has nothing to do with pricks."

Or Lisa who is out working the street almost every day and who has up to eight customers a day. "Ugh, the whole thing is sick. I close my eyes and ears. I cut out everything to do with feelings. It's never, never okay. It would be totally different with a lover. I'll stop when I get a steady boyfriend."

One method of turning off is to consciously think about something else. Elisabeth: "Otherwise you can just stop thinking. When I was working the most, it was just to get money for drugs. What I thought about during the job was if I'd manage to score, how much money I needed and so on."

Shirley, an English prostitute: "I think it's a natural thing. We often discuss it in work and laugh about it, not laugh at the clients but the things you can be thinking of when you're having sex with a client are so ridiculous – like I'm thinking how many calories I've had that day or something totally the opposite. I'm definitely not thinking about sex. The nearest you come to thinking about sex is the money. You're usually thinking, 'It's 20, oh good.' It sounds a bit mercenary but you're usually thinking, 'This will meet that bill.' That is usually the closest you'll come to thinking about the act" (McLeod, 1982, p. 39).

Being high is an effective aid in blocking consciousness in prostitution as in the rest of society. Pia: "I have to be a little stoned before I can go through with it. I have to shove my emotions completely to the side. I get talkative and don't give a shit."

Elisabeth: "You switch off your feelings, you have to do it. You have to switch off for as long as you can. And you can only do it by drinking or doing drugs. And then you need money for drugs again. It becomes a vicious circle that's hard to get out of, if something else doesn't suddenly happen. It hardly ever does."

Kari: "I have a beer or a couple of Valium. Then I relax more. I get more open and friendly too and then I get more money."

Jane: "I've taught myself to switch off, to shove my feelings away. I don't give a damn, as long as there's money. It doesn't have anything to do with feelings, I know that. I couldn't care less whether they enjoy it or not. It's like something pulls me down. At the same time I'm telling myself, 'Jane, don't do it.' It's something cold, it's money. Occasionally I wonder why I'm there. I want to be somebody else. I want to put an end to it. I feel I'm really hopeless. It's when I'm on a binge, when I drink beer first. I need more money. Everything feels numb, it's like I need something more. I become another person. Really it's against my will. The walk down to the car is empty. Then the car's there. Then it's the trick. Afterwards, I want to blank out the whole shitty mess."

"Necking is gross – forget it"

A common way of protecting the self is to reserve certain parts of the body for uses other than prostitution. To my question as to whether there was anything the customer isn't permitted to do, Katherine makes a dramatic gesture across her shoulders "My boundary is here. He's not allowed to kiss or caress me. He's not allowed to touch my hair either. He's paying to stick his weanie in, nothing more."

And Hanna says, "Necking is gross – forget it."

The most common restriction is the mouth. I ask Kari about kissing. "Definitely not, not on your life. I cough and say I've got a cold. I don't want them around my face. But I can suck them." And Lisa, "I only do normal stuff, just a regular lay. I've gotten offers for whipping, but I just say no. I can't stand kissing either, then I turn my head away. It's revolting."

Other studies of prostitution also demonstrate the mouth's inviolability. "Like most of the girls, I personally refuse to let a client kiss me on the mouth. . . . I make a distinction between my vagina and my mouth. I think it's only normal, we've got our dignity too"(Jaget, 1980, p. 167).

I shudder to recall the hypocritical discussions we had in my Christian youth group when I was young.

Where was the line for a good girl? We all agreed that the boundary was the throat.

The mouth was permitted.

Breasts and lower down were not allowed.

In prostitution this boundary is inverted. The body parts' relative worth is reversed. Genitals are allowed. The mouth is taboo. Evaluated in terms of the usual double standard this is an odd, twisted system of values. A woman's greatest virtue is in fact her virtue. In the past especially, a bride's virginity was her most important gift to her bridegroom. The value of women as wives was sharply reduced if they were raped. A kiss now and then during the long summer nights was always acceptable, particularly if no one knew about it. In spite of various sexual revolutions this bodily value-system remains applicable. You can kiss lots of people. You only go to bed with your chosen lover.

After considering it more carefully one realizes that the prostitute's bodily value-system is nevertheless logical. Customers are preoccupied with buying entry to the vagina, in part because in everyday life women's genitalia are less accessible than their mouths. When genitals and intercourse lose their value, another value is put in their place. It's not strange that it is the mouth that is allotted this sacred position. The mouth is the organ we use in the first all-absorbing relationship we have with life, the relationship with the mother. The mouth is the means of acquiring life-sustaining nourishment. The mouth is the instrument of speech. The mouth is the most important channel of communication with other people. It is the mouth, not the eyes, that is the mirror of the soul. A study of the mouth says more about a person's mental state than a study of the eyes. Cold sores cause more immediate personal irritation that most sexual diseases. The mouth is closely linked to identity. The mouth is particularly well-suited to assume a sacred position.

"Always remember your mouth's your own. When he's shot his muck you've got to go back and kiss them bairns" (from the novel *Blow Your House Down*, Barker, 1984, p. 160).

Almost all prostituted women demand that the customers use condoms, even for blow jobs. Its rational explanation lies in the prevention of sexual disease. Simultaneously the condom serves as a physical barrier between the customer and the prostitute. Another related protective mechanism is to shy away from some sexual variations – variations that are experienced as loathsome and degrading. This applies particularly to oral and anal sex.

Jane: "I can't stand blow jobs. I had one and it was more than enough. He smelled like shit. I told him, too, when I got out of the car – 'God damn, you smell like shit,' I said. He took forever too. It's disgusting when they pull out their filthy prick." Inga: "I won't take a banana in the ass or them shitting and pissing on me. I prefer hand jobs. But it's the john who decides what we're going to do."

Anna: "I don't let them screw me. That's special for me and my girlfriend. Most everybody screws. I can't deal with it. Well, when I'm high. Then it doesn't matter what they do with me. It doesn't have anything to do with me. But not from the back. I never let them fuck me from behind."

Make it quick

Jane: "The first trick of the day is the worst. Waiting for tricks and the first trick, that's what's hard."

Inga: "The worst is if I have to wait for the first trick. Then I get nervous and come down. I ask if I can have some money, 'then we can do it afterwards.' Pretty often they go along with that. I get a little extra if I'm nice and sweet and the john is satisfied. I can wrap them around my little finger. That's good, because then I get home earlier than planned and then Elin doesn't have to wait. It's also happened that I've gone out to get money for two bags and I've come home with four bags. I'm active. I hum, I'm in a good mood. And I always wear straight clothes. Then I get tricks faster and often a little extra. And I can get 50–100 crowns extra if I listen to the john and feel sorry for him."

Ester: "I don't stand there longer than ten minutes if I don't get a trick. I get incredibly depressed and irritated. I get the urge to slash their tires. One time I kicked a dent in car."

Quick and crazy. What's important is not to have enough time to think about it. Waiting gives time for second thoughts; it's painful. But most important is that the trick itself is short. For the less time a john has, the less chance he has to be invasive. Let the contagious period be as short as possible. Rare is the prostitute who prefers a long trick. In this way prostitution resembles typical piecework, earning as much money as possible in the least amount of time.

For the woman it's smart to play turned on and to give signals that the john's performance has given her a lot of pleasure.

Ida: "They want to play big lover. 'Did you come?' 'Can I come now?' Oh yes, a long time ago, darling. Lovely. So just go ahead and finish" (Halvorsen, *Hard Asphalt*, 1987, p. 240).

Jane: "You wouldn't believe how I've learned to fake it. I've gradually learned special tricks. It has nothing to do with feelings. I say something like this: 'What a marvelous body you have. I like men like you.' But it's false. When you really care about someone, the length and thickness of it have nothing to do with it."

Ulla: "I'll do blow jobs, but never without a rubber, yuck. It goes just as fast when I suck. When I have intercourse I move around just a little. Then the customers get more turned on, so it goes faster. Otherwise, it's so gross; besides, I get sore if it takes too long. I work hard enough and am not about to let some perverse shithead use the whole darned day. I hate it. It's my job, I say."

Mona: "If it takes more than 15 minutes, then it's a long time. A half-hour is an extremely long time. You're sitting there completely dressed – you only pull down the one pant leg. I don't call it sex. I think about other things, try to pass the time, breathe a little faster to get it to go faster."

Anna: "If they ask me to talk dirty, to say such-and-such, then I'll try. I can moan and pretend I like it if I'm threatened. Or if it drags on too long. Then I moan and say dirty things if I'm in the mood for it. Or else I say, 'Come on, hurry up and finish.'"

Anita gives this answer to the question of what makes a "good whore." "Good whores are those who sacrifice themselves a little, so he can have a good orgasm. I was like that too, before. Now I can't be bothered to make the effort anymore. I only do it if there are big problems. If a john is impotent, I have to use my skills. I can appear very sensual if I feel like it. I can be shy, careful, and sweet, or hard, brutal, and indifferent."

Mona: "The nicer you are to a customer, the less time it takes." Liv Finstad asks what it means to be nice. "It means not to be impatient. And to squeeze the right places. The ones who rag at the johns and tell them to hurry up get the opposite result. It's unprofessional. My own slogan is 'take it easy.' I'll do the job. The whole thing doesn't take more than five to ten minutes."

Moving around as if you're "there," breathing excitedly, expressing your desire, squeezing the right places and creating a relaxed atmosphere – the tricks for getting him and the time to go more quickly are simple, well-tested and effective.

Hiding your true self

Prostitutes usually don't like customers to ask about their private lives. "It's none of their business." If they have to answer, they prefer to come up with a story they believe the customer would like to hear, like that of the poor student who has to supplement her student loan and who believes that prostitution is a good way to combine work and pleasure.

A number of prostitutes take their customers to their home, like E. from France did. Others refuse to have them cross the threshold.

Inga: "I won't have them here at home. Elin and I have the attitude that our home is private. A home is a home."

There are also more literal ways of hiding one's private self. Some prostitutes avail themselves of working names, all or some of the time. The customers don't get to know their real name. Some hide themselves behind wigs and special "whore clothes." This serves more purposes than just hiding the private self. The fear of being recognized or the attempt to play up to the customer's wishes for how a whore should look are good reasons for using wigs and other clothes. However, we believe that these devices can also have a second, deeper function.

Eva: "I cut all ties. I burned my clothes, destroyed the answers to my ads and got rid of the wig. I had nightmares for a long time afterwards. I had a nightmare of getting into a car. Then the man in the front seat turned and took off my hair. It was the wig I had used to hide myself."

Without making too much of the symbolism, it's probably reasonable to see Eva's burning of the clothes as primarily a ritual farewall to the identity she had assumed.

Sociologist Erving Goffman has described life in what he calls total institutions. Prisons, psychiatric hospitals, monasteries, and convents are all total institutions. People who come to total institutions come there to be changed. This change is attempted through breaking down experiences of the "civilian" self, the self-image. In the vacuum that arises a new personality is erected with a new self-image. The nun shall be liberated from all wordly ties to ascend to higher unity with God. The prisoner shall put his criminal role behind him in order to become a rehabilitated, useful member of society. In order for this to succeed, all ties to the "civilian self" must be severed. The induction rituals in total institutions serve this purpose. One gives up one's civilian possessions; the nun receives a new name, the prisoner a number. Personal clothing is turned in. The prisoner gets a uniform, the nun her chaste habit. Things that recall the old life are removed (Goffman, 1961).

Prostituted women's defense mechanisms present an interesting parallel to such induction rituals. New clothes, a wig, another name, make-up. The purpose is the same: to lay aside one's civilian self. Not in order to be a new and better person such as the nun or the prisoner is assumed to be, but because the attack on the civilian self in prostitution is so massive that the self can only be defended by "putting it away for a while." The public self, the mask, will have to do.

In the same way we can understand the extensive washing and showering after an act of prostitution. The washing goes far beyond the dictates of hygiene.

Elisabeth: "If I could have sold encyclopedias and gotten a lot of money for it, then I would a hundred times rather have done that. After all, you *sell* your body as a prostitute. A lot of times you stand there washing yourself for several hours afterwards: you wash yourself internally and you almost feel like pouring the soapy water down your throat to rinse yourself out afterwards. You *do* get dirty internally. Your head gets dirty and your body gets dirty." Washing serves to remove all traces of the public self, of the whore, so that, pure and spotless, you can again step into the civilian self.

Interestingly enough, only a few like E. go back and forth between bathing and showering. By far the majority shower. To bathe is to surround the body with something comfortable. To shower conjures up other images. Not to surround, but to remove. Hosing the filth away.

In total, the prostituted women we've interviewed have taken part in several tens of thousands of tricks. It's very very rare that they have orgasms. Roughly calculated, 10 to 15 of these tens of thousands of tricks have produced an orgasm for the women. When it happens it's more like an on-the-job accident, like a purely automatic physical reaction, devoid of feelings.

Anna: "It's happened to me a couple of times when I've been doped up. But it doesn't make it any better afterwards; more like the opposite."

Like other job mishaps it's best if they're hidden from the employer. "Luckily he didn't notice anything," says Ulla. (See also Jaget, 1980, p. 128, where a prostitute describes it similarly.) This too is a part of the prostitution game's logic. Pretend you're having an orgasm when you aren't. Pretend you're not having an orgasm when you are. Don't expose anything of yourself. Keep your distance. Emotions are to be postponed for an indefinite period of time.

Dry hustles

The customer pays to empty himself in the prostitute's vagina. Perhaps the simplest method of protecting oneself is to cheat the customer of what he's paying for, to rip him off. It's also called a dry hustle. The large majority have done it once or, more often, many times.

Anna: "I change my mind in the car really often. For example if I've said yes to a screw. Then I change my mind. I make up things so I can split. That I'm hungry and that I can't do anything before I get something to eat. So we drive to a snack bar where I can take off. Or I say that I have to get out and pee and then I take off. If it looks like I can bum some money without turning a trick, I make up some story or other and ask for 50 crowns."

Jane: "If I'm in the mood, you wouldn't have to give me a penny to cheat him. I remember one. It was actually a customer a friend of mine had. He lived in retirement housing on the East Side. I went with her. He was impotent so he just masturbated and felt us up. We got 500 crowns each for that. He was loaded with money. He had it in a bureau. He had 10,000 crowns, because he was going to buy something for his grandchild. I had these super-strong sleeping capsules. He poured us some beer. Then I asked him to get some more beer from the refrigerator. While he was out, I put the capsules in his drink, then we chugged them when he came back. He showed us an inflammation in his balls. Then he slept. We carried him into the living room. We worked open the bureau and took the money and ran. Later when we were there we said he was going to get his money back. But he'd forgotten everything, he was so senile. We didn't give a shit so long as we got the money."

Cecilie: "What did you use the money for?"

Jane: "Partying, messing around, clothes, a hotel room."

Inga: "I have to work almost day and night to scrape together enough money. It's such a bitch. If I see that a guy has a lot of dough, I try to pick his pocket. I was only reported once. The case was dismissed for lack of evidence. There are three or four at the Bank Square who just steal and cheat and don't turn tricks."

The johns rarely have a leg to stand on when they are cheated.

Randi: "I had one who was stinking drunk. He was the director of _____ [a city institution]. He was so drunk that he just kept writing out checks to me. In the end I had to help him to sign them. I let him keep one check. The day after he reported his checkbook stolen. He probably didn't remember anything. I told everything to the police. I even told them he'd sat on the fence up by the fort jerking off and complaining because he had such a little prick. They laughed their heads off. I only said what was true. I said that they should interrogate him before he filed charges. He was a terribly respectable citizen. When they called him he was embarrassed all right. He said that everything was fine and there was no problem and they should just forget the whole thing."

Randi has a good laugh as she tells me this story. She says that she's fooled a lot of johns. For instance she might take the money in advance, and then invent something that will allow her to get away, like needing to shoot up first. I ask if it's okay to cheat customers or if she has any scruples.

"Why fucking not, when you're so bad off. I try to get 300 for a screw. Sometimes I have to go all the way down to 200. Those scums'll want it for nothing pretty soon. I've worked hard enough for money. I don't give a fuck. You feel so small when you're on the street. Sometimes I have to stand there a long time, up to three hours. Lots of times I've just walked. It's really horrible. Like Friday evenings when the cars just drive by and honk and stare."

Customers to avoid

Some prostituted women protect themselves by refusing certain groups of customers. Lesbian customers are very infrequent, but there are exceptions. It says a great deal about the battle to keep emotional distance that every single lesbian prostitute we interviewed reacts visibly when questioned about whether she could imagine having female customers.

Marie answers the question about female customers thus: "No, thanks but no thanks. I have too many feelings about women. It turns into something really different. I can't deal with it."

Ellen: "I would manage to keep the same distance to a woman, but it would be more disgusting."

Pia expresses herself this way: "It would be dirtying something that I think of as good. It would be acting against myself; it would be prostituting myself."

Eight of the 26 women we have interviewed define themselves as lesbian. Because of inherent weaknesses in the snowball method, lesbians are probably over-represented. But there is good reason to believe that prostitution, all things being equal, is a less painful solution for lesbians than for heterosexual women. It's easier for them to keep the necessary emotional distance from the customers.

Some prostituted women also avoid young men. "I was with a 20-year-old once. It was disgusting. What are they doing there? Normal straight boys shouldn't have to resort to that kind of thing," says Randi.

In bad literary representations of prostitutes' lives, it's not unusual to find a prostitute waiting for her dream customer. The prince on a white steed who'll take her away from the degradation of the street, marry her, and make her an honest woman. Only one of those we interviewed had been lovers with someone who had first been a customer. This doesn't necessarily mean that there aren't more clinging to that dream. But we believe these are the exceptions, the reason lying in the very fact that the women don't *allow* themselves to have feelings for customers. Falling in love isn't part of the repertoire they offer as prostitutes. It's simply not relevant. If something like that happens, the connection must be dropped. "Once I met a baker. I liked him a lot. He wanted me to move in with him, for us to be together. Then I had to say to him that I liked him a whole lot but that it could never develop into anything since I had met him on the street," Jane tells us, sadly.

A., a French prostitute, explains it like this: "Often girls can't show this sort of interest in the guys, in the clients. They'd feel they were prostituting themselves even more, renting out a bit of their head and their heart into the bargain" (Jaget, 1980, p. 74).

Elaborate defense mechanisms: a summary

Instead of speaking of the two defense systems – not touching and not participating – as Olsson does, it is more precise to speak of a whole set of defense mechanisms that all serve the same purpose: non-participation, maintenance of distance, protection against the invasion of the self. Our material has revealed the following defense strategies:

- *Blanking out*
  Thinking of something else
  Getting high
- *Retaining physical boundaries*
  Avoiding kissing
  Avoiding touching special body parts
  Avoiding certain sexual variations
  Demanding condoms
- *Keeping the time down*
  Getting the trick quickly
  Choosing the spot yourself
  Pretending he is sexy
  Pretending to breathe excitedly
  Moaning and saying dirty words
  Moving around
  Pretending to have an orgasm
  Not pressuring the client
- *Hiding yourself*
  Not talking about your private life
  Not taking the client home
  Using a false name
  Wearing a wig

Wearing different clothes
Hiding orgasms
Washing afterwards
- *Dry hustles*
Taking off
Stealing
- *Avoiding customers you could start caring about*
For lesbians, not taking female customers
Not taking young men
Not having steady customers
Dropping likeable clients

The system is extensive and to some extent scheming and ingenious. None of the 26 we interviewed availed herself of all of these techniques. Far from it. They select a few, nor do they use all they select all the time. It depends on how they feel and if they're "in the mood." But the overwhelming common thread is this: during every act of prostitution almost all of them strive to keep a wholly necessary distance. Many apparently bizarre or peripheral details of prostitution thus acquire a deeper meaning. The strategies contribute to safeguarding one's own sexual abilities, as Olsson mentions. But the intention is more extensive that that: it is necessary to safeguard one's emotional life in its entirety, to avoid every form of closeness and intimacy. Through an extensive "pretend-you-are" game, they strive to protect their true self. In this way prostitution develops its own distorted and eerie logic. In the most famous Norwegian erotic novel, Mykles' *Song of the Red Ruby*, Burlefot's friend asks why love is expected every time one makes love. The prostitutes' message is the opposite: never love when you make love. While elsewhere in society it's seen as wrong or irresponsible to sleep with someone without having strong feelings for him, in prostitution it is wrong or irresponsible to have any positive feelings at all during sex. From the women's standpoint the sex trade is a grotesque masquerade where nothing is what it seems to be.

Is there anything good about it? What ties the women to prostitution

The prostitution debate is riddled with myths. Myths about hot and passionate whores, myths about the disabled customer, myths about prostitution as a charitable act performed by happy female samaritans. We have felt a responsibility to participate in these debates. We aren't researching for a filing cabinet, but in order to contribute towards changing society. The contrast between the rosy myths surrounding prostitution and the ugliness of its reality makes conveying this abomination a high-priority task for social researchers.

Nuances easily disappear in shallow debates. This has a price *outside* the political struggle. Social work becomes more difficult. In order to carry out useful social work among women who prostitute themselves, it is absolutely necessary to know what it is about prostitution that ties the women to it. Which aspects of a life in prostitution need to be replaced by alternatives outside prostitution, and how can social workers and others help the women to achieve these changes?

Their own boss

We have earlier described how the money is central for the women in prostitution. Why can't the women do as other people do and earn money at a respectable job? Of course, they *can*.

The correlation between a poor education, bad jobs, and prostitution is heavily underlined in the literature (see for example Schiøtz, 1980; Larsson, 1983; Persson, 1981; Finstad et al., 1982; Jaget, 1980; McLeod, 1982). The "straight" job possibilities for the majority of prostitutes often involve underpaid routine labor, inconvenient work hours, and drudgery. In other words, the jobs demand immense resources from anyone who is going to carry them out over a long period of time, as is true for most working-class jobs. But the connection between the lack of attractive jobs and prostitution is not as automatic as the literature would imply (see for example Jaget, 1980; McLeod, 1982). Prostitution is not the typical solution for young women faced with unemployment or unattractive jobs. As we have previously described, the road into prostitution is a gradual process. Women who take the drastic step of prostituting themselves have through their own experiences and the cultural milieu acquired a view of their personal value and their bodies that makes prostitution an alternative to other forms of support. It is this combination of self-image and an oppressed position in class society that can be fateful.

The women we interviewed were quite young when they started: an average of 15½ years. On the average the girls had little experience with adult working life before they prostituted themselves for the first time. That does not mean they hadn't worked.

Working-class youths, perhaps more than other teenagers, use vacations and bright summer days to acquire a little extra money. As these girls did.

As adults, the women have, at any rate, *attempted* to get a firm foothold in the job market. With a couple of exceptions they all had many jobs before the time of their interviews. This emphasizes the shifting, cyclical nature of life in prostitution. Prostitution, institutionalization to dry out, then a life on the run, more prostitution, attempts at being like others and getting a job, working a few days or weeks, prostitution, institutionalization . . . a restless cyclical dance in search of a niche for survival.

The jobs they have had are like most jobs for women – few occupations to choose among; poorly paid routine jobs with little opportunity to influence their working situation. Four types of jobs are particularly frequent: cleaning jobs, sales jobs, untrained jobs caring for children or the elderly, and waitress jobs in cafes or restaurants. Pia's working life is quite typical. "First I was the errandboy, as they called it, in an office. That probably lasted six months or so. Then I worked washing for the elderly and I've worked in a store. In between I've had short cleaning jobs. They've been shitty jobs, all of them."

Why did they quit? Anita says, "My jobs have never lasted long. The longest was three months. I can't stand it anymore. It's too fake. Like, you stand in a shoe store and you have to say to the customer 'oh yes, Madam, they suit you very well.' When they're *such* ugly shoes." Anita is 20 years old. The social welfare office has applied for a permanent disability pension for her.

Kari works as an apprentice in a beauty parlor. But she doubts she'll manage to hold out for six months until summer. "My boss is awful, he knows I work on the street, so he thinks he can treat me like shit. He keeps to boys himself – he thinks that's a completely different thing. I can't change my job either; he'd just call up the new employer and tell. They're afraid the customers will recognize me." Kari understands the political economy of her position: "Anyway, it's exploitation, that's what's going on. He earns 5,000 crowns a week from my labor. All I get is 400. He has got me right under his heel."

But even when the jobs have been poorly paid, the women generally don't stress that. They blame themselves when they can't manage to hold onto a job. Ester: "I'm too weak." Hanna: "I'm so lazy. I'm way too easygoing to work hard." Mona: "There was too much drinking and partying." Lisa: "I can't get up in the morning."

There is one thing that hurts. People talk. Life has placed the label of whore on the women beforehand. When they make an effort to find a place for themselves, they come up against the whore stigma. It's not thrown in their faces – on the contrary, the usual experience is that there is whispering and nodding in corners. This doesn't necessarily literally mean whispering – some of the women can "feel it," as Ida Halvorsen says. In the Oslo Project we ran across this time after time. Take Margrethe. She wanted to work with children and was proud and happy when she got a job in a nursery school. She had problems getting up in the morning, so we drove her to work every day for a while. The pay was lousy, and for criminologists spoiled by flexible work-hours, it was difficult to get up at 6:00, five days a week, no matter what our mood or the weather, and set out for the opposite side of the city. But not for Margrethe. She got along very well and told wonderful stories of how she was mastering the job and how the kids liked her. Until she began to "feel it." An older woman at the job gave her a weird look. After a few days Margrethe became convinced that they were talking behind her back. Nothing concrete, but Margrethe was certain, she could "feel it." No matter what we said, the fear of looking her co-workers in the eye was, after a while, greater than her pleasure in the children's affection. Margrethe quit.

Many women relate similar experiences. For example, Jane has had countless brief jobs. "But then they start to talk about me and I quit on the spot. I can't even face going to get my shoes. All over this city are pairs of shoes that belong to me."[2]

The problems are not over, even if you talk about your previous life. Even with the nicest co-workers – perhaps particularly with them – the margin for making mistakes is narrow. Most mistakes are attributed to your earlier life. Elisabeth wrote to me: "The whole time I've had this job I've walked around on pins and needles. First I was afraid the others were going to expose me. Later, after I'd said something, I was still afraid. I was afraid of making a mistake and they'd see it as a consequence of my earlier life and not as a mistake that anybody could make."

Ida and I have often talked about this: that the whole time you're being reminded of who you were and therefore who you are now. Ida: "Cecilie, if you're late for work, then you're late. Stupid, but that's that. If I'm late, Mrs Nissen thinks, "Poor thing, it's not

---

[2] Due to the climate in Norway, it is common to remove your outdoor shoes and change to indoor shoes. Thus, Jane had left her jobs so quickly that she did not even stop to collect her extra shoes.

strange that she's late. She hasn't learned to watch the time – of course she didn't need to – where she came from."

All in all the women's relationship to work is, to put it mildly, problematic. It you hang around with other prostituted women, you avoid the fear of gossip and exposure; you earn much more; you decide for yourself how hard you are going to work; life can be combined well with partying. Because at least today, it's easier just to go with the flow. It's going to be different soon.

Plague or cholera

For those who see themselves as hooked on drugs, there are not many alternatives to prostitution. Drugs are too expensive. The alternative is various forms of income-producing crime. Some people resort to prostitution because they can no longer deal with the consequences of crime.[3]

Randi has been on the street for three years. She is on heroin. She tells how she started on the streets. "I was completely desperate for money. I had been doing break-ins and fraud before I really started hooking. It was a tough scene and I got totally paranoid about jail. I have three suspended sentences and I've been held in custody at the women's prison. Now I'm on probation. I'll do anything to stay out of prison."

For some, however, prostitution and crime merge together. Some prostituted women commit a number of crimes on the side, usually by picking the pockets of the johns. Prostitution and crime become two inseparable parts of life on the fringe.

Shared knowledge and friendship

Cecilie asks Eva: "Did you get to know the other women down there?" Eva answers: "I used to talk some with them, of course. But they didn't like me; I was a bit different from them. I remember one time, a woman came over to me and started asking me questions. I didn't want to tell her where I went – I had my own special place – but I gave her some general advice. She asked if I had been there long. Her first time was the day before. A little while later, I saw her again and she knew everybody down there. It turned out that lots of the others had been at the same girls' home she had. It only took her a few days to become a part of the scene. How's a person

---

[3] Prostitution itself is not illegal in Norway.

supposed to get out of it then? After a while you can't just say 'I don't want to do this anymore.'"

We earlier described how the introduction to the street often occurs with another woman. On the street the women find their social sisters – often they've been brought up in the same institutions. For others, the downtown milieu can be a tempting alternative to difficulties in their home environment. Ester: "I didn't like school. There were just a bunch of snobs at the school where I went. So I came down to the square by the train station to find other friends than the snobs in my class. Some of it is mutual friendship. Sometimes we discuss things – everybody has to do their part. We're straight with each other."

The various milieus downtown are also arenas for leisure time. The women wander between the street, restaurants, and cafes. Many are bingo addicts. You can relax and be yourself. Nobody minds. Alone or with someone, it doesn't matter. Kari: "Whores aren't accepted in society. In my free time I can't go where the little snobs go. I go to the offbeat pubs and nightclubs – the places where there are lots of shady characters."

Though people hang around together both on the street and in their free time, there are limits to what should be talked about where. The overlapping of people in the two arenas is not complete.

Randi: "On the street we don't ask about private lives and stuff. The little there is, is chat about johns and stuff. And sometimes it's the opposite. I've met women from the street in other situations. But we never talk about the street then, it's too disgusting." The two lives shouldn't be mixed.

When it comes to minimum prices and customer violence there's solidarity among the women; it is in everyone's interest. The solidarity also finds expression in other areas. Very young girls are chased away from the district. This may not always be an expression of solidarity: very young girls get tricks more easily and, besides, they draw police to the street. But now and then solidarity is the motive for chasing them away.

Kari: "Where I go, there are 40 to 50 regular girls. I know the others enough to say hi. We chase off 15-year-olds. It's not because of the competition. But that's *too* disgusting. Men prefer kids."

Solidarity in the downtown area can also find expression in attempts to stop others from becoming addicted.

Randi: "When I was 13, I warned two young girls in the subway – they were in the middle of fixing. I showed them my arm full of needle-marks and said that's what would happen. One of them just laughed at me, the other one listened."

Jane: "There's friendship. Lots of them are really nice. We're on the same level. I don't feel like a prostitute with other prostitutes. But people can be really two-faced down there too. One time I ran into a junkie I knew. He tried to tempt me with some really good hash even though he knew I was on antabus. But there's the opposite too. Some guy I met at Egertorvet tried to trick me into my first shot of morphine. It almost worked. But another user who was my friend got really mad and told the guy, "You're not going to hook one of my friends!" The guy answered, "She's a whore, isn't she?"

When you are first addicted, solidarity gains other meanings. Then, it's central to share and share alike. There's no space in friendship for thinking that you have all the right answers. Elisabeth: "I think that friends help each other to get through what one of them wants, that is when she's decided what she wants."

A place to belong. A place where people are like you. A common front against the super-straight joggers and fitness freaks. All the same, many prostitutes are fairly critical of the milieu they themselves are part of. Laila: "What we have in common is being against society. That's what it is, being together against society. But inside it's often a rotten and deteriorating mess. You're all right as long as you can handle stuff. The environment seems attractive to outsiders, but it's often bluff, a lot of them are friends if it's worth their while."

Within the larger groups, people that say "hi," closer groups form. Inga: "I know everyone who is at the Bank Square. I don't known how many of us there are all together, but one time I counted 15. We're a clique of five women who usually work together. We're friends and we talk a lot together." The propensity of girls to find a best friend also persists. The chosen one you share everything with, from drugs to customers. The one you protect from other women on the street. Jane: "My girlfriend and I just turned a trick. She's so slow with her tricks – she takes such a long time. I go with somebody, then I do a quickie in the street. When I get back, my girlfriend's fighting with two ladies. They say we have to split. "This is our spot,' they say. 'What are you talking about?' I say. 'I've been working here for six years. I was inside and just got out, that's why you haven't seen me.' I don't know how I managed to hit on that, but anyway, they took off."

Inside a niche on the fringe of society: this applies to most of the women. But there are two other patterns: lone wolves and commuters. Randi: "A lot of them disappear for a while, and then come back. As a rule I work alone. There are some I talk to a little bit. But I'm not down there to look for friends. I want to get it over as quick as I can. I pretend that I'm standing there looking in a window and am glad as hell when someone picks me up."

It can shift with time. As a young teenager, Anna was part of the Stener Street gang. She dropped the street when she started vocational training. She stayed away almost three years. Then she slid back into it again, without quite knowing why. "On Stener Street part of the point was really the other girls. Now it's completely different. I work alone if I'm going to turn a trick. I hang around in several groups – old druggies and the people at work. You can't mix them. In some ways it's dangerous. It's too easy to change groups, to run from one to the other. But I experience lots of different things that way. I like different kinds of people."

Elisabeth, who is a social genius, moves in several very different circles. "It's not good to have several groups. Somehow it becomes too handy. But everybody has that, really. Even those who seem like they're just hanging out down there. Everyone takes a break, or else they'd be dead. It's not possible to be there year after year. If nothing else they're in an institution from time to time. People in institutions are careful about giving out their private addresses. You get afraid of being used. And everybody needs a little private life."

The environment can be all-absorbing for days, weeks, even months. But not forever. Not all the time. Nonetheless, many women experience the street life as positive – it is, at any rate, better than the alternative. It is still a temptation when the women are trying to break out of prostitution. It's easy to slide back to the environment and the rules that you know, the place where you don't make mistakes, where you aren't talked about or laughed at.

To be your own boss and to feel a sense of belonging to an environment – it's not difficult to understand how these things can tie women to a life of prostitution. But there are also other, more complicated advantages to a life of prostitution – and they are advantages primarily because prostitution is so vile. This sounds paradoxical. In the rest of this chapter we'll let the women expand on this paradox.

Power over men

Eva: "It gives you a feeling of power in your job too; everyone likes to be admired. So you could say there's something positive about the job. When I was down there and lots of cars honked at me and I could say yes or drop it. I learned fast that I didn't need to go down there as a beggar – it's the woman who decides. After a while I learned that I was the one made the rules; there were enough people to choose from. If people didn't want to follow my rules that was it."

Elisabeth: "I don't know if I can manage to explain it completely to you. It's so double. The customer has power over me, he's bought me, and I have to do what he wants. But in a way I have power over him, too. I can get him to react the way I want. I'm the one who has control in the situation, he is too busy being horny. I'm the one who has the perspective, not him."

We believe that several customers also experience the prostitute's power over them *on this level*. She controls his immediate need to be satisfied. He is dependent on her. Elisabeth does not have power over men in areas other than the sexual. She has this in common with many women. When sexuality is the woman's only means to power, she would have to be extremely strong *not* to use her sexuality as a means of power. Simultaneously, the use of sexuality as a means of power forces on women an instrumental relation to their sexuality. Sexuality is used as means to reach a goal outside of sexuality. Prostitutes' experiences here become a magnifying-glass which clarifies the general, less dramatic character of the traditional woman's role.

Acting out

Anna: "In one way there are other things besides the money. I can act out other stuff. I can be tough and rowdy, do a bunch of shit and smart off. Get them all worked up. I like it right now. But I'm not really like that. Sometimes I'm just scared."

Acting out doesn't need to be directed towards others, it can also be directed toward oneself. As Marie says: "Either it's just lack of money. Or else it's because I make myself sick. Like yesterday. Elisabeth and I had been talking about how we grew up. It got too heavy; there was so much oppression. I don't want to think about it, that I've allowed myself to be put down like that. I feel sick and have to switch over to something else. I get so many feelings. I get empty and sad. It becomes a kind of revenge against myself – it has to do with destruction. It's when I feel the pain and nausea. It helps right then. The feelings are blocked out. But it's not enough with a trick."

Elisabeth interrupts: "Sometimes there's something about the filth of it pulling me down; it's a way of walking all over yourself."

Marie elaborates: "It's different if I work just for money, or if it's to block out the nausea. I have different things going on inside me. It's never all right to go just because you need the money. But it's somehow all right to go when I go in order to be destructive. I'm more 'never mind.' When I'm in a 'never mind' mood, I'm different inside. I behave differently too. I get another tone of voice and another way of acting."

Elisabeth: "Like yesterday. You sat right down and pissed right on the street. You, you're so shy you don't normally even dare show me your breasts in our bedroom."

Marie: "After a 'never mind' trick I can feel tough afterwards. I feel I'm living again afterwards."

Elisabeth: "Yeah, I know what she means. I take that 'never mind' attitude along with me. When I go to a gay bar afterwards, I know that I've done something a lot tougher and harder than just going to a gay bar."

Elisabeth and Marie begin to bicker a little about an episode the day before. Elisabeth fills me in. "We were sitting at a cafe talking with a retired carpenter. He was really sweet. Then Marie asked if he wouldn't give us 30 crowns for the taxi." Addressing herself to Marie, Elisabeth says, "You can be a whore when you work the street, you don't need to be one elsewhere too."

Marie: "Boy, I thought you understood. I couldn't stand sitting there and seeing a guy being so nice. And then there was a guy next to him who was staring at us. He got more and more of a devilish look in his eye."

Who dares to speak of women with few resources? How many others have the courage to look so deeply into themselves?

The buyer's trick – an entire project

Many women express surprise at the customers' behavior. What's the sense in something so simple that is over in a couple of minutes? But there isn't necessarily complete agreement between what the women sell and what the customers buy. The coming together of prostitutes and customers is the coming together of two parties, each with their own point of view. Dissimilar points of view give a different quality and meaning to the content of their meeting.

During the summer of 1984 a study was carried out that takes a closer look at the behavior of customers.[4] For five days in June we had people in cars parked in two places in the backstreets of Oslo. They attempted to record the license numbers of all the cars that drove by. In addition, all contact observed between the drivers and the prostitutes was recorded. In all, 8,664 observations were made, divided among 2,834 cars. Prieur and Taksdal describe something of the mood of the district:

"You're struck first by the heavy traffic – a continuous stream of cars driving slowly by. You notice quickly that many of the same ones return, circling steadily. After a while we see some of them negotiate with some women, just a few pick up the women. While many just drive . . . .

"At lunchtime it can sometimes be completely empty of women, and there are never more than a couple out at the same time. During the evening it's never quite empty; as a rule there aren't more than a handful at a time, but we've seen up to 15 women at the same time. Few of them are picked up quickly even though there are many cars circling. The is a large turnover among the women; you don't see many of the same ones from one day to the next. All in all we must have seen over 50 different women in the course of the five days. . . .

"We tried to construct for ourselves a picture of the population of cars. We won't maintain that it was much different from the Norwegian car population as a whole. But we were struck by some extremes. It seemed that there were many expensive, good-looking cars. And it seemed that there were many specially equipped cars, typically 'masculine,' with special paint jobs, tinted windows, louvers and spoilers, or else 'cool' cars with interiors of imitation fur. Putting a lot of money into a car does not necessarily signify high social status. It can also be a part of the male image and what the man needs in the way of equipment to check out women. Some of the more absurd elements were trailer trucks, that made several trips around the streets, and a tow truck with a wreck in tow – its driver also negotiated with a woman" (pp. 86–8).

Three groups of men

PEEPERS There can be many reasons to drive a car through the red-light district. Observing cars circling around and around in an

[4] The study was part of a preliminary project for the customer investigation. The study is described at greater length in Prieur and Taksdal, 1986, pp. 86–101. The method and margin of error is also clarified.

area that has lots of empty parking places gives one reasonably good reason to believe that the cars have something to do with prostitution. In order to avoid confusion with other traffic, we limited our analysis to those who circled five times or more. There were 332 cars in all. Cars that had driven around five times or more were recorded as peepers.

NEGOTIATORS   Men who made contact with prostitutes were classified as negotiators. There were 103 men who were observed negotiating with prostitutes.

CUSTOMERS   Forty men out of the 103 negotiators picked up prostitutes. (This is a low estimate of the number of customers.)[5]

There are clearly several reasons to approach prostitutes other than the intention of becoming a customer. Let's look a little more closely at the behavior of the 332 men we call peepers.

On average the peepers spent an hour and four minutes in the district during the course of these five days. The average is pushed up by a few men who spent large amounts of time – the record is over five hours. Several of the peepers were regulars. Probably 40 percent were observed there on two or more days. The peepers don't necessarily spend a long time on the street every time they are there. They may go by, take a swing or two around and get a look, and return the next day.

103 men were observed negotiating with one or more women. They used approximately the same amount of time as the peepers; on the average, an hour and one minute. The majority of negotiators only negotiated once. But 15 of the 103 entered into several negotiations. Eighty-two negotiations did not end in an act of prostitution. Some drivers pushed their peeping status one step further: knowing you can if you want, you pull back at the last minute. But the majority probably have a simpler explanation: the negotiator and the woman don't agree on the price, act, or location.

Forty men in the district were observed as customers in the course

[5] There is an overlap between these three groups. Half of the negotiators drove around so many times they also belong to the peepers. And all the customers were first negotiators.

of these five days. The 40 customers had driven around from 0 to 34 times before they were observed as customers. On the average they drove around four or five times. The way they spent their time varied considerably. Some picked up a woman right away. The slowest man took four hours and ten minutes. On average they took half an hour. The man who took over four hours had circled 34 times in the district before he settled on a woman. The length of the trick itself varied from 15 to 50 minutes for the customers we saw returning.

Peeping

It's not a shortage of prostitutes that creates peeping. Even when there are a number of women standing and waiting for a customer, the cars drive around and around without their drivers making contact. Why?

The most obvious explanation is that the men don't find a woman they want a trick from. Arthur: "Sometimes I went down there to find women I'd done it with before, women that I liked. And if they weren't there, it could be I gave up. Lots of times I drove around and didn't do it because I didn't see anyone I liked. What I was looking for was a face and way of acting, if they seemed friendly and open."

Does this mean that the customers are picky? Prieur and Taksdal describe it this way: "Some of the most run-down women could be out the whole evening without us seeing that they were picked up. Others were picked up as soon as they arrived. One evening a great-looking woman in tight clothes come wiggling down the street, acting out the myth of the whore, swinging her arms, smiling, and offering herself. Three cars stopped immediately; two waited while she negotiated with the first. One evening we saw two stray schoolgirls seeking shelter from the rain under an underpass. Four cars stopped immediately. Of course the girls didn't quite understand why, so the men kept standing there waiting. But other times we were surprised at how long even pretty and well-dressed women could remain standing while lots of cars circled around" (1986, pp. 95–6).

But peeping can also have its own sexual value. Several women tell of men who drive around and look while they jerk off in the car. During the research project a prostitute came over to those who were recording information. She had begun to be irritated by their proximity and wondered what they wanted. After having learned their purpose, she said, "They're not all johns, you know – all they do is drive around and around here while they jerk off... I'll tell you what they're doing, they're just using up gas!" (p. 91).

Accessible women, all lined up. The market of possibilities. This alone can be exciting. Frank has picked up prostitutes on the street. But he also drives through the backstreets to take a look: "Well, it's just wonderful. I drive down to see them and then I say to myself that now I'm going to do it. A 'yes' is all you need, and then the whole thing is set in motion. Especially when you've got the money, you have every possibility, it's only that word. It's really exciting, at the same time you know that you won't do it, but you don't think about that, because of the excitement. Some of them are so pretty that it's strange you don't do it. I see girls like that at the beach too, but here you know you can have them. All you need is money. That feeling drives you crazy."

It may also be that some of the peepers experience powerlessness instead of an intoxicating sense of power. They want to make contact, but don't dare. What if they're rejected? What if they're not even good enough for a whore? The women possess goods that the men must humiliate themselves by begging for or paying for. The feeling of powerlessness towards the women can merge with a desire to see women humiliated. The women stand on the street with their provocative sin and shame on public display. The customer sits in his car protected behind glass and steel.

The number of peepers is much higher than the number of customers. This means that far more men than just the customers have a concrete, visual relation to prostitution: it becomes images on the retina that can flash by in situations and places far removed from prostitution.

We have seen that some men look at the women but then go home because they don't find anyone suitable. Other men perhaps don't dare to approach the women. We have also seen that some men find an intrinsic sexual value in peeping. But it is also conceivable that some men find sexual value in peeping as a prelude to the act of prostitution.

The recorded figures provide a new picture of what it is to be a customer of a prostitute. Earlier research on this has primarily been based on the women's experiences. For them, the whole thing seems to be a simple, hurried, two-minute fuck – basically quite a meaningless event. For the customers it's different. A trick is an elaborate project. Though the trick is quickly over, preparations take time. Being a customer is much more than paying a few hundred crowns for a speedy sexual release.

It's *supposed* to take time. The prelude is a feeling of forbidden excitement, a feeling of power, the joy of the hunt. Morten, a customer: "I think I understand the guys who drive around and around. A lot of it's that it is a taboo – that's the reason it's exciting. You see it on the Reperbahn [red-light district in Hamburg, Germany] – it's the tourists who walk around and around there, not the locals. Men can drive around and maybe feel that they're hunting prey night after night before they shoot the shot that kills. It's partly about power, the hunt appeals a little to feelings of power. In the first place it's having power over the situation, that you control your own drives and yourself. At the same time there's something that Cecilie Høigård also mentioned [in a video about prostitution] – that shooting a bear becomes a bigger exploit the longer you're hunted the bear."

Sexologists have demonstrated that normal intercourse is usually over rather quickly (Kinsey et al., 1953, p. 626; Kinsey et al. 1968, p. 580). Foreplay can take longer. But foreplay prior to regular intercouse, too, can be a solitary affair. Fantasy images or strangers can be used to build up excitement before intercourse with the steady partner. From the customer's perspective, prostitution doesn't need to seem so different from other forms of sexuality.

The experience of being a customer becomes a project that unfolds: from a thought that crosses the mind like a possibility and a temptation, to a determination that slowly solidifies – yes, I'm going to do it – to the drive down to the district, titillating rounds where the fantasy can play freely with living pictures, and finally, the release of tension. In a certain sense the customer is paying for all this: it is the possibility of a trick that lends color and quality to the foreplay. And foreplay isn't necessarily only about physical excitement. The mental excitement, using item on the streets to find the "chosen one," negotiating with several – all this makes prostitution resemble more typical pick-ups, "where one sends signals, evaluates the response and then gradually approaches" (Prieur and Taksdal, 1986, p. 100).

Seeing the customer's behavior as an entire process is something new to research on customers. In the international literature we've only seen this described in one source, in the form of an important quote in Jacobsen et al. (1982), when a man prostituting himself as a woman in a Copenhagen massage parlor is asked:

"Aren't the customers ever disappointed that it almost *always* takes such a short time?"

"No, because the process is a long one for them. It begins to simmer in their heads when they're sitting in their office, for example. Then they go and get themselves excited. Maybe they think about it the whole day, so their visit to us is actually just the culmination and conclusion. Therefore they feel that the payment covers everything from when the desire started until they come, in here" (pp. 109–10).

What is he paying for? How customers experience the trick

We have described the contents of a trick as it is experienced by women in prostitution. How does a customer experience a trick?[6] Does he, for example, know that he is fucking what Eva calls an icicle?

A great way to earn money – maybe

Sometimes it becomes obvious. The women's piecework attitude can be hard to deal with. Frank: "I was together with one, she was really pretty. It was in the winter, cold and awful. We drove out to the wharf, and she was the one who sucked and was trying. But then she started to complain, 'Hurry up already.' I said, 'No, wait a minute.' So she moaned a little, 'so fantastic.' Then she started again with 'aren't you finished yet?' So it didn't work."

Henry: "Mostly I go to the Bank Square. They're cleaner and older; I don't chase after young kids. And older women are more controlled and have more practice. The young ones hurry more; I've gotten old enough that I want a little more time. To be honest, it happens that I don't finish. 'Come on, come on, hurry up,' the younger ones say. You notice that they're waiting for the next man. It's no good saying anything about it."

Most customers are searching for something that resembles regular intercourse. Then the sexual act is reduced to a one-sided release – his. But if this becomes too blatantly clear, if affects his ability and desire.

Therefore the women do what they can to make the whole process less transparent – acting aroused, groaning, breathing, moving.

[6] A good deal of the material in this chapter originates from the Norwegian customer study: see n. 4.

The women believe that men are easily fooled. But not all men are.

Rune: "I don't believe they experience sexual pleasure from being with customers. It's just money they're after. They moan and groan like others do, but I think it's mostly acting. When you feel their bodies they don't seem especially excited. They haven't reacted to being touched down there."

Harald: "Everything like that from their side is a game, empty gestures – but I've never paid much attention to it. I know it's just a game. And I see it as completely natural; it's the way it should be."

Se some customers see through the game. A few stop being customers for that reason. Others continue. On the other extreme we have customers who are convinced that the women are part of it.

Hugo: "I think it's wonderful to feel that a woman is coming."

Annick Prieur asks: "Do the prostitutes you're with usually come?"

Hugo answers: "I've had the experience twice that they've said they don't want to. Otherwise they probably have. When a woman comes, more happens than just in the cunt – you can notice it, on her stomach and different other places. I don't think that I'm one of the more easily fooled that way. It may have happened that she's been pretending, but in that case, it was well done. If we've done it mutually, then I've come first and then she has. By then we've talked a lot beforehand and I don't think I've been fooled – it's all seemed honest and above-board."

Extremes are, as a rule, infrequent. It's our impression that insecurity and doubt on the part of the customer go hand in hand with a dream that yes, perhaps, maybe . . . .

Yngvar: "I don't know, they wail a little, but whether they come, I don't know. They're old hands at the game, after all. There are a lot of them who want to cuddle first, yes, I'd say that most do."

Frank: "It comes in waves. In the beginning I'm only interested in myself. I'm going to enjoy myself. But as soon as you are physically enjoying yourself, then something pops up in the man, I don't know if it's the lover or something like that . . . There were two of them who said to me that they started out doing it to earn money, but that it was a great way to earn money. I think that some of the young girls could be enjoying themselves, that it's good sometimes."

Tore: "I feel she's enjoying herself, but I don't actually know what is faking and what is reality. But right then I don't think about it. But anyway I suppose that she's feeling it. But the first one I was with said she had strong sexual needs, and why shouldn't she get something in return, huh? But I've often wondered what kinds of sensations they can have after working three of four years. Maybe they lose the feeling. I think of a machine, it suffers wear and tear after a while. Then I wonder if the same thing happens to women. The body is built up of fine parts that might be damaged. I have also thought about the emotional life, whether it can be kept up or whether it's lost. I know of course that if you work with heavy things in you hands that you lose the feeling in them, and then you can pick up hot things without burning yourself."

And Ragnar: "Yeah, you can never be totally sure. But when you've come, then she asks me if it was good for me and I answer 'yeah' and then I ask her the same thing. Or she asks if I came and I answer 'yes' and she says, 'I came too.' Women's orgasms – that's something men can't really understand . . . . It can't just be for economic reasons, there must be other things that come into it, too, that they have strong sexual drives and want experiences."

Not fantasy *or* reality. But fantasy *and* reality at the same time, ambiguities and possibilities, layer after layer of contradictory images. It's not at all strange. Few of us have crystal-clear, noncontradictory images when it comes to the more meaningful areas of life.

And it is precisely in the sexual domain that fantasy is used to deepen and strengthen reality. During regular sex, pictures can flicker through the brain – pictures of other people, other sexual organs, other situations. At any rate, for some of us, now and then. The boundary between fantasy and reality is erased. Fantasy becomes a part of the experience. A comparison with masturbation makes it clearer. There *is* a market for inflatable dolls and for realistic vibrators. Sexuality is laden with pictures and imitations. Prostitution can be understood as the last link in a chain of always more lifelike and expensive aids to fantasy: from pornographic photos to mechanical simulations of a woman's sex, to peep-shows and finally to prostitutes. Pretending as if . . . get turned on by the sexy breathing and passionate movements of the prostitute . . . be *in* the fantasy and *in* the images. Afterwards it's not easy to sort out which is which.

What the customer wants from prostitution

Men's motives for going to prostitutes are as countless as grains of sand. They go because they desire to be dominated, to dominate, to have anal sex, oral sex, to experience excitement, to be passive, to be active, to get deeper human contact, to be an infant, to be a parent, to scold and be scolded. And much more. The research literature is full of long lists of motives, yet these are not very illuminating. Prostitution is about men's sexuality.

It's important to maintain the connection between men's "usual" sexuality and men's experiences with prostitution. Prostitution magnifies and clarifies some of the characteristics of masculine sexuality (see for example Høigård and Finstad, 1988). But if the end result is exclusively a catalogue of the entire panorama of motives for male sexuality, then the structuring of the question and the methodology are wrong. If one primarily wishes to chart men's usual sexuality, then prostitution research is a detour and a skewed point of departure. The approach to the problem should probably be different. Why do some men seek out prostitutes in order to act out their sexuality? What qualities does prostitution have that make some men specifically choose prostitutes?

The customer's relationship to women outside of prostitution, as we described in chapter 2, helps us part of the way down the road to obtaining insight into why men go to prostitutes. But only part of the way. We also have to look at what prostitution gives the customers. There were few of the interviewed customers who didn't see some distinctive and attractive sides of prostitution that made them choose *precisely this way* to get sex.

SEXUAL ACTS Many customers placed emphasis on particular sexual acts when they described what they wanted from their prostitution encounter. The acts aren't necessarily very deviant or special; most are acts that very many would see as common elements in a varied sex life. The similarity with the type of sex shown in pornography is often obvious, and some also state that trying out some of the ideas they got from pornography is what prostitution is all about. Tom, a young husband, says: "Yeah, I've been able to try out what I've read and seen. I want french, and to come in the mouth and between the breasts. I don't get that from my wife. There's more I'd like to try, that I've seen in movies. There was a Japanese movie, and there was this guy who got a soap massage from three girls."

When these men tell of what they got out of prostitution, they emphasize what happened, the actual acts, and what the woman looked like.

NEW WOMEN   To have sex with *new* women is also an important motive. This desire is easy to fulfill in prostitution. Johan had never been with anyone but his wife before he started to go to prostitutes: "It's because of curiosity – when a guy stayed virginal in his youth, then he thinks of what he missed by following the straight and narrow. It's fairly banal and simple, getting a little excitement with different figures. . . ."

The customers place a particular emphasis on the pleasure of a new woman; they aren't especially preoccupied by being with a specific woman. Most important is having this type of experience. It seems to be a matter of dreams, of expectations as to how life should be – and how they themselves should be. Present as a backdrop to their activity is a picture of masculinity where experience with many women is central. As with Mads, who tells of all kinds of "flings" and rounds it off with "Gosh, what kind of a guy is it you're talking with? This all seems pretty bad." He pretends to be embarrassed, but his proud smile is poorly hidden.

A DIFFERENT AND EXCITING EXPERIENCE   Many say that they were curious as to what prostitution entailed. It *is* different to just pick up a woman and then pay to have sex with her. For a number of customers there is also something more. Prostitution can play on the myth of the horny, pleasure-loving whore, and on the picture of women who are experienced and skillful in sexual matters. Vegard gets turned on because the women walk the streets, they're "bold."

"A bold girl dresses a little temptingly, that's it I guess, that she walks, and she looks horny out on the street, right?"

"Is it because she walks out on the street?"

"Yeah, yeah, that's exciting."

Frank, too, talks of excitement: "It's the excitement, that I drive there and find a girl who's good-looking. It's exciting to stop and to hear her steps in high heels. When you've discovered her and – well, the most exciting thing is when you've parked the car and then, maybe in the rear-view mirror, you see that she's coming over, you hear the steps – oh my god, that is so exciting that I get . . . I start to sweat just thinking about it. Then you drive 50 meters down to the bridge at Akershus. And you do it there, so you could be discovered any moment. It's so exciting."

Curiosity, excitement, and a desire for totally different experiences – these motivations are far more prevalent among the majority of the customers than among the customers in the interview material.

They are motivations primarily reserved for those who have only been customers once or perhaps a few times (see for example Månsson and Linders, 1984; Winick, 1962; and Holzman and Pines, 1982).

EASY AND NON-COMMITTAL The features that are described above deal with which experiences prostitution can give the customers. The features that remain are more geared towards what it is about the relationship to the prostitute that makes prostitution attractive.

Almost half of those interviewed pointed out that prostitution is an easy and/or a non-committal solution. Of these, over half are married. For those who are married, their appreciation of its easiness and lack of commitment goes hand in hand with not feeling unfaithful – at least not so unfaithful as they would have if they'd had a relationship which engaged them emotionally. Also, prostitution is easier to hide from the wife. And prostitution is direct. Thomas: "If you want to be sure to get a number, you know what you should do. Get out of sitting in a bar and acting important and talking all night, and then there isn't any more. Then you're stuck."

Prostitution is full of paradoxes. Though the majority say that they go to a prostitute among other reasons because it is non-committal, they also say that they want warm girls, increased intimacy, and understanding. They complain that prostitution is cold or say that they get an empty or negative feeling when they realize that it is only money that lies behind it. This is particularly true for the older husbands.

ONE-SIDEDNESS Paying for it also makes it legitimate to lay aside any expectations of one's own performance. Enjoying oneself is in focus. Some customers want to avoid the mutual sex act: they strive only for a climax. Ivar's pleasure in the fact that his needs come first resonates in his lyrical account of a massage parlor: "It was obvious that she was a professional, that she was trained in what she did. It was, you might say, carried out in a way that male customers would find agreeable. They give you a wonderful massage, they're really good. There's music there; they massage you up and down your thighs, scratching and tickling you. They start tentatively and then get increasingly more intimate. Stroking your thighs, over the stomach and chest and soaping your penis. It's beautiful. They're well-groomed and refined and agreeable. They're not sloppy junkie whores. They're professionals. They don't get any pleasure from it, it's just routine. But it's a professional routine." And Jack says: "'Cause she's a prostitute, I dared to let myself flow more with the sexual energy. I didn't need to pretend like anything, or be considerate to her. I abandoned myself to my own needs and satisfied myself, I wasn't the one who was supposed to give her something."

Sexuality can be tedious. Demands for profundity, stamina, sexual technique, for intimacy and emotions – it's good, for once, to relax with a self-centered climax where the only demand that's made is on the wallet. For some men, prostitution plays the same role as masturbation within the framework of a steady sexual relationship: as something a man (or a woman) occasionally experiences as simply pleasurable, neither dramatic nor ecstatic. Orgasms are so many different things and they all have their distinctive qualities.

Martha Stein, who observed customers with call-girl prostitutes through a one-way mirror and a peep-hole, also noted this one-sidedness. She described the majority of the customers as passive and interpreted this as the customers abandoning the active male role. She felt this was encouraging for women's emancipation. Prieur and Taksdal comment on it in this way: "This doesn't ring true. The customer can take a vacation from demands regarding initiative and activity, but he simultaneously takes a vacation from mutuality. It's impossible to escape from the masculine role and into the customer role. The customer role is a masculine role, regardless of whether the service he is ordering is to hit or to be hit. It is his desires that are in the center, it is his desires that dictate her behavior" (Prieur and Taksdal, 1989, pp. 174–5).

Prostitution can give the customer answers to totally conflicting desires. Prostitution can give both self-occupied pleasure, and the feeling of intimacy and warmth. The reason is that one of the most important things that the customer buys is the power to interpret what is sold – the power to live in his illusions.

AVAILABILITY   Arne explains what a woman being "whorish" entails: "Willing, that you can get a hold of her, also, that you know that you have her. That you can grab her and pull her with you." He has control.

Prieur and Taksdal comment on the meaning of one-sidedness in this way: "The district becomes a symbolic arena, where the man can obtain confirmation that women exist for men. They stand here displayed and available. The men themselves sit protected behind armor and glass. When wants and dreams can't be realized in everyday life, then it's good to know you can turn to the district. 'You don't need to come home one night and be disappointed. You can sleep with a girl if you want,' says Frank. Therefore, it's important that prostitution exists even though you don't make use of it and perhaps also for many more than those who would even dream of making use of it. They all have emergency exits. Going down to take a peek is like checking that the door isn't locked. It's reassuring." (1989, pp. 177–8).

Natural differences?

Availability is fundamental for all prostitution. Women can be bought, that's what it's all about. All customers make use of this, whether they formulate their motives as wanting particular sexual acts, new women, or exciting experiences, or because they also have a unique attraction to prostitutes as an embodiment of availability.

Availability elicits a feeling of power. But prostitution's availability is also a picture of many men's feelings of powerlessness in relation to sex. Many customers interpret sexuality as something men take and women have. The male sexuality is experienced as a strong unmanageable urge. It is different for the woman: she can mete out sex as goods in an exchange.

This view of sexuality's genderedness sheds light on the connection between usual sexuality and prostitution, on customers' views on prostitutes, and on important tensions in the masculine role. We will now take the opportunity to let a man give a longer presentation of his experiences as a customer. Arthur's account contains several of the themes we have dealt with in the preceding pages.

Arthur has a managerial position in industry, is married, and has three children. He is handsome, a little on the short side, with beautiful dark-blue eyes. He was a customer on the streets for many years, often several times a week. At the time of the interview he had stopped.

"The first ten years of marriage were very bad sexually. I can say that I missed warmth. Occasionally, for some strange reason I thought that I could find a substitute down there. There was something or other I was looking for. I didn't go for women who had attractive figures or faces. What I went by the whole time, was if they were sweet and nice. Most of them were hard-boiled. There were times I liked someone, and then I drove down there to look for them. And if they weren't there I might drop it. I talked a lot with the girls, especially with the regulars. But there were a lot of them who could barely be bothered to answer if you talked to them. I decided that talking was pretty important too, it's a form of contact too. I didn't pick up women who seemed cold and unwilling. But I didn't pick them up just to talk; it was a combination of sex and contact and warmth I was after. As a matter of fact there were several times when the sex was completely immaterial, but I did want value for my money in a way; after all I'd driven down there for sex.

"Luckily, I've managed to get rid of that bad habit now. I realized eventually that it didn't give me anything, that's why I quit. I've asked myself why I went there. I decided after a while that it was my fault that my wife and I were so bad in bed. I'd read too much about sex and about sexual techniques, up one page, down the other. But that's totally secondary. There was no warmth in our relationship. It took a long time before I figured that out and it took a long time on the street before I asked myself why I was there – maybe three years. Besides there was the excitement of going down there. My wife found out one time, fairly early on. She took it quite hard. Her reaction was that the worst thing about it was that I had paid for it. I believe she's been suspicious of me a couple of times since then. I'd never dare discuss it with her – she'd have a violent reaction if she knew I'd been down there more or less regularly.

"I'm not exactly afraid of a divorce, but more of destroying a relationship that's a little tough to begin with. There are other things that make it difficult at home as well. But it's easier going with prostitutes than being unfaithful with women friends.

"It's much worse having a relationship on the side. This way it's casual – it happens today, but it's forgotten tomorrow in a way – though of course it's not. Some people believe that anything is acceptable, but neither of us is an adherent of open marriage. A diversion now and then doesn't need to mean anything. But a regular relationship – I wouldn't dream of that, it has to do with feelings. I'm afraid of losing my wife, even if there are times when I think that divorce is the only solution. But I don't want to; I think a person should try as long as possible. It's as much for her sake, not just for the kids. I believe that the nuclear family is the only work-able solution for the time being, and we must try to preserve it as long as possible; after all, there are no norms for anything any longer. The simplest and easiest solution is to drive down and get laid. My interest wasn't great enough to put any work into getting involved in an affair.

"On the average there's a big difference between men and women when it comes to drives. Nature hasn't made them the same, men have a greater urge. Even in a good relationship it comes up and then it's clear that the man wants to more often than the woman. The first ten years of our marriage when we had intercourse I'd often wondered why the hell I was doing it – it was such a failure. I insisted in order to impress my will on her. I don't do that any longer, I don't do that just to get laid; she has to want to too, or there has to be some kind of contact at least. You have to know a person to get something out of sex, that's what I've realized.

"I've thought a lot about why I went down there. It became a kind of obsession, like smoking, driving there to see if there was anyone there. Often I just drove home again. The problem with our marriage for me is that I miss warmth and love outside the bedroom. I don't think she understands that. We don't talk much together. I have problems opening up, she doesn't understand what I think and feel. I don't know if I understand her any better, well, maybe in terms of some things. She knows me, she knows how I react, but she doesn't understand me. Our temperaments are so different. She says things like, 'Now get out of the house and go do this and that.' That's especially important, that the tone of voice in our home isn't a pleasant one; when I was growing up we never used that tone. It's really a sharp tone of voice. But I guess it's the usual tone in the town she comes from. She uses that voice with the kids too. The kids and I get hurt. I love my wife, I know she needs me too, but at the same time I often wish she'd go to hell. She's incredibly hot-tempered and irritable. She can go around being in a bad mood for several days and then I get in a bad mood and don't say anything, and then she gets in a bad mood again. During those periods there's no point in even touching her. My body doesn't fit her rhythm. My needs are stronger than hers, they've always been."

Cecilie later asks Arthur if he thinks he's handsome. Arthur answers: "No, absolutely not. I have dry hair that sticks out in all directions; my teeth aren't particularly attractive, and then, I'm short and skinny. That's bothered me all my life. I don't believe my wife finds me attractive. She did say I have beautiful eyes, without me having seen that myself. But it's been many years since she said that."

It sounds unpleasant, all of it. If Arthur's wife had told us about her life at home, we would probably have heard another story. Perhaps we would have heard about Arthur's lack of responsibility for the children and for doing the dishes, about how exhausted she was at the end of a tiring day, about Arthur's lack of understanding of that and his monomaniacal desire for sex, about Arthur's reticent behavior. The point is not to divide up guilt and innocence, but to present Arthur's experience of the marriage. This experience gives us several ties that connect prostitution and established relationships. Let us expand on this.

If Arthur is correct that men, for the most part, want to have sex more often than women, there is nothing that certifies that this is *natural* in a biological sense. There is no pure, true sexuality, unaffected by other people and society. The sexuality of human beings is indeterminate, amorphous, capable of being shaped in many ways. The real, undisturbed and pure human sexuality does not exist, Referring to the behavior of chimpanzees and other primates is hardly sufficient in understanding the end product.

"Object-relations theory" is the unfortunate label for a direction in psychology that is steadily gaining ground (see for example Dinnerstein, 1976; and Chodorow, 1978). This direction is relevant to our work because it suggests answers to the dissimilar experience of sexuality that the two sexes have. It would take too long to give a thorough presentation of the arguments here. We will content ourselves with saying that these theories attempt to explain how men, through their early upbringing, are given a vulnerable sexual identity, and have difficulties in acknowledging feelings of dependence and intimacy. Intimacy that isn't linked to their sexuality becomes a threat to their fragile sexual identity. Boys are thus socialized to translate feelings of intimacy into sexuality. Girls' psychological development is different. Women don't have the same problems with their sexual identity as men. Instead, women have problems with defining their boundaries, with differentiating between their own conflicts and needs and others' conflicts and needs. Women more readily define themselves through their relationships with others than men do. We are socialized into two sexes on a collision course – a collision between the masculine anxiety for intimacy and the feminine proeccupation with feelings and interpersonal relationships. The result, stated more directly, is the male fixation on sex and the female fixation on soul-sharing. Perhaps the typical conflict between her "lack of desire" and his "inability to talk about the relationship" finds much of its psychological resonance here.

This earlier socialization chimes in almost too well with men and women's later experiences. Many men don't understand why women complain about being seen as sex objects. "Well, I think it would be great if anyone looked at me as a sex object." Most women have probably heard that or something similar from men. And in one way of course it is great, for women as well. At the same time being a sex object is something that is probably experienced differently by women and men. Why?

Historically women's societal position has been largely tied to raising children and taking care of the home: to the reproduction of humanity. The value of a women has been her value as a reproducer. To be a woman, to be womanly, continues to be tied to reproduction and sexuality, to a completely different degree than manliness is for men. Few of us have an uncomplicated attitude to this: who wants to renounce her womanliness? The courting game at times dramatizes these problems in the woman's role. Being chased after, being a sex object, becomes a confirmation of our value. Women become something men make use of or don't make use of. Women's sexuality becomes a stock-in-trade she can portion out to men or not. Women's sexuality becomes like a gift to the man, something he receives or something he must beg for, pay for, or take by force. The woman owns something the man wants. This gives her power in this area. But simultaneously the sexual game labels women as exploitable objects, devoid of individuality. This confirms that we either lack something or are deprived of something. We are deprived of individuality. In its place we receive a function: she who satisfies male sexuality.

For men the role of sex object implies the opposite. They get something in addition to what they have. In addition to the resources at their disposal by virtue of participating in various spheres of life – work, politics, art – they are acknowledged to be sexually attractive. The different ways men and women have been socialized give the same phenomenon – that of being a sex object – different meanings for the two sexes. And if object-relations theory has any validity, then this difference is being strengthened. For men, being a sex object is a positive confirmation of their vulnerable point, their sexual identity, while women receive negative confirmation of their vulnerable point – their identity as a unique individual.[7]

We have moved far from Arthur's view of sexuality as something

---

[7] Influential theories about sexuality and control of sexuality are most often neutral in relation to social gender. In the above discussion we have indirectly argued tht theories of sexuality must be gender specific.

pure and spontaneous, something nature has arranged so badly that men want sex more often than women. It's important to recognize that a number of customers in committed relationships experience such a difference in strength of desire. We have suggested an alternative explanation to the biological. The socialization of girls and boys into women and men, and the two genders' different conceptions of what it is to be a sex object, can create the experiences of differences in desires. Some men solve this by becoming customers.

Bad can also spring from good

Whenever we begin to explain phenomena that are regarded as social problems, as social ills, we are quick to point out other ills as causes. Juvenile crime comes from broken homes, unemployment, lack of a social network. Schizophrenia comes from distorted forms of communication in the family. But does it need to be that way? Beethoven's great musical production in his last years is occasionally attributed to his deafness. And everyone knows that hungry writers are the best. So we know that something good also can come from something bad. Yet it can be reversed as well: something bad can come from good.

Prostitution is something bad. The behavior of customers is bad too. This is a common theme in recent Scandinavian prostitution research. In Swedish studies the activity of the male customer is explained by the masculine sex role, upon which little positive is found to say. The stereotypical masculine sex role is described as a role where the central idea is to treat women as anonymous beings. This attitude makes women into instruments that men can use to affirm their masculinity in front of other men. Men use women as a way to achieve a feeling of being a winner, a conqueror, a man among men (see for example Månsson and Linders, 1984, pp. 21–51). We see it in a slightly different way. *The masculine sex role is far from unambiguous.*

In sociology a role is usually defined as the set of expectations the environment has towards a person in a particular position. For some roles it's probably more fruitful to define them though the tensions and contradictions that characterize the role.

The masculine sex role is a difficult role to fill – the expectations of what it means to be a man are contradictory. It is clearly part of the masculine sex role to be the active agent, the conqueror, the one who decides and provokes. The isolated orgasm, independent of who gives it to him, and the use-and-discard mentality with regard to women are *one* part of the masculine sex role. Thus a part of the man's sexual training becomes a qualification for being a prostitution customer. There are probably few men who haven't at one time or another – perhaps often and to a completely different degree than women – practised and acted out these oppressive characteristics connected with the male sex role. But this doesn't mean that these characteristics are the usual or dominating characteristics of male sexuality. For men, as for women, positive sexuality has to do with warmth, love, trust, the wish to be loved and to love as a whole person. The oppressive characteristics are more like sediment, *within* the role; acted upon occasionally they stand as a contrast to other aspects of the male gender role.

To be a man is also to be a person the woman can lean on, trust, be protected by. To be a man is also to be an adult, realizing one's responsibility for home and family. Don Juan conforms to some expectations of the male gender role, but is in strong contrast to other expectations of the same role. In his account Arthur strongly emphasizes that it is wrong of him to abandon his wife and children. They need him. Henry's description shows how contradictory traits of the male role exist side by side: "It can all be summed up by saying that the wife was operated on for cancer. They took out everything, so she has no more feeling down there. My body needs it. If I'm going to get some of it, I have to pay. What else is there to do? My wife feels nothing. I gotta have living blood, to say it like it is. I love my wife and I won't divorce a woman because of sickness. We have too much together, you could say we've grown together. I'd never let go of that lady."

It is time to weave the threads together. Some men live in committed relationships and simultaneously visit prostitutes. We have briefly outlined some psychological and sociological suppositions as to why women and men have different relationships to sexuality. In some relationships this expresses itself in the man experiencing a stronger desire for sex than the woman. But an unsatisfied need for sex is not sufficient reason to end a relationship. It breaches, among other things, the convention that men should be women's stable, reliable sources of support. Going to a prostitute takes care – no matter how inadequately – of certain sexual needs that have been created by the male gender-role. At the same time prostitution doesn't entail an emotional betrayal of the partner. Going to a prostitute, is in other words, *not being particularly unfaithful*. Paid sex with publicly available women has nothing to do with emotional

engagement. Understood in this light, part of the customers' behavior is an adaptation to a life situation where contradictory tensions in the male role become apparent.

The customer – a loser in the male role

The male role contains many conflicting features. But there is one
feature that, more than any other, defines the male role: men's
dominance over women. We will forgo discussion as to the historical foundation for this dominance. More important for our purposes
are the changes in form that this central characteristic has under-
gone in our time. As an ideology – far removed from being practised
– equality stands firm. This, however, has not let to men relin-
quishing power. Power has become more concealed. The Norwegian
psychologist Hanne Haavind formulates it in this manner: "A modern woman can do everything, but only as long as she does it
subordinately in relation to the men she deals with. The chances for
her being positively acknowledged as a woman, i.e. that she will be
appreciated, are greatest if she herself contributes to this subordination appearing as something other than subordination.... In other
words, men and women have a joint project in making his dominance and her subordination appear as something else – as their
personal relation to each other.... What is new is that the obviously
aggressive or authoritarian men are more easily rejected as personally unsuccessful examples of the male sex ... A positive masculine
man dominates not only because he is a man, but because he has
personal qualities that are appreciated by the woman or the women
he deals with" (Haavind, 1985, pp. 38–9).

In our time, men's dominance over women is expressed as a
demand that women's subordination should be silent, invisible, and
self-chosen in relation to the men we associate with. Not all men
are successful in this type of subordination of women. Prieur and
Taksdal comment in this way: "But when he succeeds, it is a much
greater victory. It is seen as defeat if he uses force or money to
obtain control. A successful man can tolerate being together with a
woman with her own will and her own judgments. He can tolerate
her judgments of him – they are, of course, positive. But what of
those who don't succeed in this? They can resign to their defeat – or
seek out women who don't come forward with their own desires
and judgments. A prostitute is paid to be this type of object" (Prieur
and Taksdal, 1989, p. 230).

The prostitution customer shares the generally accepted goals of the male role: objectification and subordination of women. But the customer uses normatively illegitimate means to obtain this goal: instead of women's "voluntary" subordination he resorts to money's tyranny.

4

After Prostitution

"I've left my body on the street:" Delayed damage to the women

In chapter 3 we described the extensive defense mechanisms used by women in prostitution – defense mechanisms which served to maintain emotional distance between the women and their customers. Scandinavian prostitution research is almost unique in its focus on, and systemization of, prostituted women's ingenious and elaborate defense mechanisms. Using this as a starting-point the next logical step in the analysis of prostitution is: do their defensive strategies work? What are the long-term consequences of trying to hide yourself and turn off your feelings?

These are questions of the greatest significance. They have scarcely been dealt with in earlier prostitution research.

Katrine believes the defense mechanisms work for her. "Prostitution has changed me. Some people think that's negative. Personally, I think it's positive. I get fancy and stuck up. You see, I know what I'm worth. And that's a lot more than simple wine whores, who go to bed for a night on the town with cheap red wine. Not to mention married women. They sleep with their husbands one night a week so they can be supported. It's vulgar, it really is, and so hypocritical. They are the first ones to attack what they call the 'bar sluts.' I get particular when it comes to men, I despise them more quickly. I think that's positive. My girlfriends talk about this one and that one being cute. Then I can cut in and say, 'Yes, that's on the surface though. What do you think his underwear looks like?' That makes their jaws drop."

Katrine is alone in evaluating the consequences as positive. The others feel more like Brenda in Pat Barker's novel:

"Gradually Brenda learned to switch off. She never managed to do it completely, there were always times when she came back and found herself lying under some sweating hulk, and then she wanted to cry out in horror, No, it isn't me.

"But these times became less and less frequent. If anything, she started to have the opposite problem. She couldn't switch herself on again during the day. Everything seemed to be happening on the other side of a dirty glass. But it was worth it: a skin had formed over her mind, and she was free inside it" (Barker, *Blow Your House Down*, 1984, p. 47).

Apart from Katrine there was one other woman, Frida, who initially said she felt that it was possible to separate prostitution from her emotional life. Later in the interview she told us that things were really not quite so simple: "You get a little damaged emotionally after a while. What gets to be difficult, is bringing in your emotions." *All* the other women we interviewed described how, in the long run, it was impossible to preserve yourself and your emotional life when you prostitute yourself. In other words only one or two of those interviewed did not report definite difficulties in maintaining the separation between the public and the private self. It becomes difficult to find the on-switch. It becomes difficult to wash the grime off the window.

Part of the price paid for prostitution is the destruction of the woman's sex life. Eva has a simple and understandable explanation as to why. It becomes, quite simply, boring:

"The worst is that it's not as bad as people make out. Down there you block it all out, you get totally sexless, that's a fact. But you can't function with a man, it won't work. It just won't work. So Fredrik and I didn't have a sex life at all. That's the price you pay when you go there, but it's not something that you can suspect beforehand, it's something that just comes gradually. After a while you notice that it bores you. Imagine you're a baker, who bakes bread all day. Then you come home and your wife says, 'Come on Hans, bake me a loaf.' I can't take doing the same job when I get home . . . I'll tell you something. When I got home at night, I just spread out the hundred crown bills on the table. I had them wadded up in one of my pockets, the rubbers were in the other one. I didn't go around carrying anything, I didn't need to use any makeup down there, I didn't want to have ID on me, and I didn't want anybody taking a purse with the money away from me. So I put the hundred bills down in my pocket. Then I came home and folded them out, stacked them up. I'll tell you, I couldn't remember then the men I'd been with, not even on that night. I couldn't remember them at all. I just remembered the cars. They weren't people to me, they were hundred crown bills. But even though I looked that professionally at the whole thing, it affected my sex life. It is something that touches you anyhow."

We are in our bodies – all the time. We *are* our bodies. When a woman prostitutes herself, her relationship to her body changes: it is as if she is moving through life inside a boil or clothed head to toe in a rash:

Anna: "Prostitution changes the girls. I feel it myself. I notice it in terms of guys. I can't be together with a guy when I'm going down there. I feel like everything about my body is just rotten. I can't stand an okay guy using my body in the same way. Then I tell him to go to hell. I would throw up if a boyfriend started with sick talk. I was together with this guy for a year and a half. But it won't work now. I'm not keen on a sexual relationship. My body's not mine when I'm going down there. Anyway, I'm such a shit. There's nothing that's okay with a relationship when I'm such a shit."

Marie was involved in a lesbian relationship with Anita before Marie herself started working on the street. She talks about the experience from the other side: "It was tough for Anita to make love. Sometimes I had to say 'Hey, remember, I'm not one of your johns.' Her emotional life got ruined. I didn't think about it, that she had johns, I just didn't have any feelings about it. I just thought about how she was ruining herself. We were together about a year, but it got too heavy. Anita lived in her own world. She was cold, in a way."

The ruined sexual life is accompanied by deep self-contempt. Anna has a rotten body and feels that she is a shit.

Elisabeth's description is somewhat similar: "Sometimes you feel that it's you that has the control. You're the one that makes yourself available, it's you who takes the money. But fairly often you stand there and throw up afterwards, you feel like a piece of shit. You can't look people in the eye, and it's not the kind of thing that you go around and talk about. I can talk about lots of other things – I can talk about drugs, that I've been locked up and that I've done burglaries, but I don't talk much about the prostitution that I've done. There's a bunch of people that I deny it to. It's like it's the worst of anything. Maybe you've beaten up people and you've been totally criminal, but being a prostitute, it's the worst of anything. You're a piece of shit, and you make yourself sick. You get pissed off, and you get bitter. You don't see it as sex, you see it as something awful, something disgusting. I've thrown up during sex, just started throwing up without thinking that it's been awful. It's just happened."

Adjusting to life outside of prostitution by renouncing lovers is both a defense mechanism and a damaging by-product of other defense mechanisms used within prostitution.

Anita has solved this in her own way: "I can't change my feelings. Well, yeah, I've become more 'never mind.' I don't give a shit. In terms of men, my sex life's ruined. Even though I'm living like a lesbian, I'm not really a lesbian."

Some count on finding their way back to their sexuality when their prostitution is a thing of the past and their memories have faded. B., a French prostitute: "I don't think I could stand a guy now, I couldn't stand him twenty-four hours a day, because I don't want that anymore, at least not for the time being. I think I'd have to stop for a while, and then maybe later I could start going out with men again. I stopped going out with men from the moment I did my first client; and yet before, I liked going out. I liked going to night-clubs – I loved dancing, for instance. Now I've become very wary, I don't believe anything I'm told. So whatever he might tell me, I'd be thinking. 'It's all a pack of lies' or 'It's only to get me into bed.' I think back to the job, because I know now that the only thing that matters to men is bed. That's primarily what they're looking for, that's what bothers them more than anything. . . . and since there's money to be had for doing that, I'd say to myself, 'If it's just for that, why not make him pay like the others?' After I've stopped, when I meet a guy, I think that I'll revert to the old ways, but I'll want to get to know him first. I won't have sex with him straight away" (Jaget, 1980, p. 89).

Eva and Fredrik managed to "revert to the old way:" "It passed after a while. It straightened out." Not everyone manages to straighten out. The wounds are too deep, the injuries too extensive.

One sign of damaged sexuality is that the ability to have an orgasm is lost. While interviewing them, we did not ask the women if they were capable of having an orgasm, so we have no quantitative information on this point. We have only our impressions. In time, we grew to be friends with a number of women, and the women were also each other's friends. The loss of the ability to have an orgasm turned up frighteningly often in conversions. It appeared to be a common experience. There is also another factor with regard to these conversations that is alarming. While bitterness and contempt towards men can be understood in light of these women's special experiences with men, it appears as though their public identity continues to grow as if it were a cancerous tumor, eating away more and more of their private selves. Boundaries are erased. Strategies and techniques adapted while in the world of prostitution obtain a place in the lives they live outside of prostitution, and after prostitution. In terms of their partners, the women felt that most lovers were incapable of accepting their lack of appropriate physical reactions. There were only a few, partners of an exceptional caliber, who could live with this without themselves experiencing major emotional difficulties. This is probably not an unreasonable assertion. As a means of protecting her partner the woman "pretends" as she did in prostitution. He mustn't be wounded. Orgasms are faked. Simultaneously, she experiences her playacting as troubling and demeaning. She has to get it over with quickly. Suddenly she is back to rapid breathing and erotic pelvic movements. Several of the women related, with bitter irony, how they convinced their lovers that he was the first one to give them an orgasm since they left prostitution. He was immensely overwhelmed by the miracle.

It is easy to understand how these reactions can create a breeding ground for self-contempt, contempt for a partner, and for the relationship in its entirety. The fact is that it is more difficult than usual for women who are ex-prostitutes to establish normal stable relationships.

The shifting boundaries between "whore" and "me" can also be difficult in less demanding and crucial situations. Eva: "At the time I differentiated very strongly between M. [her real name] and Eva. I'll tell you a story about when I was at a restaurant with a girlfriend. There was a man at the next table who asked if we could do him a favor. He was leaving on the train a little later and would like very much to have some company. In the beginning he was taken with my girlfriend. I changed personalities, I began to ask him about his work, told him how smart he was and so on. They can never resist that, so he was infatuated with me the rest of the evening. I went into the role of Eva. That's the only time I've done that in my private life and I felt terrible afterwards."

Eva is adept at making the separation between M. and Eva. It is harder for most of them. And it is not just feelings connected with sexuality that are destroyed. One's entire emotional life is attacked. The vocabulary tells it all. Corrupt, hard, and cold are words the women use to describe their own emotional lives.

Hanna: "It's a rotten life. You get hard and cold." Inga: "I'm bitter, I think I've been abused. The whole way I am changed, I get more tired and burnt out. My feelings are changing too. I've gotten hard."

Randi: "I was warned beforehand. They said I shouldn't start down there. But I can never learn from other people's experiences. I had to feel the misery myself. I'm completely paranoid. People judge you the minute they hear it. When you're getting to know some people you think are pretty okay and they get to hear about it. You have to put your feelings away. Don't think about it. I was warned beforehand. I don't dare even think about having a boy-friend. Because then all I think about is what I did yesterday. Frustrating. It's not healthy to hang around down there. It's never all right. If you can just sit and talk, then you don't get those scruples. But after all there's only one in a hundred who only wants that. I wish I hadn't had this experience. I've gotten incredibly cold. The mentality, you've got to get rid of everything from down there, I can't use that experience for anything."

Like Randi, many are paranoid that someone will find out that they prostitute themselves.

Eva: "That was my big nightmare the whole time – being recognized. It was the worst thing about the street. The other method, through ads, was much safer in terms of that. You could screen the customers. Imagine, once I got a long letter from my brother-in-law, answering an ad . . . It would be a catastrophy if anyone found out about that now. If anybody knew about it, I don't think I'd get any pleasure out of the things we've bought. It's like sitting on top of a big mountain packed with gold. What's the sense of sitting there if no one will come to you? . . . You somehow start to despise yourself when you work down there. It's completely normal. But it shifted back and forth some, it varied how I saw myself. And you can imagine how my self-respect used to swing. If you start despising yourself, it's not long before others start despising you. Even if I didn't want to admit to myself that I did it, it was obvious anyway . . . It's totally different [life then and life now]. It takes a lot out of you to go around being constantly afraid. And when you've bought what you want, what happens then? Besides that you're changing the whole time, without noticing. You tell yourself that you're just as good as everybody else, but you don't really think that; you're as good, but with a minus sign attached. Imagine if my girlfriends knew what I did, or imagine if they knew here in the restaurant what we're talking about, what I had been, then I wouldn't be welcome here. Fredrik sees it differently; he believes that if a person is just successful then everything's fine, but I don't agree with that. When I have girlfriends over, they can tell others how well I live. And then others will say, that's not so strange, think where the money came from, think about what they did before. Then I might as well be sitting on a cardboard box. They say money doesn't smell, but it depends on whether you know that it smells. I think we're all a lot more dependent on other people's esteem than people would want to admit and believe."

The accounts of self-disgust are numerous. Anna said she was a slut. Elisabeth feels like a piece of shit. Pia puts it this way: "When you're a junkie you don't need food or friends or sex. You don't need anything. But I'm disgusted by myself afterwards when I've worked down there. I only feel indifference towards the customers, I don't despise them. I am the one I despise afterwards. I eat my heart out every time I think of it."

Other people's disgust, the disgust of the customers, and self-disgust merge into a great wave of hopelessness.

Elisabeth: "They see you as a whore, never as someone they'd want to know, never as someone they'd want to be seen with. It's fine with them to come to work and say they've been and had a fuck and paid such-and-such a price, and they exaggerate a little when they tell how great it was. I'm nothing and no one they feel connected to. I'm only the genitals that they use. They could just as well have bought themselves one of those blown-up dolls. I'm nothing – I'm just a piece of shit. Some men pay me to sit and talk with them afterwards, but they would never look at me in the street. There are lots of customers who just pass right by you in the street – they have never seen you before. Not because you've got 'whore' written on your forehead, but because they know I am and so then I'm a piece of shit. Then I'm no one there's any reason to know. I'm only someone they can screw."

Ida sums up her reactions like this: "I was wrong. Once again. It's not easy money. I can't point to anything in particular. Not any single thing, or a single customer. Not the violence. It's more the regular, daily tricks. It's so massive. Small, unnoticeable scratches. Each scratch helps to separate my body from my head. The feelings I had, I've left behind on the street. They're lying down there.

"Sometimes I dream of being like I was before prostitution. Of feeling something. It's like I've burned up a hundred crown bill and am trying to make a new one out of the ashes. It's gone. Only my head belongs to me now. I've left my body on the street" (Halvorsen, *Hard Asphalt*, 1987, p. 206).

Elisabeth wrote to me, having read the first draft of this book. "It's embarrassing, but sometimes I long to be back on the street. Cecilie, please don't imagine stupid things like a life of irresponsibility and so forth. It's not that. What I long for is the laughter, yeah, that's it – not being alone, not having to pretend. And here comes what you wrote with just that, about longing to not have to *fool* people. I don't know whether I should laugh or cry, but the feeling comes back over and over, not all the time, but over and over. The feeling of pretending to be nice, smart and proper, when you know inside yourself it's not true. You're none of these things. You're lying right in people's faces when they believe that. The exams you take, you don't have any right to them.

"I want to write some shameful secrets. I use tampons all the time. Even when I'm not having my period. It's because I'm afraid of stinking. I never sit too close to people. I wash my ears ten times a day because I'm afraid guck is running out of them. Cecilie, along with *not* wearing nice clothes, *not* covering up blemishes or *not* using make-up to hide ugly or spotty skin. Everything is always double. Wanting to accept my filth on the one hand. Letting others see it, letting them be disgusted by it, letting them help me get rid of it. And on the other hand, being the pure, odorless person who stands up at meetings and says smart things. And you're so fucking marvelous because people are thinking about my 'old life.' At least for me what you've written is true. Imagine being so divided that you almost write with two pens and speak with two tongues. But that's just the way it is."

Finally, we'll allow ourselves a longer quote from Randi. In a remarkable way she puts into words what can happen to the women's emotional lives in the long run.

"I've got a certain amount of hatred. I'm vindictive, it's a big handicap for me. I feel so split up. I'm also a person who has a job and an education. The other person speaks very cultivatedly. I can't glue the two people together into a whole that functions normally.

"I can fall in love. But it soon reminds me of the street. That they are in some way only with me to satisfy themselves. I start hating myself, my body is filthy. I can get incredibly depressed by it. And when I'm in love I also become suspicious. I think of all the happy, decent girls. I'm just a disappointment. The people I'm with, they never smile. They get depressed. My relationships never last long.

"I've had two abortions. Because I didn't want a child to grow up in my hell. I have to get out of it first. But it would have been nice to have someone to give something to. Then I'm living. But I can't manage to accept anything. Praise is just fake. I don't want to be bought. I don't want to accept presents from anyone. After all I was bought the whole time. I don't want sympathy either. It's just fake. 'No reason to feel sorry for somebody who caused her own problems.' That's what they really think. Now I'm just playing games with myself. I have an incredible amount of aggression inside me. Some people say it's easy money. Easy. If you really think about all the shit, about all the oppression you've swallowed....

"I've tried suicide a lot of times. One time I took 50 milligrams of Truxal [a sedative, available only with prescription] and then 40 milligrams. I drank some wine and laid down. I woke up at the hospital. I was really furious when I woke up. As if I'd done it just so that people would feel sorry for me. The psychologist there was a real nitwit. I signed myself out after a few days. All I had was the feeling of having disturbed them in their job. When I drink, I hate myself. One time I stabbed myself in the chest with a knife. I kept pressing on it. It was as if I sat and dreamed. It got too painful. But in my subconscious I know that I'll go through with it next time. I'm too much of a coward when I'm sober. I shouldn't drink. The only revenge I've had is that I'm going to get even with myself.

"Actually, I want to go to school and start all over again. I don't know what kind of school that should be. I could imagine working with people, yes, with young people. That would be really all right, I think. But I'm not used to making plans. I live one day at a time. My plans have always been just vague ideas. What happens, happens. It's a little too little to fill my life with just myself. If I'm just going to live this one life, it's a little too little. When I'm going to cut out the other. To be honest: I'd like to move away from the city and be completely different. Be satisfied with myself, like myself. That's the only goal I have. It's more important than a lot of furniture. Be satisfied with myself. Now I hate myself. That's the only feeling I have left."

Prostitution as violence against women

Prostitution tears feelings out of the women's bodies. The necessary emotional coldness from the public prostituted "self" spreads and takes possession of large portions of the private "self." It is virtually impossible for the women to have a love life while they're tricking. This effect can last for months, even years after prostitution itself is a thing of the past. The relationship with a lover is destroyed by his natural desire for a sexual relationship. Memories of countless, faceless customers pass like a panorama before her and make sexuality loathsome to the woman.

Other feeling are burned out of the body as well. Prostitution is a game played with feelings. Pretend you are favorably inclined, absorbed by the customer, hot, and excited – when you feel indifference or perhaps revulsion and hatred. Feelings have their price; they can be translated into money like all other wares and are therefore, ironically enough, *worth* nothing in themselves. Feelings are an illusion.

Self-respect and self-image are also destroyed. To sell oneself "voluntarily" – that is the worst, most offensive thing a woman can do. It's frightening to see what a burden of guilt, shame, and self-disgust former prostitutes drag after themselves for years. No matter how well they master their new lives, at the core they experience themselves as really only "cheap whores." That friends maintain otherwise only shows that the woman is able to fool new friends. We ourselves have been brought to the edge of despair several times by this.

The impoverishment and destruction of the women's emotional lives makes it reasonable, in our eyes, to say that customers practice gross violence against prostitutes. The customers' *physical* violence against prostitutes is also massive, and it too, of course, creates anxiety among prostitutes. When prostitutes talk about the damages of prostitution, however, it is not the traditional violence they emphasize most. Fractured jaws heal, split lips will mend. Even anxiety dulls and fades. Regaining self-respect and recreating an emotional life is far more difficult. It is as hard as reconstructing a hundred crown bill from ashes.

The women's reactions to prostitution have many similarities with the reactions of women who are survivors of incest and rape. The feelings that are burned out of the body, self-disgust, guilt, the sense of being a split personality, are also central in descriptions of these women. Information about such types of emotional reactions to these forms of sexual assault has attained the status of established facts. This is not true in prostitution research. This is *new* knowledge.

This is the most important discovery we've made in our research. In our prostitution research we have confirmed and elaborated some impressions we had at the outset – like our impression of the women's total social destitution. Other impressions have been weakened or disproved – like our ideas regarding pimps (see chapter 7). But the idea that prostitution constitutes a gross form of violence was not even a vague impression before we began our work.

Prostitution is a central, classic subject within the sociology of deviance. A massive bibliography is easily composed. In retrospect, it is striking how absent this unquestionably central theme is in previous research. There are indications, in quotes from prostitutes (see Jaget, 1980, pp. 88, 101, 107, 145, 150–2; McLeod, 1982, p. 41), but they have been overlooked.

The reasons why the map is uncharted this area are in part the same reasons that "the general public" does not consider the concept of violence when referring to prostitution. One of the most important aspects is difficulties in conjunction with the concept of "voluntary choice." Even for a sociologist solidly armed with knowledge about society's structural pressures, it's difficult to understand how women could more or less "willingly" subject themselves to gross violence.

Secondly, it is the *sum* of prostitution acts that give them their destructive effect. Each individual customer, each individual trick is a grain of sand in a sand dune. Thus, the individual customer does not appear so responsible, nor does each act seem so vital.

Both these factors are linked to the fact that prostitution's destructive effects often do not appear until much later. As with concentration-camp prisoners, damage does not occur after the first shocking experience or even after the second. It can take years before the full impact of the damage is known.

A third reason lies in the methods used to gather knowledge. Prior to the newer Scandinavian research of the 70s and 80s, the primary method used in prostitution research was analysis of official documents. Though satisfactory for descriptions of background variables and other statistics, it was ill-suited to conveying emotions and experiences. The combination of in-depth interviews and of maintaining close contact with the women over a number of years has given us the opportunity for new insights.

The final reason lies in the protection given us by the limitations of our imagination. The everyday life of prostitution is distant from most of us. And here, our imagination is a poor assistant. Negotiate a price with a stranger. Agree. Pull down one pant leg. Come and take me. Finished. Next, please. It becomes too ugly to really take it in. The imagination screeches to a halt.

Sexuality as a means of exchange

At the beginning of this chapter we raised the question of whether the defense strategies used in prostitution work. The in-depth interviews show that these strategies do not provide satisfactory protection. After a while the women experience difficulties in connecting their sexual to their emotional lives. This must mean that their sexuality and emotional lives have nonetheless been used and worn, and that it is not possible to totally disconnect sexuality and emotions from prostitution. The women bring their bodies and their feelings to the job, however much they try to minimize the risk.

Several times in this book we have traced the connections between the role of the prostitute and the female role. The similarities are there. But they can easily be exaggerated. Prostitutes' experiences and destitution are so overwhelming that important qualitative differences between the two roles become apparent. Yet a study of the role of a prostitute can – precisely because of the role's exaggerated characteristics – show us meaningful traits in the female role. Earlier we alluded to the way that women's powerlessness and oppression in a number of social arenas can make the use of sexuality as a means of power over men seem an obvious solution. A woman can use her sexuality as a tool for achieving something else outside of sexuality. A new piece can now be added to the puzzle. More women than just the women who have prostituted themselves use, at times, techniques like simulated orgasms, passionate words and moans, and thinking about something else in order to protect themselves and get sex over with as soon as possible. Prostitutes do this so often that it has extreme consequences for them. Therefore it is a mistake to draw a direct parallel to the situation of other women. However our analysis still warns of the dangers connected with using sexuality as a means to an end outside sexuality. Such an abuse can corrode sexuality itself.

Modest dreams: The women's hopes for the future

To save up a lot of money and then give up prostitution and live a normal middle-class life is not a dream that is widely shared among the women. It is too unrealistic. In our material only one woman has actually managed to carry it out: Eva. Over the years we have learned the fate of quite a number of prostitutes – both those we interviewed and some we did not. We know of none other than Eva who managed it. Certainly, in all of Oslo, there must be a few more, but we have seen enough to know that there are not many of them.

We asked the women how they wanted to be living in five years. Afterwards we asked them how they thought they would be living in five years. The answers speak for themselves – about prostitutes' lives, about their dreams and values and expectations of what life has to offer.

Anita: "I'm against society. I don't want to be a member of society. But I don't want to be a bag lady either. I've thought of starting to sing blues." Anita *can* sing blues. All the same, this becomes a little too heavy for her and she retreats by adding, "But I can't stand all the fuss about recording."

Ester also has a political creed when she speaks of the future: "Society's fucking crazy right now. Steen [a well-known social-democrat] and the other conservatives are making things totally crazy. They'll end up making the decisions until they're 80 years old. Then it will be too late for us young people to decide anything. It's impossible to get rid of prostitution. In 1990 there'll be twice as many who work the street. People who're to lazy to work, who see that they earn money just as easily on the street. It's no problem if they have a girlfriend who knows about it. It's not a good thing. I'd like to see a society where the heterosexuals decide how they want to live and where homosexuals can live how they want."

Ester also has more practical desires that have to do with work and education. "I really regret it, I could have been a senior in high school now. I'd like to study social work or be a psychologist." Elisabeth interrupts and says that she can still do that, she's only 18. Ester: "Yeah. But I have to give things a rest for a year, I have to cut out hash for a year and pull myself together." Elisabeth: "Well, you're smoking now. You were high yesterday and you were high when I came today." Ester laughs a little despairingly at herself.

When they dream about the future, the majority of the women mention professions that are concerned with people. But they mention more modest, less focused things than Ester: housekeeping for the elderly, assistant nursing, something to do with people or with animals. Their desires are for work that contains human warmth and a sense of belonging.

The other main group of work fantasies has to do with areas where the women have already picked up certain skills: working as a hairdresser, in a cosmetic shop, or a clothes boutique. Only one would like a more masculine craftsman's job for herself. All in all, ambitions for work in the working class or lower middle class predominate. The dream of being wealthy and middle class is not at all relevant.

Their other dreams also express the desire to belong and to live a normal life with a secure relationship to other people. Anna, who grew up with a single mother, is the exception when she proclaims, "I'm not going to get married. I'm not big on kids now, I'm not sure how I'll feel later. But I'm not going to be alone with a kid anyway. The father's going to take the kid if I'm alone."

The other women draw other lessons from their troubled upbringings: happiness is the nuclear family. Several express themselves in the same manner as Hanna: "I want to marry a good guy. Someone I love and who loves me. And have lots of kids and a home."

Inga dreams of her own particular form of nuclear family. She admitted herself to a drug clinic for detox and drug withdrawal after she had given birth to a baby boy. She wanted and intended to keep him. Nothing meant more. But: "I was so stupid that I told the hospital that I'd shot up. They hadn't noticed anything. But I thought that if I was going to deal with this, I had to have help and then they had to know how things stood. The doctor discharged me the same day! Now I can't get the boy back before I've managed for a year. It's unfair. We want out of it, Elin and I. Everything I earn goes to drugs. We have a hard life. But the only thing I want is for Elin and me to have a good life. We have plans to cool it and maybe go on a vacation together. And then we want the boy. We want to be home alone together as much as possible."

Marie's wishes take a different direction than the others. "What I'd like for myself is to have nature back. That I'll manage to experience it again – I actually like nature a lot. And like yesterday, when Elisabeth and I were at a concert, it was really nice."

Ulla does not want to look as far as five years into the future and talk about work and family life. The short-term needs are more urgent. "I really want to get off drugs, because then I can visit my mother in west Norway. And then I'd like to go to the dentist. I haven't been for ages, drugs are bad for your teeth."

Socializing outside the interview situation tells its own story about the women's lives and what they long for. Marie, Elisabeth, and I drink coffee one morning at my apartment. After a while I have to leave to mail a socialist journal I am editing to the subscribers. They ask if they can come along. Sure! We go down to the office and fold and staple along with a psychologist who works in the editorial department. Afterwards they say a little disdainfully that he was a typical psychologist. Marie: "He used words I didn't even know existed."

After the job is done, we go to a cafe. Anita sits down at our table. We discuss socialism – Anita doesn't like it. "It won't be free."

Marie thinks of it differently. "Those are the people who want the public health service. So I'm a socialist for sure."

Then we talk about what is more beautiful – spruce or pine or birch. We don't agree on that either. Then we talk about the future.

Marie: "I want something completely different. Prostitution is just an excuse not to live. People forget that it's a part of society down there on the street. It's society's rejects. I want to do something else. Like a little while ago, that was something useful, when we were doing the mailing. It's good to be together with people like you who have some interests, who have something that is meaningful. The life I live is so tiring. That's because nothing happens."

Elisabeth: "Straight people probably think it's strange that this is tiring. We sit around and kill time at cafes, like now. But it's tiring to sit and wait for hours for something to happen that never happens."

Marie would like to use her life to help others who have also been rejected by society. "I get mad seeing all the people who are chronic patients in institutions. I feel powerless and then I get aggressive. I think that books and all that studying destroy the people who work there. I don't have any feeling for them. They're so incredibly narrow, they're far too quick in accepting a diagnosis of sick or well. They say that I'm a borderline psychotic – that doesn't exactly make me any healthier. And no one gets better from being labeled chronically ill. I'd like to work in an institution, I think I have something to contribute, because I know inside me how it is for them."

Anita dreams of totally different things. She talk about the little red house at the edge of the woods that she wants to have. Elisabeth and I get up to go to the restroom. I make a comment on the difference – that Marie talks about what she wants to do, while Anita talks about what she wants to have. Elisabeth criticizes me because it is all too apparent that I have more empathy for Marie's future dreams than for Anita's. "You know what, sometimes you're a real snob; just so you know. That's prejudice – it shows you don't understand anything. When Anita says she wants to have a little red house in the woods, it actually means what she would like to do. Remember that she has never, never had any home. That's what she says she wants then. She wants a place where she doesn't have to put on make-up, where she can relax with her own things. Do what she wants and not what others tell her to do."

All in all the women's dreams are hardly demanding. A regular job, a place to live, a normal family life. Will they ever achieve them or is it too much to expect of themselves and of life?

The women are rather doubtful about getting the future to match their dreams. "You can hope anyway," and "Take it one day at a time:" expressions that don't exactly bristle with enthusiasm and spirit.

Lisa: "I've thought of cooling it for a while now. But I want to get away from it. I have to think of my little sister, too. I'm really afraid for her, that she'll take after me. I don't want her to have a life like mine. If I could only get up in the morning. Besides, I'm used to going through a lot of money."

Hanna: "I'm an optimist about the future. Well, both I guess. Totally seriously, deep down, I think I'll be working on the street. Even if I get a job, too. It's disgusting, but it's easy money."

Anna: "What do I want in five years? To have an apartment with two rooms and a kitchen. I've only got one room and a kitchen. It's not mine; I've only got a six-month lease. Also, that I've gotten some education and an okay job. I don't want to just work, I want vacations. But not such long vacations. That's scary, 'cause I get so laid back."

Where does Anna believe she'll be in five years? "There's a big possibility that I won't completely stop walking the street. I do make the decision myself. But I don't make the decision when I go there. I often think, now I'm going to be able to stop. It's really never all right. Anything can happen, anything's possible. I don't have any confidence in myself that it will be that way. Even though I want a whole different life. But it's most likely that things will be like they are now. Or else maybe I'll have a little more, like a two-room apartment."

It's a lack of confidence in themselves that makes the women as pessimistic as they are. They put absolutely no blame on society.

They could have had more confidence. At the time of the interviews three of the women had moved on from their lives in prostitution. By the time the Norwegian edition of *Backstreets* was published in 1986, there were an additional ten who had left the street. In other words, exactly half of those we interviewed were now out of prostitution. The other half are still drifting along.

What helps?

The education explosion among Norwegian women in the last 20 years has also affected women who have prostituted themselves. Eight of the 13 women who put prostitution behind them have gradually obtained some degree of education. There are four who have completed vocational training and received a degree during the last couple of years. Education has been the ticket to good, average jobs. There are also four who have graduated from high school and are in the process of obtaining higher education. One of them has completed a bachelor's degree.

At regular intervals alarming reports have turned up in the Norwegian newspapers that students have now begun financing their studies through prostitution: getting a student loan has become that difficult! It's true that the steadily worsening loan situation undermines the equal right to education. But there is little basis in reality for the notion of the poor student who has to work as a prostitute to earn enough for her daily expenses. It is true that the police have registered several women with student IDs. We know the majority of these women. They are women who've been in the life for years, but who are now trying to make a place for themselves in the world of education. Naturally enough, this is not unproblematic for them. They have their difficult times, which often involve relapses to drugs, alcohol, and pills. This is occasionally financed in "the old way" by prostitution. Prostitution is thus a sign of a life they are trying to put behind them, rather than an expression of their status as students.

This is important. When people think of a "relapse" (to drugs) or "falling back" (to prostitution) they associate it with dramatic and fateful events: that at the first sign of a relapse, all hope is already crushed and everything becomes as it was. This is a damaging notion. It can function as a self-fulfilling prophecy in which the woman and those around her expect that she is now irretrievably back "in the life." That's not how it is. The majority of the women in our study who have turned away from their earlier lives have experienced relapses; some of them will have problems with this in the future.

A home, education, work, a steady lover, a child – it appears that it is the normal things that help. The common denominator for these things is that they give the woman a new sense of belonging. After a while she finds friends on the "straight" side of society, friends who can compete with the feeling of belonging she had in her other life.

For several women who have put prostitution behind them, it is quite easy to point to two or three new friends who have clearly been very important during the women's good and bad days.

Established social services have played a decisively positive role for only two of the women we interviewed. For the most part the women have managed to leave prostitution on their own, with good help from new friends.

5

Indoor and Outdoor Prostitution

A shifting market: Different types of prostitution

The public debate on the issue of prostitution often distinguishes between street prostitution and high-class prostitution. The preconceived notions are something like this: on the street they are ragged and drunk. The high-class prostitutes indoors have a much better lifestyle than their poor sisters on the street. The customers in high-class prostitution have a higher social status than other customers. Street prostitution is vulgar. High-class prostitution is of a totally different nature, more closely resembling usual sexuality. To the degree that it distinguishes itself, it is likely to be in the form of titillating refinement, subdued lighting, red velvet, champagne, and ingratiating, sentimental music.

In segments of Swedish prostitution research, a pyramid is used as a model to illustrate divisions in the prostitution market. The point of departure for the prostitution pyramid is a description of social status. The base of the pyramid has the lowest status, the tip the highest status. Mobility within the pyramid is low (see Borg et al., 1981, p. 454–8; and Persson, 1981, pp. 46–53). How accurate is the division between street prostitution and high-class prostitution in reality?

Overlapping milieus

The Swedish prostitution researcher Stig Larsson's work on "the sex trade" (1983) builds on impressive quantitative data. Below, we have simplified and summed up his table of women's experiences with different prostitution milieus.[1]

---

[1] This information was assembled on the basis of the first 96 women in the assistance project in Malmø (from Larsson, 1983, p. 161).

Only street	29
Only club	1
Only studio	1
Only other milieus	1
Both street and club	4
Both street and studio	6
Both street and other milieus	15
Both club and other milieus	1
Three or more milieus	38
Total	96

We see that not more than a third (32 women) have experience with only one prostitution milieu. Twenty-six women have experience with two milieus, 38 have experience with three or more milieus. In other words, two-thirds have been in two or more prostitution milieus. Larsson therefore dismisses the pyramid model that other Swedish researchers have developed.

These figures show that there is a large overlap between various types of prostitution. One problem with Larsson's quantitative information is that we are not told much about the facts behind the figures. Perhaps they show that the women stray into strange milieus only rarely, and then hastily return to more familiar ground. The numbers seem a bit too overwhelming for this to be probable, but as a hypothesis it is conceivable. A more likely variant is that the women, at least for a specific period of time, confine themselves to a single form of prostitution – though they might change forms over time.

Our qualitative material provides a foundation for advancing this discussion. In-depth interviews shed light on the more common forms of prostitution in Oslo: street prostitution, hotel and restaurant prostitution, and prostitution through the personal ads. Our interviews obviously don't offer the same opportunity for a sharp numerical division as Larsson's extensive quantitative data do. Nonetheless, let us first summarize the distribution of the 26 women we interviewed. Twelve have only street experience. Five have experience in two different forms of prostitution and nine have experience in three or more forms of prostitution. Thus, at least half of the women have experience with two or more milieus. The tendency is the same as in Larsson's material, though not as marked. The street is almost always included when there are mixed forms of prostitution. This pertains to 13 of the 14 who have experience with two or more types of prostitution.

What sort of people are the women who only work the street?

Does their lifestyle vary from the others? Drug and alcohol problems are somewhat more prevalent for those who only work the street. We have not – in spite of persistent searching – found other differences between them. There are no systematic differences in variables such as social background, education and work experience, or length of time in prostitution.

The material from the interviews can provide some information as to how the overlapping occurs, and it provides valuable information regarding how the women experience the different forms of prostitution.

In our interviews there was only one woman who has a pattern of strictly adhering to one type of prostitution and then totally switching to another. Eva worked the streets for several years, then broke with it abruptly and started advertising in an Oslo newspaper. For a short while during her advertising period she was also a call-girl on the periphery of the sex clubs. She says: "You can divide my career in two. One part was down there and the other was through the personals. They're two different things."

Katrine worked in sex clubs for a very brief time. She didn't like it and went back to The Rainbow restaurant. The remaining 12 who have been in several milieus move back and forth. It appears that it is coincidence that determines the form of prostitution. Karin, for example, has oscillated between the street, hotels, and ads in *Dagbladet*. At the time of the interview it was over six months since she had placed the usual type of ad in the personals: young woman with own apartment seeking well-off man. She still has customers from the 40–50 answers she received; she uses them to fill gaps left by street customers. Occasionally she also works out of a hotel. Thus, her main emphasis is the street, and the street is supplemented with customers from other forms of prostitution. This is the most common pattern for those who have street experience – the street weighs the most heavily. However, there are also examples of the opposite.

Literary clichés flourish of the woman who starts out as a high-class prostitute only to slide downwards and end in the street gutters. However, both Larsson's material and our material reveal that nearly all women begin directly on the street. A typical career in prostitution can look like this: a debut on the street, followed by street prostitution for a year or two, then street prostitution supplemented concurrently by prostitution based in hotels and restaurants.

The women give different answers as to whether there are differences in who works where. Naturally it depends upon one's personal experience. Katrine does not have street experience. She makes a sharp distinction between herself and street prostitutes and believes there are great differences in who can work where. "It's not very often that street prostitutes come into The Rainbow – it's more demanding. We leave them in peace when they come, but they usually disappear quickly. They find out that they don't belong there. You have to offer more when you work at The Rainbow – you need clothes and make-up, you have to have style. Street girls are too sleazy. Besides, there's no drugs at The Rainbow. You have to be able to make pleasant conversation. Occasionally women from The Rainbow will work the streets. Both . . . [three names follow here] work the street. But it doesn't happen very often."

Frida, on the other hand, only works the street. "There's a prostitution hierarchy. It's hard for street prostitutes to get into The Rainbow, for example. You have to fix yourself up and have some style to be let in. But street prostitutes mostly wear jeans and sweaters. Besides the prostitutes in The Rainbow get unpleasant if a street prostitute goes in there. But sometimes a prostitute from a place like The Rainbow will turn a trick on the street if she needs the money real quick."

These descriptions are the exceptions. Among the women who work several places there do not appear to be any barriers between the different forms; they drift back and forth. This does not mean that they cannot still have an identity linked to a certain form of prostitution. Jane has worked a lot on the street. But she has also worked out of countless bars and restaurants. Nonetheless she talks as if she is a street prostitute. "At restaurants the clothes are more elegant, that's okay. But it's dirtier anyway. There's more friendship on the street. At the restaurants there's a lot of competition. It's all about looks – you have to be thin, poised, and be able to speak nicely. It's more for grown-up women. Still, you see it all over them. I'm not real popular. They call me a street whore and a sleazy kid. 'Is that what your pimp says?' I answer back. But I don't like to go to the bathroom and run into them. They're overdressed and super-elegant. Anyway you see how pocked their thighs are when their skirt rides up. Some of them have stomachs." *Them* and *us*.

Elisabeth and I discussed this last summer. Elisabeth has always defined herself as a street prostitute; she did at the time we interviewed her as well. Yet at that time she also had extensive indoor experience, at the usual places. The overlapping was complete, and not at all periodic.

Elisabeth: "I think, 'I've worked the street.' I don't think about having worked indoors. I hadn't thought about it before you asked, I've only thought that there's a difference. Even though I spent a certain amount of time at the SAS hotel, for example, at the same time as I was on the street, I still thought of myself as a street prostitute. I didn't think about the times I was other places. I can never say that I've worked indoors, even though I have. It's because the street meant most. After all it was the street that was my spot, where my people and my friends were. Even though I was indoors, it wasn't my spot."

Cecilie: "That's a little strange, you have been quite a bit indoors too? Does it have anything to do with your self-image?"

Elisabeth: "Yeah, obviously; there's nothing strange about it. There's nothing mystical about bringing outside opinions with you. You bring the classic stereotype of what you are when you're a whore and what is more high-class, and that the ones who work indoors are posher. Well, I wasn't. But at the same time when you're in the life you take whatever chances you get. I've roped in customers almost anyplace."

Many women only work the streets. And some women undoubtedly only work indoors, though we only have an in-depth interview with one of them in our material. And some women work several different places simultaneously. It is still worth noticing that a few of the women who have shifted among different milieus link their identities to a single type of prostitution.

Choosing a type of prostitution

The women's choice of a type of prostitution at any one time seems a little random. Like Elisabeth they often take the chances that present themselves. But at the same time there are clear advantages and disadvantages connected to the different types of prostitution. The choices are also a result of what seems most (or least) frightening to the woman. Eva describes it this way: "Street work is simple in a way – you don't give anything of yourself down there. You have to give more of yourself when you do the personals. That was the huge nightmare the whole time [on the street] – being recognized. That was the worst thing about the street. The other method, through the personals, was safer that way. You could screen the customers. I feel more secure with the personals, but there are other things that go along with it. There are other ways of doing things –

you have to take off all your clothes, for instance, it's not enough just to pull down one pant leg. The customers do pay a lot better, and they expect more. I had to play-act more, while on the street that's not expected at all. You can imagine that if you pay three times as much for something, that you expect it's going to be three times as good. The possibility of being recognized was much less with the personals. I never answered those who gave the number to a telephone booth, I preferred to answer people who gave a business number where I could ask for them. And I was more likely to choose telephone numbers on the other side of the city. You could say I got security, but in return I had to play-act more."

The heavy strain of indoor prostitution is that you must give more of yourself, as Eva describes. The more customers pay, the more of yourself you sell. Anita has indoor experience from bars and hotels in addition to the street. She says: "It's actually more tiring than the street. It's a lot more work. There are the old men you have to talk to and drink wine with. You have to be more professional, have sexy underwear and stuff. You've got to give more."

And Ulla: "You can't keep the same distance. It's obvious, you spend lots more time on the same customer."

Katrine's reason for preferring to work indoors is the security. "Personally I'd never dare work the street. Now I have the opportunity to check out the customer over a drink, and I get tips from the other girls. If a customer gets a bad name, all the girls will put their purses on the chair next to them to show it's taken. The bartender can be a help too; he can tell you discreetly if there's a certain man we shouldn't go with. You can also get by on one or two tricks; I only turn one trick an evening. But to tell the truth it's not the sex that's the worst. The worst is the fear of getting a nut, and what goes on before the sex. And foreplay is a lot longer at The Rainbow."

Indoor prostitution has a different character from a hasty backseat ejaculation. Indoor prostitution is intended to resemble a normal encounter between a man and a woman. There's supposed to be conversation, flirting, toasting, and romantic glances. The more it resembles the tone of a normal sexual encounter, the better. Jane: "It's different. They've been sitting around hot for you the whole evening. Then they can say, 'Now let's forget that you've gotten money for this.'"

It is precisely the similarities with a "normal encounter" that make indoor prostitution strenuous. It is the *customer* who wants this similarity, not the woman. How do you make it similar for the customer and simultaneously maintain the crucial separation for yourself? For the woman it is more difficult to use defense strategies for maintaining distance. If you make "cultured conversation," it's more difficult to be absent, to think about something else, to avoid talking about your private life. The foreplay makes the whole thing more time-consuming. Undressing completely makes it harder to hide yourself and harder to keep your distance. It all becomes more complicated and exacting.

However, restaurant prostitution does have its advantages. The length of foreplay provides increased opportunity for avoiding "nuts." Visibility within this arena makes the women's built-in warning system more secure. Moreover, there are fewer tricks. There is also more dressing up. Some, like Jane, enjoy dressing up. Others, like Anita, think it's too much trouble.

Champagne, orchids, and caviar

There is a widespread conception that indoor prostitution provides the kind of money that can lead to a life of luxury, while street prostitutes are impoverished, pitiful souls. There are wide variations in the minimum prices among the different types of prostitution. On the street today, intercourse costs 300 crowns. When the sex clubs were at their peak in the middle of the 70s, a street trick cost 200 crowns. In sex clubs a trick was 300 crowns. The club owner wanted 100 of this; thus, for the woman, the end result was the same. For tricks through the personals the price today is 500 crowns. For a restaurant trick the price is 700 crowns. These prices have varied over time, but the relationship between the prices is quite stable. Money is often used to measure social status. Measured in terms of the cost of the acts there do appear to be status differences between the types of prostitution. The prices control the selection of customers to a certain degree. The wallets of restaurant customers are no doubt thicker than those of street customers. For the women the situation is more complicated. Their total earnings are just as important as the price they receive per trick. Once again, a closer investigation reveals that one widespread conception about prostitution is a misconception.

Katrine worked The Rainbow. But like the other women, she observed: "In reality you can earn just as much on the street, because it goes faster there; you can do more in less time if you keep at it. At The Rainbow there was less sex for the money, but it took at least as long to earn the same amount."

Mona has chosen her type of prostitution by its income. "I've hooked both on the street and in restaurants. I wanted to see where it was best, and where I've worked lately has been on the street."

Prostitution can be compared with piecework. There is no hourly wage. Tricks on the street are quick. The number of customers on the street greatly varies, from one single customer in any evening all the way up to ten or fifteen. It's highly exceptional for a women to have so many customers. However, three to five customers in an evening is normal. At restaurants with "all the fuss" beforehand, one or two customers is usual. There simply is not time for more. The income-level indoors and outdoors is quite similar. The difference, to the extent that there is any, is that the women can earn more on the street if they really keep at it.

The customers' social status

The pyramid model also says something about the customer's social status. The higher up on the pyramid, the higher the status. As a starting-point it is probably a reasonable supposition that restaurant customers, at any rate, are generally "well-to-do men." Though all in all women can earn just as much on the street, the customer must pay considerably more for a sexual act indoors. At a minimum of 700 crowns a trick, a certain wallet width is necessary if this is to be more than a one-time event. The preliminary drinks and dinner must also be paid for. The women's descriptions support this hypothesis to a certain extent.

Jane: "It's a certain kind of person who goes in for restaurant prostitution. There's a difference, there are more businessmen in restaurants. More of the kind who shower first."

Ulla: "The customers at The Rainbow are a bunch of old pigs with fat wallets."

However, the Norwegian customer study showed that, for the men as well as for the women, there was a good deal of overlapping between the prostitution forms. Many customers use more than one form. There is a tendency that customers from higher social classes, with higher incomes and living in established relationships, prefer indoor prostitution to street prostitution. However, this tendency is very weak (Prieur and Taksdal, 1989, pp. 57–8).

The pyramid model is found lacking as a description of the teeming, chaotic life of the streets. The women have described how the street customers are just anybody, ranging from "blue-blooded snobs to honest working guys." Randi, who like most of the other women takes tricks indoors and outdoors, comes right to the point in her summary of their experience: "There are lots more different types of customers on the street."

An unproductive model

Every model is a simplification; therefore, there must be exceptions to every model. The model may nonetheless be useful if it can approximate a pedagogical summary of *tendencies*. The pyramid model, however, is an example of an unproductive model, at least of Scandinavian conditions, where departure from the model is not the exception, but the rule.

A view of "high-class" prostitution as more refined and more like normal relationships is very clearly a customer perspective. Vast differences between the various types of prostitution are in relation to the *customer's* perspective. Mobility between prostitution forms will probably vary from country to country. Perhaps there is greater variation between indoor and outdoor prostitution outside of Scandinavia. Irrespective of this, the model does not capture the essence of prostitution as seen from the woman's perspective: regardless of variations in the type of prostitution, women feel that they have to rent out the most intimate parts of the body to anonymous strangers to use as a hole to jerk off in. The women try to keep themselves as unharmed as possible from this massive invasion by maintaining a distance from the customer. We have attempted to show how this gives meaning to the way in which prostitution is played out. No other single factor is as important if one is to understand what actually goes on in the encounter between the participants. The women's attempt to maintain a distance is as important indoors as outdoors. But it is more difficult indoors. Regardless of its form, prostitution is a mill where the emotional life of women is inexorably ground into bits. This is probably Scandinavian prostitution research's most important contribution to the field. It is the result of years of close contact with women in prostitution both in Sweden and Norway.

6

What Ever Happened to the Pimp?

Prostitutes' views of pimps

So far we have been concerned with prostitution and its main participants, the contents of the sex trade, prostitutes and customers. But no pimps. What ever happened to the pimp? Because he is important, isn't he?

In Norway's limited debate of the 70s the pimp was totally absent. It's different in the 80s. The concept of the brutal pimp who literally kicks the woman out on the street has become one of the most important – perhaps *the* most important – explanations for prostitution's existence. The fight against prostitution is often tied to tougher legislative control of pimps. Editorial comments from readers speaking out against reprehensible pimps flourish. The Oslo police department has established a special task force against pimping.

Is the pimp the main villain, the powerful and dangerous man behind the scenes in the prostitution market? Who is the pimp? What is a pimp? We'll let the women speak first.

The women's stories

Anita: "Well, me, I don't have a pimp. But most of the women do. There are some who have a boyfriend, and then there are some who have a real pimp. I guess about a quarter of the women have a real pimp."

Cecilie: "Just what is a real pimp?"

Anita: "A real pimp is somebody who follows the woman in his car and makes sure nothing happens to her. There are pimps who have great big American cars and a lot of women at the same time. That kind of pimp has one steady girlfriend among the women and she's the one who earns the most. And then he has some other women at the same time. If he wants to screw one of them, he gets what he wants."

Inga: "I've never had a pimp. None of us at Bank Square has a pimp. Junkies don't. But there are some pimps at the other places where women who aren't high go. I know at least three of them."

Sonja: "There aren't any pimps where I go. But I'm pretty sure there are some at Bank Square."

Asking the women if they have a pimp is making a fool of yourself and announcing that you're from another planet. As green as I was on the first interview, I bluntly asked that question. I learned a lot from that blunder. The answer was a sullen "no," and the rapport we had established was broken. In later interviews the women were asked if they had a special friend. This opened things up and we could talk more freely about how the two of them lived, how they provided for themselves, what he did during the day. Gradually this led into a discussion of what they thought was meant by the term "pimp," what others thought, and how extensive pimping was in Oslo.

What do the women say about the extent of pimping? The answers cover a broad spectrum, from those who say that almost no one has a pimp, to those who say that almost everyone has a pimp. However, most of the women agreed that there was *not* extensive pimp activity in Oslo. The chief argument given by those who believed that there was little pimping was an economic observation related to drugs. Doris: "The pimps in this city can be counted on one hand. Junkies can't afford to have pimps. What they earn goes straight into their veins." There was an interesting pattern in the answers of those who believed that some pimping does go on: There are pimps. I don't have a pimp myself, many others do. There aren't any pimps where I work, but there are in other parts of the city. The pimp is located away from themselves and their girlfriends, in a distant location.

This was also observed in the Swedish study by Månsson, who interprets it as an expression of the women's desire to protect themselves and their pimp. Who wants to admit that she is involved in illegal activity and that she is being used? (Månsson, 1981, p. 135; and Borg et al., 1981, pp. 388–92). We believe that an alternative interpretation has more validity: the women have a concept of "The Pimp" which to a certain extent resembles the popular stereotype where violence, force, a life of luxury, and "stables" of women are central elements. The stereotype is also fed by the few well-known pimps in town. When the women mention pimps, it is most often the same handful of men who come up; and these elements are present, although to a varying degree. In contrast to this concept of what a pimp is, they have their own experiences. Jens, Peter, Kristian – they are not pimps, not real pimps. The stereotype does not fit them. They do not have a stable, they do not use violence, and they certainly do not live a life of luxury. Love and joint economy are quite different from slavery and exploitation. Denying that you have a pimp thus becomes a way of expressing that your own experience does not coincide with the stereotypical pimp–prostitute relationship. And the denial is the first interesting clue that the term "pimp" *is* a stereotype, remote from nuances, emotions, and everyday life. One central reason for our belief that this interpretation has greater validity than Månsson's is that the women openly talked about their relationships in such a way that it was clear that their friend *could* be arrested for pimping, under the current wording of the Norwegian penal law.[1] Thus, their denials do not afford much protection to either of them. A similar openness was exhibited in talking about other violations of the law as well. In other words, we believe that the women should be taken seriously. When they say that they do not have pimps, it is because they mean it.

This perspective poses its own very interesting research problem, namely finding out what the women perceived a pimp to be. It soon became evident that the women's concept of the pimp was complex and that they emphasized different aspects in their definitions of a pimp.

Boyfriends are not pimps. Often, the women would talk about other women's boyfriends with a tone of disdain: "He operates just like a pimp." Their own boyfriend, on the other hand, was not defined in that way. Katrine worked indoors at The Rainbow at the time of her interview. She takes pride in the fact that she's a professional and that her affairs are in order. This business of having a pimp is just a bunch of crap – she certainly has no need for one. "The only thing I take along on the job is my power of persuasion." Later she talks about her husband: "He thinks it's OK. He reaps the benefits of it too. It's my couch he's sitting on." Katrine has a steady customer who comes to her home every other month. He pays 500 crowns per visit. He was there late yesterday morning. He is a businessman who keeps a tight schedule. He always finishes in 15 minutes. When he came to the door yesterday, Katrine's husband was home.

---

[1] See the discussion of the Norwegian penal law on pimping, pp. 202–204.

Katrine took the customer into another room. When she came out again, her husband calmly asked: "Is he through already?" Katrine thinks that her husband could contribute a little more by engaging in homosexual prostitution. "It's not fair that I have to do more than my share. But when I say that, he pats his stomach and says he's gotten too fat. But then he could just lose some weight. He says it's easier for me, but that's because he's so lazy. He's let some really fantastic opportunities slip by. Once there was a man who owned a furniture store, who had the hots for him. He could have turned a couple of tricks then, and now we would have a new living room. I think he could contribute something too and take advantage of good connections like that. But of course it's easy for him the way it is." Though her husband sits on her couch, prefers that she be the one to prostitute herself, and contributes very little financially, Katrine does not look upon him as a pimp.

Lisa says: "I had a boyfriend once. But that ended. Dammit, he just sat on his ass in the apartment and waited for me to come home with the money. 'I'm under no obligation to support you,' I told him and threw him out." Later in the interview she says: "No, I've never had a pimp. Not unless we count the guy who sat on his ass waiting."

Vilhelm, who is rumored to be a pimp for his girlfriend Frida, says: "It's not pimping in the usual sense of the word when it's between the woman and her boyfriend. That's something else. There isn't much pimping now. There was more before, back in the 50s and 60s. There's almost no one who has a stable anymore. N. N. [well-known pimp] has a stable. And Mona [well-known transsexual pimp] has two or three boys working for her. But otherwise there isn't very much. The women are too independent nowadays. They work to get money for their own drug habit and maybe their boyfriend's habit. There's nothing left over. So there isn't much of that anymore."

In her excellent book about sexual slavery, Kathleen Barry estimates that approximately 90 percent of street prostitutes have pimps (Barry, 1979, pp. 6, 111). If this estimate is correct – the way the information is presented, it is difficult to judge – Oslo differs greatly from the international picture. *The majority of the prostitutes in Oslo operate alone.* Of the 26 we interviewed, half (13) had never been involved in a relationship that could be called pimping – not even when seen in terms of Norwegian penal law's very wide definition (roughly, any cohabitation with a prostitute with a joint economy; see pp. 202–204). The other 13 women interviewed have had, at one time or another, a relationship which *we* categorize as a pimp relationship under the Norwegian criminal law.

This is within their entire prostitution career. Only four of the 13 *themselves* think of their relationship as that of pimp and prostitute. And to emphasize the point even further: only two of the four describe their relationship as one involving a pimp while the relationship was current; the other two did so only with the help of hindsight, as they thought back on terminated relationships.

At the time of their interviews only four of the 26 women had a pimp – again within the broad definition.

The image of the pimp

The women have a complex definition of who and what a pimp is. Ida says: "Someone who shares in spending the money that's earned on the street. Not just one time, but over a longer period of time." But definitions along this line are the exception. It's much more common to hear descriptions of Evil People:

Vilhelm: "A pimp is someone who uses violence to force the woman out onto the street."

Marie: "As far as I'm concerned, they could rot away in jail. They are psychopaths. They steal money from people who are slowly disintegrating. A pimp is someone who begins with and continues with force. It's taking money from others."

Anita: "A pimp is someone who's married and just lives off her money, even if he has a great education. He doesn't bother to work. A lot of times the wife is working on the street, and then she and her husband get her girlfriends to start working in a club. They make a good living off of others and can go to the tanning salons. It's when he doesn't even bother to use a good education."

Once when I was out with Marie and Anita, they started arguing about what the term "pimp" implies. Their argument is a small indication of how problematic and unsuitable the term is for street life. It all started over an argument about the relationship between Inga and Elin, a lesbian couple. Both agreed that Elin is like a pimp for Inga.

Marie: "I call it just plain pimping, no doubt. Elin refuses to turn tricks herself. She says that it's tied up with her childhood and that she can't do it. That's a pretty thin excuse. Inga has to work alone. They live on what Inga earns on the street. That's just a way of defending herself and Elin. Elin takes advantage of Inga."

Anita: "Yeah, because it's just as bad to turn tricks for a woman as for a man. There's no difference." Turning to Marie: "I worked for you, too. If Elin is a pimp, then you were just as much a pimp when we were together. We lived off my money, you know. You drank off me, you lived off me."

Marie becomes furious: "Goddammit, that's not fair. I'm not going to take that. I couldn't help it, could I, if I was on sick leave? And we used my sick pay too."

Anita: "Your sick pay didn't amount to much. Just think of how much money we went through then."

Marie: "That's really low. Why haven't you ever said that to me before? That wasn't how I felt. A pimp is someone who starts with force and keeps using it. It's taking money from others. We had my money too, even though it wasn't very much. And then I fixed us up with that lady from southern Norway." [A wild story follows about the time Anita and Marie were in Copenhagen with a rich lesbian. She lavished 100,000 crowns on them during this period, according to the story.] "I did a lot of things for you, too, Anita. Remember that I was the one who took your clothes to the cleaners, things like that. And you were working less when you were with me than when you were alone."

Anita, conciliatory: "It's no wonder you had to go on sick leave from the chocolate factory – that was a hard job. It's different with the ones who could have gotten themselves good jobs because they've got an education. Those are the real pimps."

Marie: "It is true that we used your money when we went out drinking. I didn't feel like a pimp – that's for sure. But today I would have gone out myself and turned tricks. I have too much respect for people to ever be a pimp."

Marie became extremely uneasy after this argument. I spent the next two days with her and Anita. Marie kept coming back to how grievously unfair it was of Anita to call her a pimp. That she herself accused Elin of being a pimp was forgotten.

Fredrik's letter

Fredrik is also dissatisfied with the way the term "pimp" is used. He writes to me:

"I've been thinking about the use of the word 'pimp' since the last time we talked. I'm not satisfied with that word. I think it's too imprecise. When you say pimp about a person, you're putting everyone in one group. And I think that's wrong. I've looked it up in the dictionary. The dictionary defines a pimp as 'a man who allows himself to be supported by a prostituted woman.' All right, so now we know that. Just a man – not a woman? If you stay within the framework of that definition, there can be no doubt. I am a pimp, or more correctly, a former pimp. But when you see how the word "pimp" is used, or rather should we say misused, then it becomes a different matter. From time to time you read shocking accounts in the press, usually taken from out in the big world – USA, France, Italy etc. – about how so-called pimps have abused women over a long period of time and how they have grossly exploited them. When you expand the definition of pimp to include relationships based on abuse and the economic exploitation of women, then I would claim that I've never been a pimp. Some people talk about pimping as if it is synonymous with white-slave traffic and the sale of people. I've also seen that the name has been split up, that people make a glib distinction between home pimp and professional pimp. In other words, we're also dealing with absentee pimp, amateur pimp, etc. So the term 'pimp' is extremely comprehensive and not at all easy to get a handle on. We ought to come up with a new name. A name that covers the original definition of the word pimp. Naturally one could say that most pimps share many common traits, and that's true enough. But this is just like snow and ice; in a way it's the same thing, but nonetheless different. The difference lies primarily in what the income from prostitution is used for, if it's used for the common good, or not. And after that, how you treat your prostitute. There's a big difference here. Getting back to the original definition, I think we have to introduce a new word. And we probably ought to stay within the prostitution terminology; so we can introduce the gender-neutral word PROSTITUTER. A prostituter would then be defined as: 'a person (male or female) who allows him or herself to be supported by a prostitute.' In my case I would say that I have engaged in prostituter activities. I was a prostituter – not a pimp."

The interviews with the women without a doubt prove Fredrik right. The term "pimp" is extremely wide-ranging and not all that easy to get a handle on. The most important knowledge the women have provided is this: the term "pimp" is almost always unsuitable to describe the relationship between the woman and her special friend, if she has one. Because pimps are evil, manipulative, and cynical people who exploit women, from beginning to end.

That's not the way their boyfriends are.

Who are the pimps? Pimps reported to the police

The term pimp is comprehensive and it's not easy to get a handle on it. The penal code does not provide a crystal-clear definition of a pimp either. "The pimp section" (section 206 in the penal code) allows for many different types of pimps:

> "Whoever entices another to practice fornication as an occupation, or to continue with such an occupation, or who contributes to such enticement, shall be sentenced to imprisonment not to exceed five years.
>
> "Whoever promotes or exploits others' occupational fornication shall be sentenced to a fine or imprisonment not to exceed five years. The same applies to whoever promotes or exploits, for the sake of profit, the immoral intercourse of others.
>
> "A man who allows himself to be supported, partially or completely, by a woman who practices fornication as an occupation, shall be sentenced to imprisonment not to exceed two years."

Sociologists with a need to create order in the chaotic and often impenetrable world of prostitution have filled reports and books with labels like home pimps, stable pimps, professional pimps, personals' pimps, club pimps, and other profiteers (see Persson, 1981; Månsson 1981; Borg et al., 1981). We have gone through all the reported pimp cases at the Oslo police department in the period from 1968 to 1982. In table 2 we have grouped this pimp data according to the relationship between the person reported and the prostitute.[2]

THE NON-VIOLENT BOYFRIEND-PIMP This is a love relationship in which the woman prostitutes herself, usually as a result of a joint decision. He does not force her onto the street. They may have occasional spats, as all couples do, but this is not the reason she is soliciting on the street. She does it because they need the money and because she loves him. In many ways the non-violent boyfriend-pimps are the one extreme in the pimp data. In order to enhance the data and to illustrate the vast range covered by the designation "pimp," we will devote an entire section to non-violent boyfriend-pimps.

---

[2] This material is presented more thoroughly in the Norwegian edition of *Backstreets*.

Table 2 Pimp data from the Oslo police department

Category of pimp	Number	Percent
Non-violent boyfriend-pimp	7	11
Violent boyfriend-pimp	22	34
Sex pimp	11	17
Stable pimp	9	14
Sex club pimp	6	9
Other[a]	4	6
Unknown	6	9
Total	65	100

[a] The category "other" consists of two persons reported for procuring in connection with their work as hotel employees, and one person whose name was included in a report involving a friend who had a relationship with a prostitute. In addition, the category includes charges against a restaurant.

THE VIOLENT BOYFRIEND-PIMP   This is the largest group in the pimp data from the period 1968–1982. As in the aforementioned group, we are dealing with steady relationships. Perhaps they are married, engaged, or living together and emotionally involved. These relationships are characterized by violent behavior; in some instances extremely violent. He threatens or beats her in order to force her to go out on the street and earn money, or to get her money when she comes home. In the majority of cases it is the woman herself who reports her violent lover. Most of them later retract their complaints. These cases are dropped by the police.

The daily lives of prostitutes whose husbands beat them is much the same as those of other abused women. He beats her, they make up, he beats her, she leaves – but often she returns. This is the pattern of half of the violent boyfriend-pimp relationships. For the other half, it appears that filing a complaint results in a permanent break. Since violent boyfriend-pimps are the dominating group in the pimp data, they will also be given a separate section.

THE SEX PIMP   He has a brief sexual relationship with the prostitute. The connection between them is far more random than between the parties in a boyfriend-pimp relationship. The relationship between the sex pimp and the prostitute has nothing to do with "true love," or even with a long-term infatuation. Instead, it is characterized by hectic and unstable infatuation and temporary sexual attraction. They are not lovers at the time charges are filed. Typically these relationships are fleeting alliances involving young people, usually the same age, who are part of the drug scene. Threats and/or violence were reported in four of the 11 cases.

THE "STABLE" PIMP   Unlike the boyfriend-pimp and sex pimp, the "stable pimp" has several women who simultaneously prostitute themselves for him. The stable pimp can, however, have a romantic relationship with one or more of the prostitutes. Just as the non-violent boyfriend-pimp can be regarded as the one extreme in the pimp data, the stable pimp can be regarded as the other. According to popular belief, the stable pimp is the prototype of his species. For this reason the stable pimp will also be treated in a separate section.

THE SEX-CLUB PIMP   The sex-club pimp also has several women who simultaneously prostitute themselves for him, but there is no emotional attachment between the parties. The relationship between the sex-club pimp and the prostitute is similar to that of an employer and his employees – it is a purely business arrangement. This group represents less than 10 percent of the reported cases.

When we study the pimp cases reported to the police, it is the emotional attachments that dominate. Throughout the material it is apparent that the accused and the prostitute are not strangers. Often they may have lived together for years. Boyfriend-pimps constitute nearly half of those reported. When we add to this sex pimps and stable pimps (who also have a personal relationship to the prostitute), we have accounted for four-fifths of all those charged with pimping between 1968 and 1982. The purely *business* association between pimp and prostitute – as exists in sex clubs – constitutes an insignificant remainder by comparison.

However, as recent research on women in abusive relationships has shown, romantic relationships do not preclude violence. There is far more violence in the pimp data than in the interview data. Thirteen of the women we interviewed had, at one time or another, had a "pimp-like" relationship. Only three of them were subjected to violence from their "pimp," while nearly two-thirds of the cases in the pimp data report violence. Though the police data on cases filed against pimps presumably record a minimum of violence, one can reasonably assume that the data simultaneously reflect an over-representation of violence, when compared to a general sampling of pimp–prostitute relationships. Often it is a violent incident which is the immediate provocation for the prostitute to go to the police.

It is primarily the woman who personally reports pimping. Nearly two-thirds of the complaints are filed by the women involved.

As the next two sections will testify, violent behavior is not randomly spread among the categories of pimps.

Non-violent boyfriend-pimps

Nils and Mette met each other aboard a ship en route to the United States. Nils was 23 and worked as a mechanic on the ship. Mette was 14 and was travelling with her parents. They enjoyed being with each other and became good friends on the crossing. They met each other again two months later when, completely by chance, they were on the same plane going back to Norway.

It was love at second sight.

Nils went to the small town where Mette lived. Mette had barely turned 15 when she came proudly home with an engagement ring on her finger. But her parents did not share her new-found happiness. They thought Mette was much too young for love.

Nils and Mette hung around together until he had to report for duty again. Mette had been experimenting with drugs since she was nine years old. Her parents had no idea of this. Nils had also done drugs earlier, but he had managed to quit. He got Mette to quit too. When Nils went to sea, Mette solemnly promised that she would stay away from drugs.

All the same, Mette ended up on drugs. She dropped out of school. Three months after he had reported back to duty, Nils got a letter from Mette, where she wrote that she was doing "the hardest stuff there is." Nils was beside himself. He showed the letter to the clergyman on board ship; an understanding man, he made arrangements for Nils to fly home from South America within a couple of days, even though ship regulations stipulated one month's notice.

Nils and Mette rented a room in Mette's hometown and moved in together. Mette went back to school. Her father was extremely unhappy with his daughter's living arrangement – she wasn't even 16 yet. He went to the local Child Welfare Council and offered to pay Mette's share of the rent, utilities etc., provided she stay in school. The Child Welfare Council asked him if he couldn't also pay

Nils' share, since Nils was unemployed. Mette's father "... would go along with this on the condition that he receive a written statement from the Child Welfare Council stating that it gave its official approval to an underaged girl living with a man who was of legal age. He did not get this, thereby dropping payment toward rent etc." [From the father's police statement.]

Nils and Mette were unhappy in the small town. Mette's parents were opposed to their relationship, and Nils did not find suitable work. They went to Oslo. The city of possibilities. Once there, they slept in stairways. They got money for food by begging on the street. "They tried to get help from social service organizations, but the response was negative. Nils tried to get a steady job. He got work with a tire company, but quit after a week. He found the work so boring that he couldn't motivate himself to stick with it." [Nils' police statement.] Nils thought it was a drag to be an unskilled worker when he had his mechanics certificate from Oslo Vocational School.

After living beggars' lives for two months in Oslo, Mette and Nils came to the mutual decision that the only solution was that Mette start working on the street. She worked every night between 9 and 11 p.m. She did hand jobs for 50–100 crowns per trick, or intercourse for 150 crowns. She quit for the evening when she had earned 300 crowns. That was the cost per day at the boarding house they had moved into. "In the beginning Nils went 'to work' with Mette and stayed close to her the entire time. He noted the license number of cars Mette got into in the event that anything should happen to her. During the last month Nils has not gone with Mette 'to work.' She felt that she had become experienced enough to manage on her own ... During the time Mette has 'worked' on the street, Nils has lived from this income. Both Nils and his fiancée have been aware of the fact this is a punishable offence. Mette learned this from a 'colleague' almost two weeks ago, and she told Nils. Nils claims that he has never forced Mette to prostitute herself. This is something they have simply agreed was necessary." [From Nils' police statement.]

When Nils found out that what he was doing was a punishable offense, he tried to find work again. The following week he got a job at a warehouse. "Nils has been promised an apartment through his job. Nils feels that if they get this apartment and he keeps his job, Mette will quit 'working' on the street. Mette has not had drug problems since Nils returned from sea. Nils believes that he is the one who has gotten her to quit." [From Nils' police statement.]

Mette was placed in a detention cell after the police had picked her up on the street. They telephoned her parents the next morning. Her father immediately pressed charges, accusing Nils of pimping. Nils, suspecting nothing, showed up at the police station the next morning to report that Mette was missing. He was frightened because she had not come home the night before. He was immediately arrested as a suspect and interrogated. At that time, Mette had been working for five months. Independent of each other – and without the opportunity to confer with one another – Nils and Mette give identical stories of love and poverty to the police. Nils was sentenced to a 90-day suspended sentence for pimping.

Judicial policy

The story of Nils and Mette is typical of the seven cases we have categorized as non-violent boyfriend-pimps. Typically enough – and in marked contrast to the rest of the data – complaints have not been filed by the woman in any of these cases. What interest would she have in betraying her boyfriend? In one case pimping was reported by neighbors, in another by the woman's father, and in five cases the report was filed by the Oslo police department.

Five of these seven cases were brought to trial. Only two were dismissed due to lack of evidence, a low ratio that is unique to this group. Measured in terms of most criteria, non-violent boyfriend-pimps are clearly the most innocent in our police data. They don't hit the women. They have no serious criminal records. Their lives are a mess – characterized by unstable work and housing. They could hardly be any farther from the stereotype of the pimp. They seem much more akin to the guy who's down and out. The fact that the wheels of justice seem to turn most effectively against this group seems cause for concern.

The high proportion of cases that lead to trial and sentencing must be seen in conjunction with who it was that filed the complaint. In boyfriend-pimp relationships without violence, the case does not rest on charges filed by the woman. The case is not, as so often happens, dropped because she withdraws her complaint. There are other people, outsiders, who believe they have enough documentation to accuse the man of pimping. Four of the five cases brought to court ended in conviction. The most severe sentence was two-and-a-half years' unconditional imprisonment. The most lenient penalty was a suspended sentence of 90 days' imprisonment with a two-year probation period. Both of these cases involved young men who were drifters, and indeed, the sentences are lenient. But the judge was not willing to grant that Nils' case had many extenuating circumstances. "The sentence is set at 90 days in jail, which shall be suspended subject to a two-year probation period, without supervision in that the accused has no previous convictions. Beyond that allowances have been made for the young age of the accused. Other than this the court finds nothing that extenuates his or his fiancée's behavior. They had put themselves in the difficult situation they were in and therefore it seems a bit presumptuous of them to simply demand that they be supported by public welfare. It was extremely irresponsible for the two of them, and particularly of the accused, to set out for Oslo when neither of them had a job to go to or a place to live." [From Nils' sentencing.]

How things went with Nils' new job and the promised apartment, we do not know. We have tried to investigate, but have not managed to find anything out.

On the basis of police documents and what we've otherwise been able to check, it seems that all seven couples have probably survived the strain of being reported to the police and standing trial. Love can sometimes conquer almost anything.

Violent boyfriend-pimps

It was the Women's Crisis Center that got Julie to report Karl for pimping, bodily injury, and threats. Julie and Karl had been married for over a year, but they had known each other since they were teenagers. When they got married, Julie was 33 and Karl had just turned 40.

The marriage was marked by trouble and quarreling from the start. Not only was Julie abused verbally, she was also beaten. Money was a constant problem. Rent payments were high and Karl's part-time job was insufficient; the small amounts they got from the welfare office did not help much either. Julie was physically and mentally threatened into going out on the street. She did not dare to protest too much. Karl's anger was easily sparked and he could "lose control," as Julie told the police. Karl took just about everything she earned on the street. Julie had to keep a careful account of what she spent on herself. Not long before their first wedding anniversary, Julie could not take it any more, and she moved home to her mother.

Karl promised to change. After a few weeks Julie moved back in with him, because he had given his word that everything would be better. But one evening when she returned to the apartment, she found a note from Karl telling her to go to hell. Julie went to her mother's. Karl came after her. He was drunk and nasty toward Julie and his mother-in-law. It ended with Julie being beaten, driven to the Crisis Center, and then to the hospital with a broken jawbone. After she had talked with the women at the Crisis Center, Julie she would file a complaint. This happened just before Christmas.

In the complaint Julie estimated that she had earned around 100,000 crowns on the street in the course of that year. "I got a beating if I came home at night with less than 800 crowns," she told the police. If she earned more, she got "time off" to stay home and take care of Karl until the money was gone. Then she was out on the street again.

Meanwhile, Karl had another explanation. He said that Julie used drugs and that she worked on the street to get money for drugs. He admitted that he spoke harshly to her on several occasions and that he had slapped her a few times, but that was merely to get her away from the street and drugs. The episode at his mother-in-law's had been triggered by Julie – she hit him first. Karl wanted a divorce.

Karl was placed in temporary custody and Julie, still in the hospital, read in the newspaper that Karl had been arrested. She was released from the hospital the following day, and the police brought her in for further questioning. Julie said that reading about Karl in the newspaper had given her a shock, and that she did not want to go through another police interrogation. More than anything she wanted Karl out of jail. Instead of making a new statement, she withdrew her complaint. In her new statement to the police it is noted that "Withdrawal of the complaint occurs not because the plaintiff has been threatened or fears reprisal, but after consideration brought on by her own conscience." Julie returned to the police station the next day as well, crying and pleading that her husband be released. "That's the biggest Christmas present I could get," Julie said. Asked if she was not afraid of reprisal, she answered no. On the way from the hospital to the police station, she had been driven to her apartment to pick up some clothes. There she had found a letter from Karl. Julie understood how difficult things were for Karl and she could not, in good conscience, let him stay in jail.

Julie got her Christmas present. Karl was released from jail and charges against him were dropped.

Boyfriends and abusers

Twenty-two (34 percent) of the charges registered in the police data involve what we have called violent boyfriends. One man was reported four times by the same woman, another was reported twice by the same woman, thus giving a total of 18 violent relationships. This represents the largest single group of charges filed against pimps during the period 1968–82. As was the case with the young drifters, in relationships involving violent boyfriends, the two are living together and she is prostituting herself. Whereas Nils and Mette mutually agreed that, as a last resort in a difficult situation, she would prostitute herself, Julie related in the first statement she made to the police that she was threatened and beaten by Karl.

One can trace similar patterns in several other relationships involving violent boyfriends. Often the two have been living together for a long time. The longest of these relationships had been going on for 23 years when the woman reported her husband for pimping. These women have been prostituting themselves over a longer period of time, and they prostitute themselves extensively and regularly, as a rule several days a week. A number of the women have, in addition, prostitution experience prior to living with the accused – there is reliable information that nine, or half, have previously engaged in prostitution.

The violent boyfriends are older than the non-violent boyfriends. Unemployment is also predominant in this group of pimps. Of the 18 accused, only two had work at the time the complaint was filed. Information about previous criminal activity indicates that the violent boyfriends have committed numerous property crimes. Only three of the 18 have no prior record. Karl is a typical representative of this group of pimps – trying to straighten himself out after many years on the fringe involved with crime, drugs, and alcohol, but finding it difficult.

Like Karl, most of the other violent boyfriends live principally on their wife's or girlfriend's prostitution money. The money goes down the same drain the other pimp cases describe: everyday living expenses, drinking, drugs, and cars. Aside from demanding the money, it appears that the violent boyfriends have a relatively passive relationship to the actual tricks. Of the 18 who were reported, seven have in one manner or another been active in terms of the woman's prostitution – however, with actions which appear to be focused more on control than on assistance. There are periods when they monitor her prostitution, particularly when the woman expresses an unwillingness to prostitute herself. A couple of the accused procured customers, either through personal contacts or by placing ads. In contrast to Nils, who kept track of Mette's tricks, watched out for her, took down license numbers, and did other things to offer protection – actions which Mette perceived as help – the violent boyfriends usually sit at home or at a restaurant and wait for the money.

Police documents tell us that violence or the threat of violence is an effective means of promoting prostitution. Judging from the statements made by witnesses, it appears that the violence in these relationships is closely tied to the woman's prostitution and the man's dependence on her money. This is true for the majority of the violent boyfriend-pimp relationships. The woman relates that her husband/partner threatens or beats her to get her out on the street to earn money, or to get her earnings when she comes home from the street. Police investigations uncovered instances of brutal and grotesque acts of violence: beating, kicking, wounds inflicted with a knife or broken glass, broken noses, and internal bleeding have been reported. One of the women was dangled from the balcony of a tenth-floor apartment by her husband, who threatened to drop her if she wouldn't go out on the street. Another woman's husband ran into her with a car. The man typically becomes increasingly violent if she threatens to leave him. In most instances it is the woman who reports her violent boyfriend. Most of them later withdraw the complaint, as Julie did.

Prostitutes whose husbands or boyfriends beat them have everyday lives which resemble the everyday lives of other abused women. The difference is that the abuse of women who prostitute themselves is often linked to prostitution and money. But the similarity between the abuse of women who prostitute themselves and other women is the pattern: he beats her, they make up, he beats her, she leaves – but frequently comes back. This happens in half of the violent boyfriend-pimp relationships. In the other half it appears that filing a complaint results in a permanent break-up.

Judicial policy

There is a striking contrast between how violent boyfriends and non-violent boyfriends fare within the judicial system. In the preceding section we concluded that the wheels of justice turned most effectively against the non-violent boyfriends. Complaints filed against the men who beat their wives or girlfriends emphasize this point dramatically. The violence in these boyfriend-pimp relationships is brutal, often frequent and long-term. Yet while five of the seven non-violent boyfriend-pimps ended up in court, only one-third (seven out of 22) of the complaints filed against violent boyfriend-pimps ended in prosecution. Four of the accused were sentenced. The most severe sentence handed down to this group of pimps was two years and three months. This sentence was for the commission of a number of punishable offences. Only two of the indictments in this group led to the man being found guilty of violence. One of the violent boyfriend-pimps was only indicted for making threats, though the description of the events in the charges against him included gross violence. He was charged with having threatened his wife into prostitution:

> ... in part threatening her with a knife; in part holding a butcher knife against her throat; in part by in his pocket holding a knife against her with the blade up; in addition on several occasions threatening to throw her from the tenth floor and on several occasions having held her out over the balcony of said place; in addition, on one occasion having held her in a stranglehold, pushed her head under the bed, placed his heel on her neck and twisted her hair; the circumstances of these acts were such that [NN] did not dare to refuse to comply to his demands." [From the indictment]

He was acquitted by the county court and the case against him was appealed by the prosecutor. But in the appeal to the superior court the charges of threats and violence had been stripped away. He was ultimately found guilty of pimping, but not of violence or threats. This case illustrates one typical characteristic of judical practice regarding violent boyfriend-pimp cases: one rarely finds any trace of violence against prostitutes in the court proceedings. The violence disappears in its journey through the judicial machinery.

"Stable" pimps

A 14-year-old girl was found unconscious on the side of the road one Saturday night. She was taken to the police station. Her name was Linda. She said it was Erik who had beaten her.

Linda got to know Erik shortly after she started seventh grade. Linda was constantly on the go – during the afternoons and evenings she ran around downtown with her girlfriends. The Mobil station by the Postal Bank building was a particularly popular spot. That's where she noticed Erik. Or maybe it was the other way around. Erik drove a big American car and he honked and waved at the girls. Erik had sex appeal and was grown-up – almost 30. Linda was one of the lucky ones who got to sit in his car. Linda fell in love. Soon they were "going steady."

After a couple of months Erik started nagging. He wanted Linda to start hustling on Stener Street. Linda did not want to. Several of her girlfriends went there, but Linda had never turned a trick. Just been there and watched. Sat up on the wall, dangling her legs and watching the traffic. She talked with her girlfriends when they were between tricks.

Erik kept on nagging. He needed money for his car. Or rather his cars – he traded in his American car as often as others buy jeans. Erik was unemployed and received sick pay as a result of an accident at work. What he could collect in benefits or borrow from friends, family, and an overdrawn checking account, was not enough to cover his car and his daily expenses. In the end, Linda gave in. She could not take any more nagging and besides, she knew that Erik would find a new girlfriend if she did not cooperate soon.

Linda turned tricks on Stener Street for almost a year. As a rule she worked a couple of hours every evening. During the day she was at school. At home neither her mother nor father noticed any difference. Linda had always been out running around after school. Erik usually picked her up at home in the afternoon, then the two of them drove to Stener Street. When she had turned her tricks for the day, he drove her home again. He often parked his car in Stener Street while she turned tricks. Occasionally he brought her customers he had found. Linda primarily did hand jobs. She could make from 300 to 400 crowns an evening. Erik got almost all of the money – Linda kept a few tens for cigarettes, Cokes, and candy bars.

Occasionally they argued, mostly because Linda did not want to work on Stener Street. Erik lost his temper and hit her. It was after one of these arguments that Linda was found in a ditch on the side of the road. Erik had dumped her out of the car.

Erik was charged with pimping, assault, and sexual abuse of a minor. Linda and her mother – her guardian – jointly filed the complaint. Erik was immediately placed in custody. During interrogation Linda said that Erik had a lot of women working for him, both under-age girls and adult women. She thought there might be ten or twelve all together. She knew several of them.

Several of the women whose names Linda had provided testified that they had had a relationship to Erik similar to Linda's. For some it was their first infatuation, then the street. Others had already prostituted themselves prior to meeting Erik.

Erik denied that he had ever forced anyone into prostitution. But naturally he knew many of the women, he said. He hung out downtown and often cruised the district. But Linda's story was pure fabrication from start to finish. Erik stated that he was engaged and had lived with a woman for the past year and that he had not gone out with anyone else during that time.

Erik was released custody after a month or so. The case against him was dismissed due to lack of evidence.

American and Norwegian images

In the complaint filed against Erik it was revealed that he had several girls/women prostituting themselves for him simultaneously. Ten or twelve different ones, Linda thought. The case documents do not indicate how many he may have had, or how many of them he had simultaneously. But according to Linda there were others besides herself. Other witnesses corroborated Linda's view. Erik, then, is what is referred to as a "stable pimp."

A "stable pimp" is a pimp who earns money on several women simultaneously. But the stable pimp is also more. In the popular culture the stable pimp is often singled out as The Classic Pimp. For prostitutes as well, the stable pimp is the prototype. To the degree that it is possible to rate pimps according to who is "worst" and who is "best," the stable pimp is in many ways the diametrical opposite of the non-violent boyfriend-pimp. A boyfriend-pimp, like Nils, does not think primarily about his own profit. His relationship to the woman is a romantic one and she feels she is prostituting herself for their common good. Love is not the stable pimp's main concern. The image of the stable pimp is the image of a man who cleverly and cunningly organizes prostitution traffic and other shady operations. He pulls the strings. A stable pimp evokes unmistakable associations with livestock. The stable pimp's stable is not, however, made up of domestic animals, but of female animals who can be milked and thereby bring their owner cash and prosperity. He enjoys the jet set life of a playboy.

A socio-anthropological study of a large American city ghetto traces the historical origin of the stable pimp as a type. The stable pimp is the son of the ghetto, who through successful maneuvering escapes unemployment and poverty with the help of prostituted women. He is a winner (Milner and Milner, 1973). Among the ghetto's either partially or completely criminal fortune-hunters, the pimp is respected and honored. He is a hero who has realized the masculine ideal of the ghetto. With "his" women he breaks out of the slum and the stench of garbage. He is a juggler with emotions who manages his women without competition and scenes of destructive jealousy arising. The use of violence on his part is, as a rule, unnecessary. His survival technique is, among other things, to make himself interesting to the women. In this way they can be manipulated, and this pays off in ready cash. He shows the world that he is on top. Conspicious consumption, a luxurious and flamboyant life-style – these are the evidence of the stable pimp's success.

Erik has been given the label "stable pimp" along with seven other men in the police data. (One of the men has been reported twice, thus making a total of nine complaints filed against stable pimps.) However, the basis on which we give Erik and the others in this group this label is somewhat tenuous. The label is based on statements from witnesses who claim that the accused has several women prostituting themselves for him simultaneously. Those accused of being stable pimps, however, flatly deny it.

In comparison to relationships with boyfriend-pimps, stable pimps' ties to the women are far less likely to be long-term affairs where they live together under the same roof, sharing the same table and bed. Stable-pimp relationships are more likely to be marked by money, pressure, and sex, without cohabitation. Linda's pimp Erik is living with another woman. Erik's relationship to Linda is a sexual/economic relationship "on the side."

This pattern is fairly typical for these cases. The woman involved with a stable pimp has quite clearly invested more, and stronger, feelings than the man. He leads an independent life alongside his relationship to the woman who is the plaintiff in the case. She knows little about how he spends his time. Judging from his own statements, it is obvious that she is *not* The Woman in his life.

The stable pimps in our material are not large-scale pimps. Erik stands out from the others who were reported, in terms of the size of his "stable." The witnesses in his case report a large number of girls/women. Even though all of them have not worked for him simultaneously, there is nonetheless the impression that Erik's many female acquaintances have played a central role in his finances and lifestyle. In comparison, the others charged have a modest "stable." Four of those charged were accused of having two women each, and two were charged with having three women each. In one case mention is made of "several" women, but no actual number is given. The police documents make it reasonable to conclude that these pimps have small "stables." For a number of them it is appropriate to say that they have a sexual/economic relationship with two or three different women simultaneously. Moreover, it is not always clear if they have pimped for several women simultaneously or serially, that is to say one after another. In that case the designation "stable" may be inappropriate, since it can hardly be called a stable when the pimp moves from one prostitute to the next over time. The men who were originally singled out as stable pimps in the Norwegian data carry on an operation which is more reminiscent of retail than of wholesale.

The women in stable-pimp relationships describe an everyday life full of violence. Seven of the eight men who were reported threatened, coerced and/or beat them, according to the women. The last case contains no information regarding the use of violence. In seven of the nine cases against stable pimps, complaints were filed by the women. Three of them, however, later withdrew charges.

In the American literature the pimp has two faces: the sugar pimp and the gorilla pimp. The first does not need to resort to his fists to get the women out on the street, or inside restaurants or hotels. He uses his head. Sweet-talks them. Through words it becomes obvious to the woman that she should contribute her share. The appropriate combination of convincing words, authority, and consideration are especially important for the successful sugar pimp. This is the only way of ensuring that peace and tolerance rule in the stable. He cannot always beat everyone into obedience. The gorilla pimp's methods are coarse. He rules with his fist, not with his head (see Milner and Milner, 1973, among others). The stable pimps in our material do not behave in a very refined manner. Sugar pimps they are not.

According to police documents, women in stables prostitute themselves a lot and earn a lot. The police material reveals that the street is the stable pimp's most important prostitution arena, precisely as it is for the boyfriend-pimps. Most of the profits end up in his pocket. But how much the woman gets back for "entertainment," "housekeeping money," or "pocket money" varies. In most cases all money detours through his wallet before any of it might wander back to the woman. He collects the profits and then "pays" the woman a little, or even less. He might reward her with cash, or by paying for her food, rent, clothes, and extras. "I got a little money for cigarettes and Cokes and candy. I didn't get to keep more than about 20 crowns a night" – that is what Linda reported in the police material. The stable pimp is greedy.

The non-violent boyfriend-pimp relationships probably survived the strain of being reported and brought to trial. This is not the case with stable-pimp relationships. In these cases it appears that the break-up between parties is permanent. *None* of the stable pimps, however, was convicted of pimping. All the charges filed against pimps in this category were dismissed.

The city boy with grease under his fingernails

The American picture of a successful stable pimp shows a well-dressed man, with expensive cars and extravagant habits. These are not the characteristic features of the men whom we, based on the police documents, have called stable pimps.

The witnesses' statements and other evidence gathered by the police do not leave the impression that the accused live a life of luxury. There is a sharp contrast between the stereotype of the American pimp and the pimps whose records are on file at the Oslo police department. In the first place, the number of cases which can reasonably be categorized as ones involving stable pimps has been negligible during this 14-year period (1968–82). Secondly, even though police documents do not contain long and detailed descriptions, these cases seem to tell of a completely different type of man from the American stereotype. The police data do not give the impression that these men are "winners." They have little education; their employment record is at best sporadic. They are men with a history of criminal activity and drug and alcohol abuse. Only two of the accused appear to "live it up" on a regular basis, frequenting restaurants, travelling abroad, and spending a lot of money on themselves. Seen in terms of the group as a whole, this is the exception. As with the others, the stable pimp's money disappears down the drain of daily expenditures: food, clothes, rent, child support, and loan payments. But there is perhaps one area where they do distinguish themselves: cars. Erik represents, in its purest form, a subculture which worships big American cars and trades them in at a dizzying rate. Linda says that Erik used most of her prostitution money on his cars. Using the case documents to get a concrete idea of where the prostitution money goes, we see that car expenses stand out in half the cases. But even Erik – who most resembles a stable pimp – cannot begin to live up to the American successes. His big American cars cannot cover up the fact that, when it comes right down to it, he is a city boy with no job and grease under his fingernails. Things do not "swing" as much for Erik as things seem to swing for the stable pimp as depicted in the American literature.

A familiar face: The pimps that get caught

The two first paragraphs in the section on pimping of the Norwegian penal code date from the turn of the century. These paragraphs are aimed at the active pimp, who "entices," "promotes," or "exploits." The last paragraph was added in 1963 and is aimed at passive pimps, such as Nils.

The rationale for the section on pimping is interesting. At the turn of the century the chief of police in the capital city was very worried about "the extremely dangerous and audacious male criminals" who were operating with female prostitutes. He believed that an effective criminal prosecution of these men would lead to a decline in the number of felonies committed. In addition, prostitution led to an economic depreciation of buildings and property belonging to the bourgeoisie in the prostitution districts. Something had to be done about this (*Odelstings proposision*, 1914, p. 13). That laws against pimping exist in order to protect the individual prostitute is an invention of modern theory. The lawmakers at the turn of the century did not intend for the law to serve such a purpose. It was public morality that was to be protected.

The addition of the third paragraph in 1963 made cohabitation with a prostitute who was the main provider into a criminal offense. It was introduced as a means of getting around the strict burden of proof which up until that time had been required in order to convict individuals of pimping. The authorities wanted to have something to fall back on which, in spite of uncertain proof of promoting, enticing, or exploiting, could bring about a conviction. It was assumed that for some of the couples hit by this "criminalization of relationships" there had been active encouragement on the man's part. This may indeed be true, in some cases. But the other men, the normal boyfriends, husbands, and lovers, were ignored.[3] It's as if we

---

[3] This is similar to legislation in several other countries. See for example Barry, 1979, p. 110.

were to declare everyone with a driver's license a criminal on the grounds that they could break the legal speed limit. In all likelihood a great majority of the speeding violations go unnoticed, so this way many more of those guilty of speeding would be caught. Even so, the argument is clearly invalid.

Who gets caught?

Only men were reported for pimping. The majority of those reported can no longer call themselves young men – on average they are over 30. The oldest was 56 years old and the youngest was 17 at the time he was charged with pimping.

On the whole these men have had little education. Admittedly, information regarding education is lacking in approximately one-third of the cases, but where this information is available there are clear indications that the majority have no education beyond the elementary or junior high school level.

The majority of those men reported, nearly two-thirds of them, are unemployed. Those who do have work hold unskilled, low-paying jobs.

Most of them have previously been involved with the police and the courts. The criminal histories of these men present a picture of traditional criminality. Crimes against property dominate, and to a lesser degree crimes of violence. Among the crimes against property, larceny is the most common offence.

Even though the information on substance abuse is in part incomplete and inconclusive, there is nonetheless a clear tendency: few of the men reported do *not* have problems with substance abuse. The overriding impression of these men is that substance abuse is a fairly well-established part of their lives at the time complaints are filed. For most of them the problem is alcohol; to a lesser degree narcotics. However, there are a number of them who abuse both alcohol and drugs.

The police documents tell us about a familiar face in criminology. While it is true that the man who is charged with pimping is older than the average offender, he is otherwise strikingly similar to the lawbreaker we know from other criminal statistics. The man accused of pimping bears all the marks of hardship which are usually associated with registered criminals. He has little education, difficulty in holding down a job, problems with substance abuse; and in addition he has already been labelled a criminal by the courts. This result poses an interesting parallel to an earlier Norwegian study of "drug sharks" [i.e., dealers] (Bødal, 1982). Both pimps and "drug sharks" are objects of widespread stereotyping. In popular mythology the drug shark is a man behind the scenes whose clean hands deal in millions of dollars, while the health and lives of drug abusers are ruined. Bødal's study of the first 350 individuals to be sentenced under the "professional drug dealers" section (section 162 in the penal code) shows us, however, a familiar picture of losers in the legal system, where, for example, nearly all of those punished were themselves drug abusers.

The practice of the courts

What was the outcome of the 65 complaints that were filed?

Approximately two-thirds of the charges were dismissed. Sixteen of the charges resulted in a conviction. Of those sentenced, six were sentenced to unconditional imprisonment.

Who is convicted and who goes free? We have presented tables with this information in other publications (Finstad, 1984; and Høigard, 1985, pp. 127–8). The tendencies can be summarized as follows:

1 Elements of violence have the opposite effect to that one would expect: the more violence there is, the less likely there will be a conviction. Even though the numbers represented in the data are small, the tendency is clear. What we have learned from the case documents is that the police demonstrate very little concern for prostitutes who are abused by their boyfriends/pimps. The violence vanishes at police headquarters. There are eight cases where it is not noted that the complaints are a combination of pimping and battering, even though the woman has filed complaints on both counts. The police "filter" the reports themselves and the violence disappears in the process. This point is made particularly clear in the case of three of those charged with pimping, all of whom *themselves* admitted violence. The crime of battery is automatically dropped when charges of pimping are dismissed.

2 Cases in which the woman has filed the complaint are underrepresented in those cases which are brought to trial. There is a greater likelihood of conviction when someone other than the woman who is directly involved reports a person for pimping.

3 None of the "stable" pimps is convicted. In all but two of the cases in this category it is the woman herself who has filed the complaint. The fact that no stable pimps are convicted can be linked to the greater likelihood of conviction when someone other than the woman files the complaint.

4 Pimps who are involved in a relationship with the prostitute, both the non-violent boyfriends and the violent ones, are overrepresented in the adjudicated cases.

5 The courts come down hard on the non-violent boyfriend-pimps. Four of the seven cases ended in conviction.

6 Sentence is passed on four of the six sex-clubs reported. On the whole the sentences are mild. No one is sentenced to unconditional imprisonment.

The question of justice – legal justice as well – is a question of values. We define *our* values in this way: violence calls for a more severe sentence than when there is no violence. The pimp who operates a stable deserves a stiffer penalty than the pimp who is involved in a relationship with the prostitute. The fact that the woman files a complaint is grounds for a more severe sentence than when a third party reports pimping. By taking the initiative to make the report herself, she is giving clear signals that she wants to break away. Reports from third parties can obviously be founded on considerations other than protecting the woman.

Evaluated on the basis of these values – which naturally are open to discussion – the practice of the Norwegian courts is scandalously unjust. The courts are moving unequivocally in the direction of handing down the severest penalties in the mildest of the pimp cases. Judicial practice does little to protect the interests of the women.

Two main conclusions

On the basis of our data we have arrived at two main conclusions:

The extent of pimping has been substantially exaggerated in the Norwegian public debate. Three things have led us to this conclusion. First, the number of reports made to the police during a 14-year period (1968–82) is very low. Though much suggests that until recently this kind of work was not prioritized by the police, this can hardly be the entire explanation. Second, the reports from the police's own task force on pimps corroborate our conclusion. In the course of the task force's first two years of activity, it registered 664 women suspected of prostitution and 81 men suspected of pimping. In both cases these numbers probably represent a minimum, and the number of suspected pimps is even more liable to be an underestimate than the corresponding number of prostitutes. But the possible sources of error notwithstanding, these figures would hardly suggest that a majority of the women have a pimp. Third, and most important, our conclusion is supported by the in-depth interviews. Half of the 26 prostitutes we spoke with currently have or have had a pimp. This figure is based on the entire period the women have been in prostitution. At the time the interviews were conducted, only four of the women had a pimp.

The pimp is a man living on the fringe. Among the few who have a friend/pimp, in the criminal sense, there are many different kinds of relationships. It is important to emphasize that the pimp in the stereotype really exists, in Norway as elsewhere. The police data show that there are pimps who have several women, who use violence, and who cynically manipulate women. But this is far from being the dominant pattern in either the police data or the interview data. The stereotypical pimp scarcely exists as anything other than a wandering tale in the interview material. The relationships in the interview material which could be affected by the law on pimping involve people who are on the fringe, people who are drifters. The circumstances of their two lives are similar in many ways – both pimp and prostitute have had more than their share of defeats, they have been rejected at work and at school. They both have problems with substance abuse. These are relationships in which both partners are using an illegal economy to support themselves, and for which violence as *the* explanation for prostitution seems blatantly insufficient. The woman experiences the man as a lover, not as a pimp. Some of the cases in the police pimp material, too, tell of people who are living on the fringe and of love's difficult circumstances.

The pimp's functions

Pistol against her temple, fist in her eye. This is how we commonly imagine the pimp wielding power over his woman. The idea of physical coercion is what makes the relationship understandable to us. Without it we might conclude that prostitution is the woman's voluntary choice. But our increasing insight into the content of prostitution makes the voluntary choice perspective a difficult one to maintain. And so we are brought back to the idea of physical coercion.

Violence does exist, without question. Violence – and at times brutal violence – has occurred in approximately two-thirds of the pimp cases reported to the police. At the same time, the violence reported in these police cases is probably not an accurate reflection of the extent of violence in prostitution as a whole. We repeat that of the 13 women interviewed who currently have or have had a pimp, only three have been subject to violence from him. There is no reason to minimize violence. But in the majority of cases it is a mistake to believe that violence is responsible for the woman staying in the relationship. In those relationships where violence occurs, the woman stays in the relationship despite the violence, not because of it. The relationship between the woman and the pimp is far too complex to be reduced to a question of physical force. One of the main arguments of this book is that the woman and her man in many ways share similar lives. More than that, they *are* each other's lives, intertwined as sweethearts, lovers, enemies and friends, supporters and adversaries, close to each other through the shifting emotions and their shifting roles. For him, she is not just a whore. For her, he is anything but a pimp. And even when they confront each other in the context of prostitution, physical coercion often plays a completely subordinate role. The source of the pimp's power does not lie here. *The pimp's foundation of power rests solely on the fact that she feels that she needs him.* The challenge is to try to delve further into these feelings.

One way of approaching this is to analyze the pimp's functions in prostitution. We have divided these functions into two groups: functions serving practical purposes, and those of an emotional nature. One danger in dividing and analyzing the functions in this way is that the relationship between the woman and the pimp can easily begin to resemble a geometric design. It is important to keep in mind that these functions interact to form a complex relationship.

Impresario

In countries where prostitutes are actively arrested and prosecuted, the pimp automatically has an important function. In a number of American cities hordes of prostitutes are regularly hauled into the police station, and the prostitute is totally dependent on having someone on the outside who is prepared to post her bail so that she can be released. The pimp becomes directly useful in the day-to-day business of prostitution. The double standard of American legal practice – where the customer and the pimp go free and the women are hauled in – serves to provide the necessary foundation for the extensive pimping in that country. No such role exists for the Norwegian pimp. We believe this is one important reason traditional pimping is far less widespread in Norway than, for example, in the United States. But this does not mean that the Norwegian pimp cannot find useful tasks for himself.

Fredrik has a much more conscious relationship to prostitution than most; conscious in the sense that he went into prostitution as a job where the goal was to maximize profits. He played a far more active role than most pimps in Oslo. We get a good idea of the range of practical tasks a pimp can fill his workday with from Fredrik's account:

"I quit my job and made a wholehearted commitment to making conditions as good as they possibly could be for Eva in her new job. I was usually with her when she was working. I also drove her back and forth to the district. Eva was so afraid of being recognized. I figured out that I could solve that problem by equipping her with clothes that were foreign to both of us, but which were absolutely appealing in that line of work. I was the one who went to the shops and picked out sexy clothes for her. I bought condoms for her too, incidentally. It was a firm requirement that she shouldn't take any tricks without a condom."

After a while Eva and Fredrik quit street prostitution and started working through the personals. It was Fredrik's job to write the copy for the ads.

Cecilie asks if he ever gave Eva advice on how she should act. "Oh yes, definitely. When Eva was working on the street she wasn't to take any initiative toward the customers; she was supposed to let them get her attention first, before they started talking with each other. I stayed out of the actual work of satisfying the customers. That was her business. But I did encourage her to read books about sexual techniques. In addition I advised her to tell as little as possible about herself and why she was earning money this way. She told the same lies that most of them do. The one about the desperate student who doesn't have money for her studies. Applied for a student loan too late, etc. – it's the usual story.

"I was the one who was in charge of our finances. I had ideas about what we could buy. Of course I knew that she didn't like working on the street, but I mean who does? Most people have boring, routine jobs which are far from being enjoyable or challenging. Nevertheless they show up at the job every single day, week after week, year after year. Why do they do this when they don't like their job? Money – of course. I could often motivate her to work a little harder by laying out all our expenses and the purchases we should make or the repairs we have to do on the house. She was more materialistic than I was, wanted to buy more expensive things. I wanted to have a profit, I wanted to save – she wasn't as interested in that. But I thought – one day the balloon might pop and it'll all be over. I wanted us to be as prepared as we could be. The money belonged of both of us, but I managed it. I saw to it that all our bills were paid on time and I put a fixed amount in the bank every month. We each had our own savings account and I regularly put money into a safe-deposit box."

We have pointed out earlier that the pimp does not play a key role in starting the woman out. Girlfriends are more important instigators and teachers. This does not mean that pimps are *never* around when a woman starts out. Every once in a great while it is the pimp who paves the way. But his instructions are fairly simple: which streets she should walk and how much she should demand. There is no basis for placing much importance on the pimp's role as impresario in prostitution in Oslo.[4] It is most often limited to this: buying condoms and maybe a few simple instructions when she's starting out.

Bodyguard

In the section on non-violent boyfriends we saw how Nils went with Mette to the backstreets and took down the license numbers of customers in the event something should happen to her. Fredrik also had this role as Eva's protector:

"I was usually with her when she was doing tricks on the street. I sat discreetly in a car and read the customer's license number and car make and model into a cassette just to make sure the information was recorded. You never know what might happen."

After a while Eva started to work indoors in an apartment. Fredrik: "I sat in a car and took pictures of her and the customer with a powerful telephoto lens as they walked toward the apartment. If anything happened to her, I wanted to know who had crossed the line. This was also something she had demanded, that I keep an eye on her. She felt safer then."

Fredrik did take his job of providing security more seriously than most other pimps. But the subject comes up in conversation with several of the women. We recall Anita, who makes the protector-role an essential characteristic of a pimp: "A real pimp is one who follows the girl in his car and makes sure nothing happens to her."

Inga and Elin are lovers. Other prostitutes say that Elin is Inga's pimp. Yet a lesbian pimp would undoubtedly not be seen as a threat by the customer. Inga solves the problem like this: "If there's any

[4] The pimp as teacher and impresario has been the subject of a number of American studies. See for example Heyl, 1976.

funny business I threaten them by saying my dude will get after 'em. The customers often ask if you have a dude. They're afraid of getting beat up." Lying that you have a male pimp for reasons like this is not unusual.

Even though Elin does not seem menacing, little and slight as she is, she still is important for Inga's feeling of security: "I always tell Elin when we are going to meet and where. Then she can let the police know if I don't get back. It's really tough if I'm not through then. I know she's afraid for me. I go and tell her if I have a lot left and will be really late."

Elin: "You do as well as you can, Inga. It's not your fault that I have to wait. You come and tell me when you can."

There is evidence of the bodyguard role in the pimp data as well, as illustrated in the following excerpt from a police report: "N. N. drove her into Oslo and followed her so nothing would happen to her. He always followed her in his own car so she never had to leave the place alone." The bodyguard role only appears in a handful of the reports. This is probably an under-representation. A common pattern in these reports is that of a woman reporting her pimp because she, for a variety of reasons, wants to break away. In this situation it does not seem plausible from a psychological point of view that she would draw attention to the fact that he has helped her. The pimp, for his part, most often denies having anything to do with prostitution and therefore cannot point to his assistance as an extenuating circumstance. Another possibility, of course, is that the guard role is not as widespread among pimps who are reported. With the establishment of the police task force on pimping, the number of reports made on pimps who perform a guard function will probably increase. A large percentage of the action taken by the task force is, in fact, based on repeated registration of cars in the district. This is ironic. We would argue that pimps who show up and try to guarantee security are a little bit better than the ones who hang around at home or at a restaurant waiting for their money. But it is the ones who are "a little bit better" who run the greatest risk of being caught by the police. The ones who are the most visible in the cityscape are also visible to the police.

There are instances where the pimp can prevent violence. He can also take revenge. Revenge is sometimes a group effort. Inga: "It's not only exploitation. The guys at Egertorvet will also back us up. Yesterday some teenagers were harassing us – two so-called high-class couples. They threw Coke bottles at us and shouted obscenities. One of us ran up and got the boys and they chased them away.

That happens a lot. Those of us who work at the Bank Square pool our money and give them 50 or 100 crowns for that. But they do it without getting any money, too. We help each other."

Anna tells this from Stener Street: "I didn't understand all that business about having a pimp. I didn't understand it at all. Indirectly, the guys did act like pimps, of course. 'Go get us some dough. Look at us, we're out of beer and the good stuff,' they'd say. And then the girls turned tricks. There were some of the guys who were together with some of the girls – there were probably four or five of them. They acted like goddamned pimps. They never did any break-ins, not those guys. But the guys did give us something in return. There was this sleazeball who came down a helluva lot. He started shooting his mouth off and bugging the whole gang. The guys turned his car over. It can be safer with a pimp. The customers don't dare to do so much then. The guys kick them in the crotch and throw rocks at their cars. Sometimes we took off with the customer's money. If he ran after us, the boys might come, and then he didn't dare do anything. Sometimes when we took off with the money, when the customer came after us, we'd run up to a total strangers on the street and holler: 'Help! Help! Rape!' Then he took off. That was fun."

How important is the role of bodyguard? More important than the role of impresario, at any rate. But the guard role isn't particularly important either. The most important security precautions are taken *before* the trick is turned. The women screen their customers in advance on the basis of the customers' eyes, their body language, and what they say. They also screen on the basis of information from the other women. Once she has gone with a customer, there is not much the pimp can do. Violence happens quickly, as Lisa's story illustrates. Lisa hangs out with three guys. They get some of what she earns on the street. Lisa is crazy about cars, and most of what she earns goes on cars and booze. "I got a trick with a Finn. He had a big semi. In the back there was another Finn I didn't know about when I said yes. They drove way out of town. Both of them raped me there, and on the way back to town they threw me out of the truck. I was a mess afterwards, covered with blood and scabs. The boys had followed the truck, but they lost sight of it on the way."

The objective guarantee of security is by no means the most important aspect of the bodyguard role. Just the *idea* of a threatening pimp in the background is enough to scare the customers. From this perspective one could say that the unrealistic stories in popular mythology have a function. But the significance of the role lies on a different level. The important thing is that the woman *feels* safer. She is not completely alone, entirely at the mercy of the customer.

At the same time the role gives the pimp a job. He does his bit. He works as long as she works. Prostitution becomes a shared project with a natural gendered division of labor. It is no longer so blatantly obvious that in reality she is supporting them both. The pimp's role as parasite is less obtrusive. And most importantly, the fact that he is actively working to minimize her risk is a clear sign that he really cares about her.

This aspect of the role is *not* consciously and manipulatively planned by a cynical pimp. On the contrary, we are struck by how both of them *believe* that these security arrangements are necessary, in spite of the fact that their experience should indicate that he is pretty much wasting his time. But in fact the more hidden and symbolic aspects of his role as bodyguard give them both a vague and diffuse feeling that everything is "all right," "like it should be" – and they therefore help to perpetuate the pimp's role. These security precautions are a ritual that tells of responsible love.

Friends and lovers

In her book *Female Sexual Slavery*, Barry describes how the pimp cynically hooks women by pretending friendship and love: "Pimps know all the cards and how to play them. The young girl or woman he sets as a target is likely to be naive, lonely and bitter towards the family she has just run away from or the marriage she has just left. She is also likely to be broke and without job skills. Suddenly a man appears who is friendly, who offers to buy her a meal and, later, a place to spend the night. She hears compliments for the first time in ages, as well as promises to buy her new clothes and have her hair done. The romantic movie scenario is being played out and it may be days, weeks, or even months before she figures out what has happened to her" (1979, p. 76).

In Barry's description the pimp plays on the woman's loneliness, on her need to be loved, and on her need to show him that she will do anything for their mutual love. It is an extensive, calculated game where he uses pretend-feelings to entrap her in his web. We have found this type of example in the Norwegian material, too. Hanna relates: "I met Lars at a pub. He was just gorgeous. Six months later I saw him over on the west side. 'Oh gosh, is this where he lives,' I thought and rushed across the street. We walked along talking and then went to the park to get some pot. That was a year and a half ago now. Lars is the most beautiful guy in the world. I turn to butter, melted butter. If he says something, I do it. It's because of his charm. He's so good-looking. He has totally perfect skin, and *that* body and *those* eyes. Every now and then he says that he really likes me and then I melt like butter. It's strange but I've never gone to bed with him. But I've lain next to him on the sofa a zillion times. It's a tactic of his not to sleep with me. Lars gets everything from me. Money for beer, pot, beautiful clothes."

I ask if Lars has a job. Hanna laughs: "Him, no, you must be crazy. He has other girls working for him too, at least one more. When four of us girls are sitting around the table, he comes around and gives each of us a hug. He messes around with other girls besides me."

I ask if Lars gives her any kind of help aside from emotional support. "He doesn't check on me when I'm on a trick. But he's very good about being on time and at the right place whenever we've agreed to meet. And he always knows where I am. So if I don't show up, he can do something. And, yeah, he defends me, too. One time some old swine on the street started mouthing off at me. Lars lit right into him, kicking and swinging, and the man took off down the street like a porcupine." Hanna has a good laugh at the memory. She says that Lars has had a lot of run-ins with the cops, and that he's served time for writing bad checks. He has tried to get her to cash checks for him; she tried, but didn't get any money.

Cecilie: "Some might say that Lars is your pimp since he gets money that you've earned on the street."

Hanna: "No, I've never thought of it that way. Not like that. He's just so excruciatingly beautiful. It's awful that he has such a hold on me. He'll have a hold on me till I die. Of course, he has other girls, too. That's damned bitter, thinking of him with other girls. But pimp, well, may be that is the right word, but no, I don't know, I haven't thought of it like that."

Lars fits the pimp stereotype fairly well: he has several women working for him, he contributes no income, he uses the classic technique of "keeping it in his pants."[5] He does not display his sexuality casually in a relationship with Hanna or other women – that could cause a scene, trouble, jealousy. He controls himself and portions himself out in carefully measured doses. This story also

---

[5] This technique is described in several sources, for example Milner and Milner, 1973.

illustrates another of Barry's main points: the fact that the woman is speechless, or does not experience the man as a pimp, does not mean that he isn't one. The woman's low self-image and desperate desire to finally belong and be loved can give her a view of reality where turning a trick seems like a reasonable price to pay for warmth. "... she has taken on the same perception of herself and her body held by the people who have abused her over the years – the self-image of a throwaway" (Barry, 1979, p. 102).

There is general agreement among others in the milieu that Lars is a pimp. Nevertheless, Hanna hasn't thought about him like that.

Is this the whole story? Do all pimps play an elaborate game to get the woman to prostitute herself?

We don't think so – not in the United States or in Norway. In order to expand on this we will use Månsson's model of the concept of pimp (Månsson, 1981, p. 84). Månsson describes the relationship between the prostitute and the pimp along four continua.

Degree of planning when meeting the woman

Spontaneous ←——————————————→ conscious strategies to entrap her

The relationship's emotional content

Mutual love ←——————————————→ extreme psychic/physical violence

Economy

The man is self-supported ←——————→ the man lives off the woman

Number of women

The man has a relationship ←————→ the man has organized
with one woman   exploitation of several women

These continua show the broad range that lies behind the general label of "pimp." The farther to the left the relationship is placed, the less it fits with the pimp stereotype. Because each dimension is independent of the others, a number of different pimp-profiles exist. Our material contains most of these profiles. The police material tends far more to the right side of the model than the interview material. The "bad guys" definitely exist, in Norway as well. A normal pattern in the interview material where a man was involved in the prostitution – we again reiterate that most of the women are alone – is this: a man can be together with a woman because he fell in love, can live in a monogamous relationship with her – and still let himself be supported by her prostitution. The relationship between Fredrik and Eva follows this pattern. Both say that they are happily married. Eva goes on to say: "Fredrik has a number of qualities which I truly value. He is very stable and reliable. He never tries to trick me – that's never happened. We are actually two completely different people. Maybe that's why we get along so well. If I were shipwrecked on a deserted island, Fredrik is the person I would want with me. Him plus a box of books or maybe a whole library."

Cecilie: "Was Fredrik helpful to you in your prostitution?"

Eva: "Without a doubt. My God, he was the only person I talked to. If anything unusual had happened, we talked about it when I came home. I told him everything. So he was a tremendous emotional support. You pick up the practical details pretty quickly on the street. They don't make that big a difference."

Fredrik is not playacting when it comes to his feelings for Eva. He does, however, have a very conscious and business-like relationship to her prostitution. Other men in our interview material did not have this conscious relationship to prostitution. It is something they both ended up doing in a difficult period in life – as we saw with Nils and Mette.

We have shown that the women we interviewed do not see at their partner as a pimp. He is a boyfriend or a husband. And that is something totally different. Being a couple – that is, literally, sharing a common fate. What is more natural than for two lovers to help each other? Help each other economically – right now and as a plan for a brighter future which they will share. Use each other as a safe haven, where the laws of the meat market do not apply. A love relationship is a *real* relationship, far removed from the simulated emotions which go along with prostitution. In the couple's relationship the primary focus is not on sex and the man's ejaculation. Being a couple means sitting up half the night talking, confiding deep secrets, scratching each other's back, consoling one another in times of defeat, affectionate teasing, dreaming of a new day, assurances of undying love – all those things which now and then make life feel safe and worth living. Loving relationships among people engaging in prostitution can clearly have all of these qualities.

But relationships based on love don't have to be perfect; not among "normal" people either. Relationships are perhaps more often the result of the fulfillment of minimum requirements than of the fulfillment of our wildest dreams. A relationship which makes life seem a little better here and now. In a male-dominated society such as ours, the woman in a relationship will often be subject to oppression from her male partner. Relationships among those working in prostitution are similar to other love relationships, for better and for worse. Prostitutes can be oppressed by their men too – not because they are prostitutes, but because they are women.

The pimp is much more important as a friend and lover than as an impresario or a bodyguard. Both the police data and the interviews confirm this. When Inga needs a pimp to frighten the customers, she lies and says she has a male pimp. She has nonetheless chosen Elin who, in the eyes of the law, is unquestionably her pimp. We know about a handful of similar lesbian couples, in which one of them essentially lives off the other woman's prostitution earnings. We do not know of any cases where a lesbian prostitute has a male pimp even though that clearly would be preferable if the practical functions performed by the pimp were the most important.

At times it can appear as if relationships take on an even greater significance for the participants in prostitution than for the rest of us.

Jane: "A lot of them are afraid of being alone. It's okay to be together with a guy. And they feel so dirty when they're on the street that they're happy that somebody wants to be with them. A pimp is also a friend. You can live with him as a whore and without being oppressed."

Or take Nina, 21 years old, seriously hooked on heroin. She also supports her friend Leif's habit. She says that she has to take in between 3,000 and 4,000 crowns a day for smack. The reason it isn't more is that they buy in large quantities. It's cheaper that way. Nina uses almost a bag every day: "Otherwise I get sick." She works hard for her money. "I hate it, but it's my job." One evening I meet her in the district around 7 p.m. She's agitated, flustered, and stressed and has absolutely no time to talk with me. "I have to get hold of 1,100 crowns by 11 o'clock. I've been standing here half-an-hour without a trick." I hurriedly leave so as not to ruin her market. Nina is one of the women who really has serious problems. The other women can afford to pity her – hardly anyone works as hard as Nina, and on top of everything she has to support Leif, the lazy good-for-nothing. Leif is not popular among the women. They call him a pimp and don't understand why Nina works herself to the bone for that shithead. Nina sees things differently: "We've been together for almost three years now. He's the only thing I live for. He's all I got. He fed me before. He was inside eight months after a break-in. I'd rather work on the street than have him doing time."

He's all I got. Strong words. And all too often, true words. Outside, a world that looks at her with contempt; outside, a world that treats her as a hole surrounded by flesh; outside, a world that has caused her pain and defeat – is it so strange, in this freezing cold, that love warms? The one person who has picked this woman to be his chosen one among all the other "decent" women – doesn't this person have to have a unique and special significance for the woman?

In *Hard Asphalt*, Ida describes how she and Knut stood together against the rest of the world: "but the most important thing was that Knut gave me the feeling that I meant something for someone. A strange contrast maybe to all the beatings. But he beat me because he was so insanely jealous. I think that jealousy comes from being unsure of yourself, afraid of losing what you have. When he was beside himself from fear of losing me, I *had* to mean everything to him. Me, an old junkie! For the first time what I did was important to another person.

"And the months on the street had tied us together. Both the shit we'd had, and the good moments. Knut had become my family. You don't trade your father for your girlfriend's father even if he is a thousand times classier than your own. You don't choose your parents, you know – they're just there. That's just not the way it is. It's the ones you've gotten who mean something to you, and who you care about, in good times and bad. It was the same kind of thing that I felt in my relationship with Knut" (Halvorsen, *Hard Asphalt*, 1987, pp. 156–7).

Many of the relationships among those working in prostitution have endured for years. Some end in marriage. The women often have a high respect for relationships. Earlier we described how some women refrain from entering relationships, feeling that it would not be right as long as they are prostituting themselves. They have high standards of sexual morality. Being unfaithful is taboo. Prostitutes and pimps in relationships are there for each other; in practical matters, but first and foremost, emotionally. They stay together through thick and thin, which is more than you can say for many of our society's solid citizens.

We may very well think that it's a terrible situation. Profligates, shitheads, lazy bums – the invective grows on trees in the debate on the subject of the pimp. All the same, it is a fact that he is capable of giving her something others in society have failed to give her. Care, interest, the respect that comes with his having chosen her. These things are worth a lot when you have known so little of them previously.

It is important to emphasize that there are notable differences in both the extent and the content of the role of pimp in the United States and in Norway. As previously mentioned, judicial practice in the United States creates, among other things, a material foundation for pimping. Moreover, criminal subcultures and organized crime flourish to a totally different degree in the United States from Norway. Therefore, the role of pimp can also receive more subcultural nourishment in the United States. It is reasonable to suppose that pimp-relationships in the United States lean considerably farther to the right on the model on page 168. But we don't for a minute believe that the more positive profile does not exist in the United States – though it is most noticeable in its absence from serious research literature. One major reason for this standpoint is the obvious one that so many more women (and men) are involved in prostitution in the United States than in Norway. It is not very likely that variations that are found in the relatively small Norwegian prostitution milieu are not also in existence in the widespread prostitution milieu in the United States. We suspect that – understandably enough – this piece of reality has been obscured because it has been so important to illuminate the gross exploitation that is found in many pimp-relations. Moreover, our findings here are rooted in our methods. Without the friendships, without having known the couples for years, without seeing how the relationships weathered the strongest adversities, we could not have described this. Nor could we have described this if we had not seen the sorrow when everything goes wrong, as when Fredrik and Eva broke up after many years. Both had left the life of prostitution, both had completed higher degrees. Everything looked so bright – until Eva fell madly in love with a 'straight' man, and left Fredrik. Fredrik lost his hold on reality – became temporarily psychotic, lost his job, and dropped out. Now, after a year, he has just begun the laborious climb back out of his black hole.

And once again, the reactions from the prostitution milieu to *Backstreets* has been our most important criticism. Their reactions have been unambiguous: that's the way it is. Far from all pimps are pimps.

7

The Fight against Prostitution

Opposition to prostitution

This is not a book debating issues. All the same, a close, detailed description of the phenomenon of prostitution leaves us with some knowledge about the validity of a number of arguments that are in the forefront of the debate surrounding prostitution. In lieu of the usual "what-we-found" summary, we have opted to summarize by re-evaluating the aspects of this study which provide background material for evaluating prostitution. We will also point out some important demarcation lines in the international debate on prostitution.

Happy hookers?

We have male friends who are or have been customers. They have difficulty believing us when we tell them about prostitutes' non-participation in the trick. It does not seem to coincide with their experience. It is certainly possible to imagine that you are the one exception among thousands of customers. But it is a bit much – there are limits to one's irresistibility. The belief that prostitutes combine work with pleasure is a widespread notion, a view which finds support in male magazines, where stories of the happy hooker turn up as regularly as bills in the mailbox.

This study tells a different story. In chapter 3 we described in detail how the tricks have nothing positive to do with the woman's sexuality and emotional life. It is part of becoming a professional to pick up defense techniques that maintain a distance from the customer and protect the self – any effects tricks have are damaging ones, not pleasurable ones.

Moreover, all the serious literature on the subject also tells a different story. In particular, other studies based on in-depth interviews have provided valuable data. These studies have different perspectives on prostitution, from demanding recognition of prostitution as a profession on a par with other professions (Jaget, 1980; McLeod, 1982) to fighting prostitution (Borg et al., 1981; Finstad et al., 1982). Studies place different degrees of emphasis on prostitution's bright and dark sides. However, there is resounding agreement on this one point: prostitutes do not "get enjoyment from it."

The insight gained through our own experiences with in-depth interviews diverges from the notion of the happy hooker. Not *one* of those we interviewed maintained that she got any sexual enjoyment from prostitution. Some did, however, have a rather aggressively defensive attitude at the outset when it came to the advantages of prostitution. On page 47–8 we related part of Kari's story: she began by saying her life was all right and that prostitution was a fine way of earning money for her beauty parlor. She ended by telling us about her empty life and how she had not managed to save a single crown.

Who is interested in immediately exposing the grim aspects of reality to a stranger? Who wants to talk openly about her failures and defeats during the first meeting with a stranger? Very few, most likely. Why should prostitutes differ from the rest of us? On the contrary, because these women are largely seen as whores, doing something viewed as shameful and disgusting, they probably have an even greater reason to adopt a defensive position toward their own activities. Had we based this part of our research on the first half-hour's contact with the women, we might also have fallen into the trap of finding "happy hookers." Not the trap of finding the sex-drugged, ecstatic nymphomaniac from the male magazines – we did not even meet her as a facade – but the mistake of accepting Kari's first statements that her life was all right and that prostitution is okay for exceptions like herself.

The final reason for rejecting the view that prostitutes enjoy their tricks lies on a different level. Reflect for a moment: what should they be like, these women who turn tricks every day, often several a day, over weeks, months? How is it possible to rent out one's vagina to hordes of anonymous men and get sexual pleasure from it? One pant leg down, a few minutes fucking, pant leg up. Next stranger please. Again, pant leg down, a few minutes fucking, pant leg up. Next man in line please. It bears witness to a lack of imagination and empathy when the individual customer clings to a notion of her enjoyment. His frame of reference is his own isolated experience, not an attempt to put himself in her position. He's got his release; it's going to be days, weeks, or months before he visits a prostitute again. For her he is on a conveyer belt, never ending. To believe in her pleasure is, on the deepest level, to believe in an all-consuming nymphomania reaching far beyond human capacity.

A puritanical crusade?

"Sexuality is complex and finds many forms of expression. You people are so quick to oppose, would even like to outlaw, all sexuality that you yourselves don't like. You're new puritans." This is a common refrain in the Norwegian debate.

It is an instructive refrain. Instructive because it points to two completely different worlds of experience. We have shown how some customers manage to believe that the woman derives sexual pleasure from her tricks. The prostitute tells quite a different story.

There are a number of acts in which force, violence, and sexuality are all tangled together: Incest, forms of wife battering, rape, pornography, and prostitution. For the men who are involved, these acts can also be about sexuality (see for example Barry, 1979, p. 138). In rape cases the man often claims that he thought she wanted to. Though this is undoubtedly often a conscious evasion, we also believe that it can occasionally also be something more. For the man who rapes there can be a fine line which separates her titillating "resistance" and his own raw exercise of power. In incestuous families, the father can assert, and probably partially believe, that the daughter liked the whole thing and that it was a form of sexual education. In pornography a number of men see sexually aroused people and get turned on by that – women more often see degradation and oppression.

The accusation of new puritanism probably has its source in these two completely different worlds of experience. For some men, sociopolitical or legal intervention in prostitution is intervention into *the sexual arena*. It is sexuality that is to be controlled, tamed, made tasteful and acceptable. For some women – perhaps most women – these phenomena are not about sexuality. They are about violence and the abuse of power. Because prostitution is a matter of violence, the argument about puritanism has no validity.

Furthermore, the consequences of these phenomena (rape, incest, prostitution) grow and spread in the woman, destroying her sexuality. If a woman's sexuality is to unfold, blossom, give her pleasure, it must be recaptured from the life of prostitution. Prostitution is not one of many forms of sexual expression for the woman. Prostitution narrows and stifles sexuality. *That* is the puritanical consequence of prostitution.

Public brothels: sanitized prostitution?

"Remove the worst outgrowths. Make it clean, see to it the women have obligatory medical checkups, set up brothels, and impose government control." We have often encountered statements like this as we have worked on this study.

This system was in effect in Norway's capital city in the nineteenth century. Prostitution was forbidden, but alongside the prohibition the brothels survived. Brothel prostitution was tolerated, while "street walkers" were hauled in for medical checkups and frequent institutional stays. Today Hamburg's Reperbahn, among other places, is pointed to as an example worth following. On the Reperbahn lie Hamburg's two best-known brothels – the Eros Center and Palais d'Amour. The women who work in the brothels must have registration cards and undergo routine medical checkups. The police and other authorities have decided this.

Whether public brothels are "better" or "cleaner" is obviously dependent on the eyes that see. Henry, a customer, elucidates his view this way:

"There is a lot of misery in prostitution, I'm convinced of that, though of course I'm no professor. I'm almost glad for them to get off the streets. It would be better with brothels with medical checkups in a house. It would be better for people like me. Then I wouldn't be afraid of being knocked down and robbed. But it wouldn't work in Norway. Like it is in the southern states, Texas, Alabama, a lot of places. It's just like going in the movies. You pay for a certain amount of time, let's say an hour. A red light comes on on the wall when the time is up, then you have to go. And then the next one comes. It's full speed all day. They're under government control there – the doctors come two or three times a week. Then all the girls have to line up. Then they get a certificate. You can ask to see their stamped card."

You can ask to see their stamped card – that is, in a nutshell, perhaps the most important reason for public brothels. Customers can assure themselves of noninfectious merchandise. In addition, state brothels ensure that the bothersome visibility of prostitution is removed from streets and town squares. Protecting public morality was precisely the reason why the authorities in Hamburg restricted prostitutes to a special ghetto in the St Pauli district toward the end of the 1960s (Hanke, 1984). This kind of regulation of prostitution shelters respectable citizens. They avoid seeing prostitution, taking a stance on prostitution, being bothered by prostitution. Out of sight, out of mind.

But brothel prostitution is no different than other kinds of prostitution. The content is the same: sexual services are traded on an assembly line. There is undoubtedly more protection against customer violence at a brothel. And the prostitutes avoid the stress of having to find a room where tricks can take place. But prostitutes' own organizations have pointed out that in spite of this, brothels are, in many ways, *worse* than street prostitution. A French woman with extensive brothel experience recounts everyday life as it appears from the woman's point of view:

"They issued you with a special card with all your particulars and your photo on it. . . . We had to accept all the guys they sent us. Every single one of them. We'd never seen them before, they'd never seen us, except if they'd been there before. The pro never knew who was coming up, who was waiting, which client she was going to do. . . . We had a check-up twice a week. First you had to go into a waiting room, and then into another room where the cops were waiting. The medical check-up then took place in another room immediately after. . . . The work itself in the brothel was really hard. I've already explained that you couldn't refuse a guy, that we were at the mercy of the client and the madam. You felt you were gradually turning into a sex-machine, a robot, you stopped thinking, you became stupefied. You no longer existed. . . . In spite of everything, brothels in all their forms are a terrible thing for us. And all the women are dead against them. . . . You aren't free in brothels. The only thing you can do is not to go into them or else leave them for good. It depends on the girls, their frame of mind, what they're after. But from the moment you're in one, you're like a prisoner" (Jaget, 1980, pp. 62–7).

You have no freedom in a brothel. You become a prisoner. In public brothels it is the authorities who decide where and how women are going to prostitute themselves. One of prostitution's few "advantages" is precisely the fact that it gives women a certain influence over their own use of time. Public brothels must also pay their other employees. Prostitutes have to fuck to make up these wages: other people earn a living through their debasement.

But the brothels are not criticized only because they threaten prostitutes' "freedom of earning" (see Jaget, 1980). There is something more: the fact that brothels become the ultimate confirmation of prostitution as a natural necessity. This was a central aspect in the criticism put forth by Carlota Bustelo, the head of the Spanish Women's Institute (which is a government organization under the Department of Culture in Spain), after the deputy mayor in Madrid at the beginning of the 1980s suggested that a special district in Madrid should be earmarked for prostitution. The fact that this type of regulation would also break with the UN resolution against prostitution, signed by Spain in 1962, did not appear to worry the deputy mayor from the socialist party PSOE (from *La Mujer*, March, 1984). Our criticism of such suggestions is similar to Bustelo's: public brothels mean that the authorities assume that men will continue to be the customers of prostitutes and that women will continue to be prostitutes. State brothels assume that prostitution is here to stay. State brothels mean institutionalizing women's poverty and women's degradation.

Women's degradation systematized: This is possibly the most important argument against public brothels. There are also other arguments: Both past and present experiences indicate that brothels do not get rid of "the worst outgrowths." In Oslo in the nineteenth century "street walkers" flourished alongside brothel prostitution. In Hamburg street prostitution is glaring. When the St Pauli district became earmarked for prostitution, however, the desire to reduce the prostitution market was a central argument alongside the protection of public virtue. The belief that public regulation would reduce prostitution continues to be the argument the German authorities use to justify why Germany will not sign the UN resolution of 1949 (Ohse, 1984). A newer report states, on the contrary, that the prostitution in Hamburg has grown since 1982; the brothels have come as *an addition to* other forms of prostitution (Hanke, 1984). The prostitution market is not reduced, its infringements do not become fewer, "the worst outgrowths" do not disappear. Brothels might make prostitution *look* better. It is not.

Isn't it voluntary?

What adults mutually agree to does not concern the public. A voluntary arrangement between two equal parties can not possibly be a social problem, much less a legal problem.

Voluntary. Freedom. Enormous concepts raising enormous questions. Almost so enormous that they become useless as guidelines for analysis and actions. We will attempt to break them down a little.

In recent years the criteria for pinning the "voluntary" label on women who prostitute themselves have narrowed. Previously only children escaped labeling. Now prostituted women with brutal pimps and with drug problems are in the process of being excluded from the group of volunteers. Why is this? The woman whose pimp is holding a gun against her temple can choose to be shot or to prostitute herself. A possible choice, albeit a drastic one. The woman who is in danger of being beaten if she returns home without prostitution money can choose between the probability of a beating, and prostitution. A narrow and hideous choice, but nonetheless a choice. A drug addict can choose between drug money via prostitution, or pulling herself together. A choice that may not be experienced as completely realistic by the addict herself. In one way or another there is always a choice. When we are confronted with a choice in which we *"could not* have chosen otherwise," where the conclusion is nearly unavoidable, the concept of force is pertinent. The concept of voluntary choice is reserved for choices where *we ourselves* could have acted differently. There are no objective, pure, and absolute categories of coerced or voluntary actions. Actions which from one standpoint in society appear to be voluntary can be experienced as coerced when viewed from another standpoint.

This point can be further emphasized by drawing a parallel to wife-battering. The classic question in cases of battering is "why does she choose to stay?" An argument is constructed about the woman's participation and her own guilt because she knows there will be future beatings if she remains in the marriage. And of course she does know that. All the same, she "chooses" to stay. This argument notwithstanding, the notion of "voluntary battering" has a false ring.

One's position in the social structure determines the extent and outcome of choice. Let us take a simple example: choice of profession. The division of labor between men and women gives women far fewer job alternatives to choose from. In the beginning of the 1980s, in Norway, there were 93 occupations where over 50 percent of the employees were men, while on the other side there were only nine occupations where over 50 percent were women (Hagemann, 1981). Women's real occupational choices are far narrower than men's. Different placements in the social structure allow different amounts of room for choice, and differing degrees of freedom. The choice as to whether to sell one's labor or not sell it is only a realistic choice for those who are supported or of independent means. Prostituted women's position at the bottom of society does not leave them very good possibilities to choose from.

There is another complication in defining prostitution as a voluntary activity; indeed the most difficult one. In order for the woman to trade in her sexuality in the marketplace, she must treat it as an object that can be relinquished and made use of as the possession of a stranger. She must be prepared to separate sexuality from its position as a part of her own identity, her own personality. She must have learned to split herself into an object and a subject. Her own sexuality must be an object that she can manipulate and transfer.

Does it provide meaning and insight to say that this split is voluntary on the part of the prostitute? We hardly think so. The split is more likely a result of society's influences, of images of sexuality, means of support, female worth and male worth. We quoted Ida's description of how prevalent the image of women using their bodies as capital was in the circles in which she travelled (page 18). For some prostitutes, earlier sexual experiences as the victim of incest or rape have forcefully and dramatically taught them to make this split. Dividing yourself becomes a way of surviving. Earlier experiences shape the women's self-image; which things – yes, *things* – about them have some value for others and can be traded away and marketed.

It is, as we have seen, complicated to use the concept of voluntary choice. Voluntary choice assumes free people; not hardened, solidified, objectified parts of the personality. And, more simply: voluntary choice assumes that there exist good, realistic alternatives to choose among and that those alternatives are perceived as good, realistic alternatives. No one "wants" to rent out her vagina as a garbage can for hordes of anonymous men's ejaculations. Both material and cultural processes lead to some women feeling pushed into a corner where prostitution emerges as the best alternative. This does not mean that prostitution is inevitable. But we cannot define away the woman's personal experiences of pressure and the lack of realistic alternatives. Nor can we define away her relationship to her own body and her sexuality. That would be too simplified, too easy.

"Legalize prostitution"

Internationally there are many different organizations working for prostitutes' rights. Many organizations, many voices. However, one theme seems to be common to many: prostitution must be recognized as normal work. This view is maintained by, among others, organizations within the movements "Collectives of Prostitutes" and "International Committee for Prostitutes' Rights' (ICPR).

The rise of these collectives can be traced to France in the middle of the 1970s. The prostitutes went on a nationwide strike and occupied churches to get media attention. The background was that several prostitutes had been murdered in Lyon – most likely by customers. The police had done relatively little to find the murderers and protect the women. Instead the police did as they have always done: harassed and hauled in prostitutes, fined them, and rounded up their boyfriends to have them sentenced as pimps. In the course of the strike the women developed a program of action. They demanded they be recognized as citizens of equal worth, that the laws which criminalized prostitution be lifted, and that it be accepted that they carried on work which was determined by men's sexual needs. Simultaneously, the program was strongly against legalizing prostitution in the form of public brothels under government control. Also in England, in 1982, prostitutes occupied a church and made demands that were comparable to those of their French sisters. At ICPR's Second World Whores' Congress in Brussels in 1986 there was a unified demand that "prostitution [should] be redefined as legitimate work and that prostitues [should] be redefined as legitimate citizens" (from The Statement on Prostitution and Human Rights). Organizations working for prostitutes' rights are particularly strong in countries where there is legislation criminalizing prostitutes and/ or where there is active victimization of prostitutes by the police – such as in the United States and England.

In the long run these organizations would also like to see prostitution disappear. They demand active measures – such as economic assistance and housing – which would make it possible for women to break with prostitution. But the daily politics of these organizations is to fight for the right to practise prostitution in the same manner that middle-class citizens carry out their occupations, as independent small-businesspeople, without restrictions. This is expressly stated in the resolutions from the Second World Whores' Congress.

The prostitutes' collectives reject the position that prostitution is acceptable. They maintain that under any circumstances women all over the world are heavily oppressed and exploited. Prostitution is one of the many forms of women's oppression. As one of the greatest agitators at the women's conference in Nairobi in 1985, a prostitute herself, said, "I grew up in the country, where my family had a poor farm. After I quit school when I was 12, I had to work from early in the morning until late at night, bitterly hard work in all kinds of weather. My father abused me sexually, he was after me constantly. Who'd blame me for running from home, for going to the big city and becoming a prostitute? Now at least I get money for sleeping with men."

The reasoning behind improving the conditions for prostitution is easy to understand. The majority who have worked with prostitution have certainly had reactions similar to ours. We see a woman waiting for a trick, lonely. The others are getting picked up. We know that the waiting time is painful. Oh, can't she get picked up soon? Won't a customer come soon? Or: give the woman the money a trick brings in, so that she can drop this one trick. This is a real and painful contradiction. One can choose to make prostitution as easy as possible by full legalization and even introduce advertising campaigns to get more customers. At the Second World Whore's Congress the demand for prostitutes' "right to advertise" was taken up and incorporated into the Statement on Prostitution and Health.

Our policy is different. One should, in every way possible, try to make it as easy as possible for the women while they are in prostitution. One should simultaneously work to provide them with better alternatives to prostitution. A large prostitution market with increased demand would most likely result in larger numbers of women prostituting themselves, getting us nowhere.

The fight prostitutes' organizations are waging against police victimization has our full support. All laws directed against the prostitute ought to be abolished. She is the victim. A woman has the right to be a prostitute as long as society fails to give her alternatives that she experiences as preferable.

However, there is a difference between decriminalizing the prostitute, and legalizing the purchase and sale of sexual services. Legalization implies that the prostitute will have to pay taxes. It is an inevitable consequence. Far worse, legalization also implies men's self-evident right to be customers. Accepting services offered through a normal job is neither violent nor abusive. The activity surrounding normal jobs is a part of society's accepted division of labor. Legalizing prostitution and recognizing prostitution as a normal occupation would be an acceptance of the division of labor which men have created. Legalizing prostitution will not remove the harmful effects of this distinction. To be sure, legalization would probably eliminate some of the stigma and shame associated with being a prostitute. But there are more feelings in prostitution than merely shame. Women will still be forced to protect themselves against a massive invasion of strange men. They will have to turn their emotions on and off. They will be left with an impoverished sexual and emotional life. Legalization will make it easier to cover up men's gross oppression of prostitutes and to remove the perspective of the prostitute as a victim. In the long run it is men who will gain from the legalization of prostitution – not women.

In chapter 4 we have described the effects of prostitution on the woman. We, too, believe that women in our society are oppressed as a sex. But we regard prostitution as a particularly hard and brutal oppression, because it has such momentous and long-term consequences for the women. The work of an ordinary wage-earner also wears down body and soul. But prostitution's destruction of emotional life, self-image, and self-respect is so massive that the comparison with typical waged work grows thin. The long-term harm effected on women who prostitute themselves is similar to that experienced by other victims of sexual violence, such as rape and incest victims. It is therefore not mere rhetoric to counter the absurdity of the demand for legalization of prostitution with: "Legalize rape and incest. Recognize these as normal activities."

In our view, the demand for legalization implies that prostitution's "victim perspective" has not been fully considered and appreciated. Victim perspective. For some, "victim" is synonymous with weak, suffering people, devoid of resources. This is a common misconception. Prostitutes are, like other people, unique individuals. Many prostitutes have resources and personal qualities that make the average academic seem colorless and weak. Being in the position of a victim is a structural and relational attribute, separate from individual characteristics. Who talks about traffic victims as lacking in resources? Prostitutes are the bearers of the structural oppression inherent in patriarchy's need to distinguish between "good girls" and "bad girls." And they are the bearers of the long-term injuries the customers' actions force upon them. This is what is meant by "victim perspective".

By international standards, the conditions for prostitution research have been good in Scandinavia. For a decade now a number of people have been employed full-time in prostitution research. Stable research networks have been formed in which information and knowledge are passed along to new generations of researchers. In part as a result of this, assistance and support programs for prostitutes have been established throughout Scandinavia, unlike anywhere else in the world. The opportunity to follow prostitutes closely over a long period of time has led to what we have called *the Scandinavian perspective* on prostitution. Naturally we have our disagreements and arguments; for instance, we do not share the same views on customer criminalization or on decriminalization of peaceful boyfriend-pimps. But underneath it all there is a common agreement – prostitution is violence against women and must be opposed. Since the publication of *Backstreets* in Norway, there has been a steady stream of research reports, books from support organizations, and fiction in which this has been the fundamental perspective (see for example Koch, 1987; Jessen and Frigstad, 1988; Sæter, 1988). This perspective is absent from the international debate. A generation of Scandinavian prostitution researchers would quickly agree that the information we have gathered on prostitution as a distinct form of violence against women is our most important contribution to the international debate.

Our perspective on the question of legalization has another basis as well: We refuse to accept the legalization of one form of women's oppression on the grounds that women are also otherwise oppressed. We want to work to abolish oppression. Prostitutes' organizations demanding full recognition of prostitution also want an end to prostitution. But not now. That is on tomorrow's agenda. With them there is a marked difference between short-term and long-term goals. But tomorrow will never come if we do not work for it today.

Sexuality as a means – a comprehensive perspective

During the course of this book we have touched upon sexuality as a means of exchange from a number of different angles. The time has come to gather these pieces of the puzzle together and try to view them within an overall perspective.

We will do this by describing two types of acts: acts which are *unfolding* and acts which are *calculating*.[1]

When an act is unfolding, the value of the act lies in the act itself. The act is like a living, organic thing, like an affirmation of life. The act is its own end, its own rationale. It can be compared to the maturation of a seed to full bloom.

[1] This discussion is based on the analyses of the German sociologist Ferdinand Tönnies (1887). Tönnies designated these two types of acts *Wesenwille* and *Kurwille*, rendered as "natural will" and "rational will" in one English translation (Tönnies, 1955).

When an act is calculated, there is a sharp distinction between the means and the end. The act is performed as a means of achieving something completely different at a future time. There is no internal connection between the means and the end. In fact, the means may even be painful and unpleasant, in sharp contrast to the attractive goal. The person who acts calculatedly figures out advantages and disadvantages, and will not do anything without a purpose. Everything done is calculated for yield. Interests are looked after.

These two types of acts give rise to two different forms of interaction and relationships among people. We have chosen to call these forms *community* and *company*.

In a community, the predominating acts are unfolding ones, as with the relationship between mother and child, father and child, married couples, among relatives, among those belonging to the same parish, among musicians playing in the same orchestra. Community is characterized by inner bonds and mutual dependence among the participants.

In a company, calculation plays the dominant role in the acts performed. The parties are prepared to exploit each other for the sake of gain. The relationship is characterized by mutual indifference; the parties see each other as a means through which to achieve their own individual ends. Examples of such relationships include the relationship between buyer and seller at a market, between partners in a contract, between adversaries in a lawsuit.

For the prostitute, acts of prostitution are acts of calculation. Her body is a commodity she can market. She performs an extremely unpleasant act in order to achieve a goal. The goal is to acquire money. The customer interests her only in so far as he possesses money. Otherwise she is indifferent towards him.

How is it for other women? Do they use their sexuality and body as a means? D., a French prostitute, says, "Anyway, all women's lives have a prostitute side to them. For a 'straight' woman, it may not be cash she gets in exchange, but it's not so different" (Jaget, 1980, p. 127). Historically, sexuality and financial support have been closely linked for women. The link between sexuality and money is now in the process of loosening in the western societies. For steadily growing numbers of women, sexuality is no longer primarily a *means* of being supported. The conditions which make it possible for sexuality to have an intrinsic value for women as well are, we believe, on the increase. A woman's sexuality no longer derives its entire meaning from aspects *outside* sexuality. She does not need to calculate it, portion it out to the man who can best give her access to benefits outside sexuality. She no longer needs to act like a dealer at the marketplace whose capital is her body.

But women and femininity continue to be tied to reproduction and to sexuality to a degree that is completely different from masculinity for men. Earlier we warned against drawing direct parallels between prostitutes' lives and other women's lives. But prostitution can be used as a magnifying glass on some aspects of women's lives.

One way of describing the women's movement is that it is the struggle for women's right to participate in all sectors of society. The women's movement is (among other things) an attempt to break down the boundaries limiting women's development in politics, art, choice of work, economics, sexuality, free time. We do not just want to be reproducers. We want both men and women to be producers and reproducers. And we have come part way down the road. Because women have entered the public sphere and have a wider platform, their experience of individual identity and individual worth is becoming more firmly anchored. At the same time we perpetually experience attempts to push us back into the old rut of domestic duties. "Woman – know thy place." We are confronted with this in the form of religious ideology or in concerns about the dissolution of social norms. But we also meet it in more subtle forms, in teasing and good-natured jokes, in the game of sexuality or in the power of everyday speech.

Women's subordination under men has not disappeared, but has in fact taken new forms. One theory is that today women are relatively subordinate to the men *in their immediate circles*, even though they may surpass men in education, income, influence, and power. This relative subordination must appear as a personal, voluntary choice, based on individual characteristics independent of gender. (Haavind, 1985, makes an interesting presentation of this argument.) Others maintain that female subordination is deeply rooted, occurs early, and often appears as natural for both partners (see Ericsson, et al., 1985). Women, to an entirely different extent from men, continue to relate to their sexuality as something that is surrendered, traded, or not traded. The manner in which the prostitute relates to her sexuality as a commodity for trade does not differ from how other women relate to their sexuality because it is atypical; it differs because it is overwhelming and dominating.

If we consider the effects of prostitution together with theories of actions as being either unfolding or calculating, we will discover some clues as to the result of using one's sexuality as a commodity in the marketplace. We have seen that the prostitute attempts to protect her private self by simulating and hiding that self. This is typical of the calculated act. One cannot engage in such behavior with impunity. We have shown how the emotional lives and sexuality of prostitutes are destroyed. We know this, really – when the choice of friends is based on whom it "pays" to know, it is not *true* friendship. When calculation, money, and long-term objectives creep into personal relationships, things usually end badly. In a capitalistic society where the forces of the market control greater and greater portions of human activity, this is difficult to avoid. Calculated actions replace unfolding actions.

When sexuality becomes a commodity for exchange, it assumes the character of an object. You have to be ready to hand it over and let a stranger use it as his own property. When this occurs, sexuality as a part of the woman's own unfolding is destroyed. The fact that women's sexuality is (also) a means of exchange and a marketable commodity is a part of men's oppression of women. Without open force, men take away women's power through the exchange itself and through the structure of the market. An act which is unfolding is characterized by personal satisfaction occurring simultaneously with satisfaction of someone else. Women have not been able to afford being occupied with their sexuality for its own sake to the same degree as men. They have not had favorable conditions for being *sex-subjects*. This is unfortunate – for both sexes. The implication of this is that women cannot – to the same degree as men – regard the opposite sex as objects of sexual desire and sexual satisfaction. Men also lose by this. They lose because women's desires are weakened, and they lose the joy of being as desirable as they otherwise could have been. The daily gloom that characterizes some couples' sexual lives can, we believe, be partially traced back to this sociological insight.

As long as women have to create access to the benefits of society via men's use of women's sexuality, it will probably remain this way. Necessity is the mother of invention, and women use what little power they have been given. When sexuality becomes the means to an end, when sexuality is calculated, then its potential for personal unfolding is undermined. The implication of this is that women must get their *own* admission-pass; they must possess their own means, utterly and completely. It further implies that the social division of labor based on gender must be abolished. It is not sufficient to appeal to men's attitudes and "good will." It is not enough to "pull yourself together." Women must have at their disposal things other than sexuality that are of value in the social exchange, just as men do. Only then will the image of women that is the underlying cause of prostitution be erased. And only then will women's and men's sexuality be able to unfold itself completely through actions where personal satisfaction is at the same time satisfying the other.

Prostitution projects: About Scandinavian assistance programs

"There is nothing that can be done about prostitution. Prostitution has existed in every time-period in every society." The claim is so well-known that it has exceeded the limits of tediousness. It obviously functions as a defense for the "let it slide" attitude towards prostitution. It is possible to claim, and more correctly, that theft and/or murder have always existed. Which society would dismantle the police, prisons – its entire criminal justice system – on this basis? In terms of theft and murder, an official ideology whose stated purpose is to attempt to limit these crimes is seen as the obvious solution.

The lack of solid evidence for the claim that prostitution is ineradicable is not the theme for this book. We fully share the view that, given the structural limits of present-day Norwegian society, prostitution cannot be totally eradicated. In this chapter we would like to describe how the *volume* of prostitution can be reduced here and now – *without* waiting for the revolution, *without* the fundamental power differences between men and women being eradicated.

In Norway, private organizations which work among the prostitutes have existed throughout this century. In the last 12 years something qualitatively new has happened. Public authorities have entered the arena and stated that prostitution is detrimental and that there exists a *public responsibility* to fight it. There have been a total of 12 separate public assistance programs in Sweden and Norway in the last 12 years whose stated aim was to fight prostitution. The majority of them were targeted towards getting women out of prostitution. The Malmø Project in Sweden was the first, and it has served as a model for the others.

The Malmø Project

The Malmø Project opened September 1, 1977 with four employees; two male sociologists, and two social workers, one male and one female. The project had two goals: to do research, and to get women out of prostitution.

The number of prostituted women in Malmø was high at the time: approximately one prostitute per 146 sexually mature men; one prostitute for every 63 women between the ages of 17 and 35 (Fredriksson and Lind, 1980). Since 1973 the police had conducted an intense battle in an attempt to close the city's sex clubs, with great success. At the onset of the project all known clubs were closed. The Malmø Project was born as an extension of the public war against prostitution.

The employees sought out the prostitution areas, particularly Kungs Street, where street prostitution was concentrated. The goal for this field work was to establish ties to the women who prostituted themselves, and to gain their trust. As expected, there was a good deal of scepticism on the street towards these strangers who had started to hang out on Kungs Street. The employees took a long time to establish their credibility. It was important that they clearly stated that they were bound by professional confidentiality. Moreover, it was important that they were honest, kept their word, and were there when they were needed: "We tried to be as honest and sincere as possible, and we talked about our personal attitudes towards prostitution and what the project stood for. We tried to always keep the promises we made. We gave them our private phone numbers. If we had promised to help out, then we would have to take the consequences of that, even if it limited our private lives" (Fredriksson and Lind, 1980, p. 42). It was important for the employees to have an errand, not just to stand there and chat. Therefore they made an information leaflet about the project and passed it out:

> The Malmø Social Service Department has, since Oct. 77, run a counseling service for prostitutes. We have our own office at Djäkne Street 4, where we can be contacted directly or by telephone on workdays between 9 a.m. and 4 p.m.
> We do not limit our contact to women who want to quit prostitution. We also currently have contact with many women who continue in prostitution, and help them solve various problems.
> We can be reached at tel.: 99 53 53 or 99 53 54.
> Monday–Friday 9 a.m. to 4 p.m.
>
> **We maintain confidentiality**
>
> You probably wonder what we can do to help or what kinds of resources we have at our disposal. You have probably noticed that

many women are no longer at Kungs Street. We have close contact with a number of them. We help them in every way possible so that they won't ever have to return to prostitution.

We have, for example, been able to provide and assist in economic aid in order to break with prostitution. We have found housing and helped women to find jobs or to start studying. We have also been able to assist in establishing contact with psychologists and doctors. We have helped with tax and other legal problems.

A number of women have had so-called pimps. When women have cut contact with the pimps we have been there all the time, if the woman wants us to be.

We can discuss which forms of help we can offer you, if you have a pimp and want to cut contact with him. We aren't moralists who only direct ourselves toward women who want to leave prostitution. You are also welcome to contact us if you want to remain in prostitution and have problems.

The Malmø Project consciously utilized the mass media's massive interest in the project. Through the press coverage, the prostitutes saw that this was a serious project.

The concrete assistance that the project provided for acute problems was particularly important – and also useful for eliminating suspicions. The women who got help told other women in prostitution about it. After a while an increasing number of women independently contacted the project's office.

One of the learning experiences from the Malmø Project was that there are no easy solutions or easy roads out of prostitution. The women often have a whole set of problems that must be addressed. The Malmø Project established a massive service network for each woman. It might be necessary to change residence, get work or schooling, do something about drug dependency, loosen dependence on a pimp, eliminate old debts, or get the starting capital needed for a new life – sometimes all of these things simultaneously. The employees had their own contacts in the traditional public health and social services who worked specifically with these services in relation to the women. The press was continually fed interviews with women who through help from the project had managed to break with prostitution. In this way, other prostituted women were motivated to contact the project. The entire project was – with help from the media – carried forward on a wave of enthusiasm and pioneer spirit.

Were they successful? In his book on the sex trade in Stockholm, Larsson gives the following summary:

**The occurrence of prostitution in the treatment population
(153 women), Fall 1981 (limited to those who reside in Skåne)**

Have not prostituted themselves since contact with the project	54.9%
Have sporadically prostituted themselves since contact with the project, but can be assumed to have quit	13.7%
Have continually prostituted themselves after contact with the project, but can be assumed to have quit	3.9%
Have continually prostituted themselves after contact with the project, and can be assumed to have continued	16.3%
Have sporadically prostituted themselves since contact with the project, and can be assumed to have continued	7.2%
Current attitude towards prostitution unknown	5.9%
Total	**100.0%**

Larsson estimates that 111 women (72.5 per cent) have probably quit prostitution. Drug-dependent women were the group that fared the worst. It was easiest to get the young women to quit prostitution.

In the years between 1974 and 1981 the number of prostitutes in Malmø sank dramatically. In 1974 the number of prostitutes known to the officials was 300. In 1981 the corresponding figure was 60.

The Malmø Project in its original form was closed in 1983. Of course, prostitution in Malmø wasn't permanently eliminated. Later, new women were recruited to prostitution in the city, and the project has reopened, though within a smaller, less ambitious framework. None of the successive Scandinavian projects has managed to produce material conditions that were as good as those of the Malmø Project. Separate public projects for prostitutes also exist in three other large Swedish cities: Stockholm, Gothenburg, and Noorkjøping. In Gothenburg there is also a public project targeted towards homosexual boy prostitution.

Norwegian projects

In an international context the public assistance services available to prostitutes in Norway are well-developed. However, behind this fact lies a relatively difficult battle by the women's movement and women's studies to ensure the continuation of these services. As a rule, the services are very small-scale – there is no reasonable link between the projects' capacities and the number of women in prostitution. Another major problem is that the services are often

192 *The Fight against Prostitution*

initiated as trial projects (most often for a two-year period). Following the two years, a new battle must be initiated to ensure that the work is not discontinued after the trial period.

The first separate publicly funded Norwegian prostitution project was started in Oslo in 1979. It was organized as a two-year trial project with three female employees.[2] As with the Malmø Project, it had two goals: assistance and research. At the close of the trial period, an extensive report was prepared with suggestions for new services – among other things a permanent prostitution project in Oslo (Finstad et al., 1982). Like their Swedish colleagues, those in the Oslo Project worked consciously with the mass media. The following year *Hard Asphalt*, an account of a prostituted woman's life, was published. It was one of the year's best sellers in Norway. The first prostitution project and *Hard Asphalt* greatly contributed to prostitution becoming a part of public debate in an entirely different manner from previously.

Later there have been prostitution projects in many of the largest Norwegian cities: Trondheim, Stavanger, Bergen, and Oslo. Only in Oslo are the services still organized as a separate public prostitution project. In Trondheim the project was closed after one year amid protests from its clients, employees, and various organizations that were engaged in work against prostitution. Today, work against prostitution is integrated into an incest center and general social fieldwork among drifters and addicts. Trial projects in Bergen and Stavanger have also been closed and the work integrated into traditional health and social services. However, in Bergen there have, at least, been four jobs specifically allocated within the social services for work with prostitutes.

All the projects have had the same approach as the Malmø Project. The goal is to provide the women with a broad spectrum of services. In addition, the Norwegian projects have, to a much greater degree than the Malmø Project, worked with the women's relationships to their bodies and sexuality. This is because many women in prostitution have been subjected to earlier sexual abuse. Their troubled relationships to their bodies have, among other things, materialized in the form of eating disorders among some of the prostitutes. The project has had to fight for an understanding of the fact that helping prostituted women takes time. One cannot by snapping one's finger compensate for years of oppression and rebuild damaged self-esteem.

[2] Liv Finstad was employed as leader of the project.

Working at a prostitution project is for many employees not merely a job, but a way of life. What counts is being there for the women right there and then; not referring them to office hours or fixed appointments. As long as the project retains something of the pioneer spirit, this is possible. It becomes much more difficult after a while when the job becomes routinized, and the time perspective is unlimited. This problem is not specific to prostitution work; it applies to all good social work.

One weakness shared by all the projects is that they didn't manage to fully utilize women who prostitute themselves as an active resource in line with the model applied in other self-help groups such as women's crisis centers. But in the fall of 1989 a "self-help" group was started for prostitutes as a part of the Oslo Project. The group meets once a week at members' homes and discusses themes such as prostitution, sexuality and relationships. The Oslo Project also considers it a weakness that it cannot offer any assistance for non-violent boyfriend-pimps.

In addition to the projects listed above, the Norwegian Social Welfare Department has started two other projects that are worth mentioning. One is an information project started in 1988. Two women, who were once prostitutes themselves, work two nights a week in the prostitution area in Oslo informing about HIV contagion and AIDS. The other project was started in the wake of the Norwegian customer study. The study caused – unintentionally and unexpectedly – the side-effect that many of the men stopped buying women. The interview process caused them to begin reflecting over their own role as buyers, what the woman gave and didn't give, and how this must be experienced by the woman. Talking about prostitution helped, they said. Therefore, in January of 1989 independent services directed towards customers were started in Oslo. The project workers are present in the prostitution districts two to three times a week, and here they approach the men directly. The employees offer discussion and information and talk to the men about their ideas and experiences relating to prostitution. Thus far, the project has been in contact with 160 customers.

The rest of Scandinavia

There is a noticeable division between Sweden and Norway on the one side, and the rest of Scandinavia on the other. In Finland, Iceland, and Denmark there are, as yet, no publicly organized and funded prostitution projects.

FINLAND   At the end of 1986/beginning of 1987 the so-called "vagrancy law" was rescinded in Finland. The law had been in existence for 50 years, but had long been "sleeping." When the discussion on repeal began, opponents claimed that the law had a preventive effect against prostitution, and that rescinding the law would lead to the spread of prostitution. This led to public debate about the necessity of separate prostitution projects. The end result was that the police authorities were to register changes in prostitution during the period following the elimination of the law. There have been no visible changes in this picture during the three-year period that has elapsed since the law was rescinded. Visible street prostitution exists – not unexpectedly – in the capital, Helsinki. More unexpected is the fact that the estimated number of prostitutes is so small – four or five women. Prostitution is more concentrated indoors, in restaurants and hotels. No effort has been made to estimate its extent. No private organizations are involved in the fight against prostitution. The question of prostitution is a "non-topic" in Finnish public debate.

ICELAND   In Iceland little is known about the extent of prostitution. The few who have given the question any thought compare the situation to that of Finland: little visible street prostitution, some indoor prostitution. There exist no public or private assistance services.

DENMARK   In the Scandinavian context, Denmark stands out as the worst example. Prostitution in Denmark is much more widespread than in Norway and Sweden. The sex trade flourishes in Copenhagen's streets and alleys – in massage parlors, restaurants, bars, sex clubs, and on the streets themselves. The police estimate that 2,000 women work in massage parlors alone (Rasmussen, 1987). Other than the glaring conspicuousness of prostitution in Denmark, little is known about it. Researchers and treatment personnel have applied for funding for a prostitution project for nearly ten years now. The answer is always the same – decisive but unexplained refusal.

Large portions of the Danish women's movement also stand out from their Scandinavian sisters. "The Red Stockings" – the largest Danish women's organization – has felt that it was incorrect to fight prostitution. Like other organizations, the Red Stockings sees stigma as prostitution's major problem. Their political standpoint has been a desire for prostitution to be seen as just as acceptable as, for example, factory work.

But the picture brightens in the south. Under commission from the Social Ministry, a study from the Social Research Institute in Copenhagen is now in progress. Its brief is to describe the situation of prostitution in Denmark, and come up with suggestions as to how to approach the problem. It is being conducted by a private organization, the YWCA (Young Women's Christian Association), which has done the most work against prostitution in Denmark. Since 1983 the YWCA has run its own assistance program for prostitutes in Copenhagen. Another positive occurrence is that since 1988, Copenhagen County has provided full maintenance support and two permanent positions to a prostitution project. The state has contributed an additional six full-time positions to the project.

The YWCA has also started a prostitution project in the city of Odense. The project started December 1, 1989 with one full-time position. This project does not have any form of public funding.

In addition another research project on boys' prostitution was started in Copenhagen in 1988. The project is funded by a mixture of private and public finance. No form of social work is connected to the project.

The need for separate prostitution projects

It has been necessary to fight on two fronts in order to organize prostitution projects. The one battle has been fought against the authorities who allocate funding; the other battle is against some groups of professionals. Undoubtedly with the best of intentions, several professional groups have asserted that prostitution projects represent an unfortunate separation of services. Employees in public health have placed particular emphasis on the fact that prostitution is just one of the many problems that the prostitutes struggle with; therefore, they feel that it is incorrect to place too much emphasis on prostitution. Sociologists – particularly male, but also a few of the women – build their arguments on labeling theory. Roughly repeated: labeling theory places an emphasis on how a person is experienced by his/her environment and how they experience themselves. The cultural definitions of a person dictate the boundaries that exist for alternative action. If a person is labeled as a deviant – and eventually incorporates this into her self-image – further deviance (secondary deviance in academic terminology) can become the person's adaptation strategy (see for example Becker, 1966; and Lemert, 1967). A common concern for public health workers and sociologists is, in other words, the concern that prostitution projects strengthen the woman's experience of being a prostitute, with this further reducing the possibility of her leaving prostitution. This type of labeling would be avoided if the women were instead referred to traditional social services.

This objection is well worth considering. History provides enough examples of moral entrepreneurs and crusaders who have intensified a problem instead of contributing to its solution (see for example Becker, 1966; Cohen, 1985).

Twelve years of experience with prostitution projects has, however, made this objection seem insipid, abstract, and irrelevant. Let's address it point by point.

THE WOMEN'S SITUATION   Several of the projects place an emphasis on the way in which the picture drawn by labeling theory is inverted when applied to prostitution. Instead of a tentative identity of "prostitute" being strengthened by the projects, the majority of the women already have a very strong identification as prostitutes before they seek out the project. Everything becomes more difficult for the woman because prostitution is a "non-theme" in traditional social services. She may have revealed her very soul in most areas of her life, and been questioned at length on most things – but her prostitution experiences aren't touched. (See for example Fredriksson and Lind, 1980; Jessen and Frigstad, 1988; and Frigstad, 1989.) Instead of strengthening a weak identity as a prostitute, the projects provide an opportunity to break down her strong identification as a prostitute, show her other valuable things that she is, and show her that there exist roads out of prostitution.

INCREASED VISIBILITY   Knowledge about sex-related violence is unpleasant knowledge. Battering, rape, incest, and prostitution – and the prolific existence of these phenomena – provide an unpalatable message about men's continued dominance over women. It is primarily assistance projects which have served to make sexualized violence visible. The battering of women hardly existed officially in Norwegian society before the crisis centers revealed that it was so widespread that it could be called a social phenomenon.

Along with concrete assistance to the women, increasing the visibility of prostitution has been one of the projects' most prioritized tasks. The projects have placed an emphasis on educating the health care and social service networks. By systematically educating health care personnel, the projects hope that this sector will some day be capable of helping women early on in their prostitution careers.

The projects have also – to varying degrees – worked at getting prostitution into the public debate, and politicizing this debate. The combined amount of lecturing and educational activity has been impressive. The mass media have been actively utilized.

It is highly unlikely that the traditional health care apparatus could strive equally energetically to increase the visibility of prostitution.

THE FIGHT FOR FUNDING   The crisis in the western economy has reached our latitude. The welfare state is being dismantled at a rate many of us would have called politically impossible a few years ago. Even the "deserving" victim's needs no longer make it through: mental hospitals, retirement homes, welfare offices, schools, youth clubs, children's nurseries – the tempo of the closures is dizzying. Though the notion of the happy, free woman who chooses prostitution has been considerably weakened in recent years, women in prostitution are still seen as "undeserving" when compared to many other needy groups. If abandoned to traditional social services, the women would be pushed to the back of the line.

Separate prostitution projects also have a pragmatic, economic justification, independent of periods of prosperity or depression – a justification several of us have had since these projects were started. Prostitution projects contribute to *increasing* the total funding given to social services. The political reality is, unfortunately, not such that the total figure that is allotted to the projects would be transferred to social services if the projects didn't exist.

THE IMPORTANCE OF A NETWORK AGAINST SEXUALIZED VIOLENCE   In the last ten years a series of new programs against sexualized violence has risen in Norwegian society, partially as a result of a strong women's movement and a strong emphasis on women's research. We have many crisis centers, support centers against incest, separate emergency services for rape victims, and separate prostitution projects. We also have a separate research program against sexualized violence.

This has opened up the possibility of practical and academic networking. In keeping with the disassembling of the Norwegian welfare state, several of these services have also been threatened with cutbacks or closure. In this situation, collective solidarity has been vastly important. The various projects have vigorously fought for each other and made closure more difficult.

Academic cooperation is not as broadly developed. There have been successful national conferences which have taken an in-depth look at various phenomena, working to illuminate differences and similarities while simultaneously striving to define a joint theoretical model for sexual abuse. As yet, there is much to be done.

In the Scandinavian perspective, work with creating an academic network has come the farthest in the area of prostitution. Every year conferences are held with participants from all the prostitution projects in Sweden and Norway. Researchers and others in Scandinavia who work with prostitution are also invited. The conferences have been very important for the development of knowledge within the field.

Can success be measured?

There are many of us who are thankful for the Malmø Project's quantification of its own success. Larsson's data have provided a hard-hitting argument in discussions as to whether anything can be done about prostitution.

However, this type of argument also has its traps and its deficiencies. First – it needs a basis for comparison. Only in a small minority of the cases will a reliable estimation of the size of the prostitution market be available *before* the start of a project. This is dependent on the political interest in thorough information, an interest the project itself helps stimulate. It is also dependent on the project's ability to make prostitution visible by providing concrete services that the women seek out. Subsequently, it is virtually impossible in practice to quantify which changes are due to the effects of the project and which changes are due to societal factors outside of the project. What if the Malmø Project had not been able to point to a visible decline in prostitution – would the project then have been a failure? Not necessarily. There are enough other factors that contribute to a strong rise in prostitution: factors like the increased exposure of commercial sex, increased emphasis on the market as a significant regulator of social life, increases in the "material consumption" aspect of relations between people. It becomes an added difficulty that the criterion for success is so coarse: prostitution or no prostitution. This says very little about what kind of new life the women go to.

Therefore, a phenomenological analysis is more important than counting. Perhaps we can also evaluate the likelihood that the contents of the assistance led to a better life for some of the women. We know of no projects that have led women farther into prostitution or served to recruit new women into prostitution. If there are examples, they must be extremely few. On the other hand, there are very many women in Sweden and Norway who tell of how their lives have been made easier, whether or not they, at the present time, have left prostitution. The fate of these actual women is, in our opinion, the most weighty argument for the importance of separate prostitution projects.

Two suggestions for criminal law reforms

Unilateral criminalization of customers

The practice of criminal law has always been characterized by a double standard when it comes to prostitution. There have been times when it has been punishable to be a prostitute, but not to be a customer. At other times both parties have been penalized. But the punishment for being a customer has either been milder in the penal code, or the law has only been enforced for prostitutes, while the customers went free.

At one point the authors of this study publicly put forward a proposal that there be unilateral criminalization of customers. This caused heated debate in Norwegian newspapers. Opinions about criminalizing customers are as divided among prostitutes and customers as they are among the general public.

Elisabeth: "I'm totally against criminalizing customers. Then it will get harder for us. We'll be left with crazies and physical misfits."

Ulla: "Deep down I'm for punishing customers. Maybe you'll think that's strange, when I work down there myself. But I wish I didn't do it, that I didn't have that possibility."

Arthur: "I'm for the criminalization of customers but it's a question of resources. I would never have dared to take the chance if I risked being arrested. It's not unfair only to arrest the customer. The woman doesn't work there completely voluntarily; it may be because of a pimp and drugs. So criminalizing the woman is no solution."

Henry: "I have to be against that on principle." [Points to himself] "I have to take myself into consideration. It's a little too drastic to go about it that way. It could be destructive for some people, it could be destructive for those who are exposed and for their families."

Knowledge of the utterly destructive effects prostitution has on the women is painful knowledge. It cannot continue this way for long. All of us, both women and men, are victims of a socially distorted sexuality, which makes life poorer than it otherwise could have been. But a small "fringe" group carries a disproportionately large part of this burden, because certain men see the abuse of these women as an emergency solution. Prostitution is like a piecemeal rape of women. Therefore, it is our view that prostitution should be defined as a crime of violence. In contrast to other violent law-breaking acts, prostitution is a question of market. As is the case with other markets, some visibility is necessary so one can purchase and sell "the goods." Like other markets the prostitution market is controlled by supply and demand. The market can be limited in terms of both supply and demand. The supply must be limited by sexual-political and social-political initiatives, not by legislation. The demand can, in addition to sexual- and social-political activities, also be restricted by criminalizing those who represent the demand-side of the purchase.

Deterrence and punishment have shown themselves to be ill-suited in terms of limiting criminal acts committed by those on the bottom of the socio-economic ladder. Not because people from those classes are worse than others; far from it. But because certain crimes are, for material and cultural reasons, deeply integrated into their lifestyle. It is this entire lifestyle, this entire sense of class division, that must be abolished if we are to do away with these crimes. The proletarian fringes present social-political challenges, not criminal-political challenges (and they also put the abolition of social class as a whole on the agenda). Nonetheless, criminal law has always been used as a means of controlling the impoverished classes.

We take the liberty to present one of our central criminological creeds: in general the entire criminal law and criminal policy system should be turned upside down – separated from control of the lower classes, separated from control of social-political problems, separated from controlling everything that can be put in a box labeled "deviance." If we must have any kind of criminal law at all, it should be directed against "normal" people's harmful behavior, like being the customer of a prostitute.

Most customers know very little about how damaging their behavior is for the women involved in prostitution. Our suggestion for criminalization is not based upon the assumption that there is an intention of doing harm on the part of the customers. Customers are no doubt like other people – some are bad, most are OK. Our suggestion rests on the *consequences* of the customers' actions – the long-term effects suffered by the women. The majority of customers go to prostitutes infrequently. Being a customer is seldom a central role. The customer most often has other roles through which he defines himself: employee, father or uncle, treasurer of the soccer club or stamp collector. Participation in prostitution, for the majority of the customers, is not an integral part of their lifestyle.

Moreover, we believe that many customers are in the kind of social situation where the threat of criminal conviction would be effective. The very character of the act as an extension of normal behavior and the ordinariness of the customer makes this probable. With the majority of violent crimes there is a great similarity between victim and perpetrator. Both are often down-and-out, with problems relating to work and family, and often with definite drug or alcohol problems. Prostitution is different. There is a fundamental asymmetry between the victim and the perpetrator. Women in prostitution bear the common signs of the victims of violence. Their social need is great. But the majority of customers do not resemble the typical violent criminal. The customer is often an integrated member of society. It is reasonable to suspect that, given the issues discussed above, criminalization would, to some degree, restrict the activities of the customers. It is precisely in this type of situation – when the perpetrator is enmeshed in society and the act itself is not central and integrated in a way of life – that punishment and deterrence have some effect (traffic laws are a good parallel). Through unilateral criminalization of the customers we believe that a portion of the prostitution market could be peeled away, removed.

The proposal to unilaterally criminalize the customer side of prostitution rests on one goal alone: to limit the total volume of prostitution. We do not for a moment believe that criminalization will do away with the causes of prostitution or eliminate it. For this, far deeper changes are necessary. We have to simultaneously work for the short and the long term. For the sake of the women who are exposed to prostitution, here and now, unlimited patience and references to the Utopia to come are useless. Every single trick not turned is a little bit of damage not done. For every trick is a scratch on the women's minds; as the sum of scratches increases, the consequences become increasingly destructive.

Scarcely any standpoint in socio-, sexual-, or criminal-political questions is completely "pure." There are good arguments both for and against the unilateral criminalization of the customer. The conclusion reached will be a result of weighing the arguments: a kind of bottom-line accounting of the effects of the suggestion.[3] When we bring up the suggestion of criminalizing the customer, it is because a single entry in the accounting weighs very heavily with us – the argument that fewer women will be destroyed in prostitution. If this argument is valid – and we are quite convinced that it is – then objections such as, for example, the classist character of the law, the dangers of a corrupt police force, and the dangers of an underground market, become somehow rather lifeless and abstract.

Decriminalize non-violent boyfriends

The data from the reports filed with the police and the in-depth interviews indicate that the term "pimp" covers a wide range of men. The penal code can be applied to all of them. We, too, adhere to the position that pimps who coerce, threaten, beat, or otherwise force women to prostitute themselves should be punished by law. However, as it is practiced today, Norwegian legislation against pimping reaches far beyond this, due to the broad application of terms in section 206 in its entirety, but most particularly in the third paragraph. *In practise* it is currently a punishable offence to be the boyfriend of a woman who prostitutes herself. We want to eliminate this aspect of the law, which makes it a criminal offense for someone to be romantically involved with a prostitute.

Knowledge about wife-battering has shown that we can't unconditionally take what the woman says about the relationship as a starting-point. Because of her emotional ties to the man she will often conceal or trivialize the violence. In prostitution we are faced with a similar problem in cases where an emotional relationship between the pimp and the prostitute exists: she will often deny the use of violence.

This is undoubtedly true. However, as an argument *in a trial* it is irrelevant. If a man is to be tried for battering his wife, and his wife

---

[3] In Norway the suggestion of unilateral criminalization of customers has been discussed for several years now. In the Norwegian edition of *Backstreets* a detailed account is given of the arguments for and against unilateral criminalization of customers (Høigärd and Finstad, 1986, pp. 341–64).

denies that she has been abused, then the prosecutors must find other ways of proving that she has been abused. One can't just imprison any husband on the foundation that "everyone knows" that there is abuse in the marriage. Allowing another starting-point for relationships which involve prostitutes, and thereby ignoring the burden of providing suitable evidence of violence and coercion, is unreasonably discriminatory. It is also a clear breach of judicial rights: one is willing to imprison nine innocent people in the hopes of imprisoning the tenth who is guilty.

But, it might be argued, what about the money? Even though he is not coercing her, he's living off her prostitution, and surely that must be punished. As long as he doesn't accept any of her money, there's nothing to prevent him from being her boyfriend. Then everything will presumably be the way it is supposed to be.

In chapter 3 we described how a number of couples support themselves illicitly. He pushes, steals; she prostitutes herself. They live a hand-to-mouth existence; the money comes in quickly and disappears even faster; expenses and income are shared, and it's not so important who brings in the most. In some cases her income will be larger than his simply because there is big money in prostitution. And there will be cases where his work activity will be minimal precisely because there is big money in prostitution. We have often heard the counterargument that he either ought to work (as much) as every other decent person does, or he ought to say "no thanks" to her money. But living with another person doesn't work like that. Try to get inside the lives he and she lead, and it will become apparent how absurd it is to imagine strictly separate finances. Absurd for the very reasons that there is big money in prostitution, and that this money is an integrated and underlying part of a *total lifestyle* which revolves around drinking and partying and is hopelessly chaotic. Regardless of how much he works at a normal job, her income will be sky-high in comparison. In this kind of living situation, demanding that finances be kept strictly separate is synonymous with demanding that lives be kept strictly separate. It is against this backdrop that we claim that, in practise, it is impossible for a prostitute to legally have a boyfriend.

This appears to be a common experience for prostitutes in many countries. A prostitutes'-rights organization in England has made the following statement on this issue: "Claiming they want to protect us from pimps, the forces of law and order make criminal any man who associates with us by calling him a pimp. He may be your son, your husband or a friend, men who are in no way pimps as far as we are concerned. And yet the law gets at us through them. The police harass entire communities and circles of friends under the pretext of catching pimps" (Jaget, 1980, p. 23). This has also been eloquently formulated as a demand for "an end to arrest of boyfriends, husbands, sons. Arrest rapists and pimps instead." (*Network* 1983, p. 1).

The prostitute is denied most things. We see no reason why she should also be denied the possibility of having a boyfriend.

The considerations that lie behind the suggestion to legalize large segments of what today is criminally defined as pimping are in essence simple questions of justice. In this case, demands for justice and effectivity align.

The police material contains very different kinds of pimps. But the group which unquestionably dominates is boyfriend-pimps. The interview material supports this picture. It is a sadly well-known figure who rises in front of us. Unemployed, difficulties with crime, kicked out of school and the work force, problems with drugs. For the most part it is those on the fringe of the proletariat who populate Scandinavian prisons. At the same time we know that the laws and the sanctions are particularly ill-suited to rehabilitate and reduce their criminal activity. International academic literature is in harmony on one point: the function of penal sanctions as individual prevention for the proletarian fringe must be viewed as a fiasco. One fundamental reason is that penal sanctions drastically reduce a person's alternatives: they change their self-image and change other people's opinion of them. For someone who already has few alternatives, this can be catastrophic. It is one of the few absolute truths of criminology.

In the section dealing with the criminalization of prostitution customers we described why the general preventive effect of penal sanctions enforced on the proletarian fringe should be regarded with considerable scepticism. See in its entirety, the judicial system's focus on the fringe of the proletariat is a logical paradox. There is reason to question why it is that when prostitution is to be judicially controlled, the laws made are aimed toward a group for whom existing professional knowledge has clearly demonstrated that punishment and prison only make things worse. The group for which it is reasonable to suppose that legal regulation would have some amount of success in limiting the extent of prostitution, is, on the contrary, not criminalized. It isn't rational. Perhaps it's convenient?

Convenient images – harmful images

The notion of the brutal pimp who seduces a woman with love and sweet music and then, when she is helplessly entrapped in his charming web, literally kicks her out on the street, has been one of the most important – if not *the* most important – explanations for the existence of prostitution in Norway.

We claimed in the previous chapter that the organization of the criminal law in terms of prostitution was a logical paradox. But its organization is by no means a *sociological* paradox. In a sociological perspective, the end result is interesting. Penal organization in the field of prostitution points towards the fact that the rational explanations of the law are shrouded in a mirage. It is our opinion that the focus on pimps is an expression of a need to create order and comprehension in the chaotic and incomprehensible world of prostitution. Perhaps our most important contribution to the international literature is the documentation of the harmful effects of prostitution on the prostitute's emotional life and how brutal and degrading her daily life is. The question of voluntary participation has for this reason and others assumed a central place in the public debate. Who would live such a life voluntarily? The existence of a pimp becomes a heaven-sent key to unlocking explanations to this kind of question. The prostitute as the slave of a pimp – this image makes the incomprehensible comprehensible and resolves the difficult question of voluntary choice.

Other convenient images exist. Like drugs. Prostitution is seen as a dramatic consequence of widespread drug abuse. Therefore the disease – drugs – must be fought, while the symptom, prostitution, can be ignored.

Incest experiences are a third convenient image. Prostitution is a symptom, the result of earlier sexual abuse. It is incest that must be attacked. Age – or the lack thereof – is also a convenient stopping-point for our thoughts. Who is not against the prostitution of children and juveniles?

We believe that narrow explanations such as these are of little use in understanding prostitution. We have shown that the violent pimp plays a minor role in Norwegian prostitution. Though drug abuse is fairly widespread, prostitution is much older than the current drug problem we face. Many prostitutes have had earlier experiences of sexual abuse, but far from all of them. Juvenile prostitution is seriously harmful; so is the prostitution of adult women.

Some prostitutes are slaves controlled by other, evil people; some are the victims of their own experiences of sexual abuse or their own immaturity. Young people lack perspective over the consequences of their own choices. Each one of these factors serves to narrow the group of "voluntary prostitutes."

All these factors have one common element: they make it easy to oppose some *types* of prostitution, without having to take a stand on the fundamental and threatening question of "voluntary" adult prostitution. Fight prostitution controlled by pushers and pimps, fight prostitution which exploits incest-victims or children. But leave "voluntary" prostitution alone.

These images also serve other convenient objectives. The roles of pimp, pusher, and child-abuser are outsider roles. They do not relate to *our* daily lives – they do not challenge our own sexual fantasies, our own gender-role patterns, our own personal practises. The roles are securely placed on the other side of a wide chasm which separates all ordinary normal citizens from the "dregs" of society. The roles are an excellent illustration of *Evil* as a motivating force – and therefore no threat to the way we arrange and conduct our own lives. The painful connections between prostitution and our daily lives are obscured. It is the outsiders who are guilty, not us.

The outsiders have all the qualifications to be what Christie and Bruun call *the good enemy* (Christie and Bruun, 1985). The stereotypes of the pimp illustrate this well:

1 He is different from us. The stereotype of the pimp with his violence, his stable of ladies, his big American cars – it is easy to dissociate ourselves from him. He is not like us, he's impossible to identify with. We can attack him without attacking ourselves.
2 He is weak and cannot fight back. The way is open for criticism. No pimp steps forward, beats his chest and defends his role. And no member of the enlightened public has any self-interest in defending him. Attacks on him are therefore completely free of charge.
3 He carries the vagueness of anonymity. The picture is out of focus. Few people know pimps personally. He is therefore unusually well-suited to be the recipient of all kinds of evil qualities. There is no corrective within easy reach, among those we meet and relate to on a daily basis.

It is interesting to compare these three qualities of the pimp as "the good enemy" with the customer. In that the good enemy must be different from ourselves, must be weak without the capacity to fight back, and must bear the vagueness of anonymity, it becomes quite understandable why the majority of customers are unusually poor and unsuitable enemies, and why the suggestion to criminalize the customer has been viewed by many as an unbelievably man-hating provocation.

Focusing one's explanation of prostitution's existence on the role of the outsider is characterized by the hunt for the single, *real* cause. This hunt is also a search for *the real problem* that we must "do something about." We, too, would like to "do something" about pimps, drug pushers, and child abusers. However, we have tried to argue that the causes of prostitution are complex and exist on many different levels of society. Emphasizing the role of the outsider obscures the societal criticism that lies in the very existence of prostitution as a phenomenon. When the image of the outsider is not blocking our perception, we have to recognize that a number of young women today experience prostitution as the least of numerous evils. This says a good deal about their other alternatives.

And without the image of the outsider, criticisms of the way sexuality is organized cannot be muffled by convenient theories of causation. Just what are the concepts of human worth, female worth, and sexuality in our society that make prostitution possible? Not the pusher's, the child abuser's, or the pimp's concepts, but ours. Our fantasies, our sex roles, our patterns of sexuality, our images of women. Shielded by a collective disgust over *Evil*, which is on the opposite side of a wide abyss, which separates "us" on the inside and "them" on the outside, we can remain untouched by all these difficult issues.

No reason for disquiet. No reason for worry.

Everything can continue as before.

Everything must be different

Disquiet. Worry. There are many of us who do not want everything to continue in the same way.

The women's movement and women's studies are often criticized for being too preoccupied with sexual violence and abuse. But in a special sense it *is* right in this context. Studies of sexual power and of sexuality as a medium of exchange help us to understand our own, at times trivial, lives, and to understand what can be different. Life does not have to be as it is now. It is not the case that "that's the way it is – that's life." From knowledge visions can arise. Visions of other possibilities. Possibilities which today are crippled: possibilities for love, work, friendship. A study of prostitution can give direction to new ways of living and relating. Ways in which women are no longer compelled to use their sexuality for economic reasons, nor men to hunt on the sex market. Ways where we live in profound togetherness with others, and our acts are a sincere and splendid unfolding of life.

Everything must be different.

Everything *will* be different.

Appendix: Sources of Information

We have been conducting research on prostitution since 1979. The field is not what might be called easily accessible. Most of the rules in the book of sociological method are of little help.

Instead, we have had to resort to fitting bits and pieces together in a jigsaw puzzle. At times we have felt closer to the role of a detective than that of a sociologist. The pieces in the puzzle originate from many different sources. In this appendix we will clarify the various channels we have utilized in our research on prostitution. Like most sections on methodology, it is boring. Those not interesting in methodology can safely skip it.

Case filed against pimps at the Oslo police department in the period 1968–82

We received permission from the Oslo police department to go through the documents on all charges filed against pimps in the period indicated above. In total, there are 65 such cases.

The first year for which it is possible to track down charges filed against pimps at the Oslo police department is 1968. During a reorganization of the police department that year, previous archival material was disposed of. It was in 1981 that computers were first used in registering complaints and charges, thus making it possible to locate material through the code-word "pimping." Prior to this the only guide to the filing cabinets was a variety of code-words like "prostitution" and "fornication." In our material a number of cases were incorrectly registered as pimping. We assume that the opposite has also occurred, and that some cases involving pimping have been incorrectly registered under other code-words. We have meticulously double-checked and questioned in detail central police personnel involved in the investigation of pimps. The number of lost cases can hardly be large. However, 65 reported cases is the minimum figure for the period. The size of the file on each case varied widely, from a couple of pages to weighty stacks. The files can provide information on the charges, interrogation of the accused and the complainant, testimony by witnesses, and investigative data, as well as the history of the case as it made its way through the legal system. The job of analyzing this material was primarily performed by Liv Finstad; the material is referred to as "pimp data."

Task force reports

In the task force reports we see prostitution in Oslo as it appears through the spectacles of the police force. In 1982 a task force of six officers was established to investigate and curtail the activity of pimps. Since that time the task force has conducted routine surveillance Monday through Friday. The surveillance is scheduled for periods of the day when there is reason to believe there is a fair amount of prostitution. Spot-checks have been conducted to verify this. The surveillance is primarily conducted by two officers in a car. The strength of these data lies in the painstaking observation which has taken place day in and day out over a period of years. Enormous research resources would be required to produce similar results. However, the data are primarily an expression of the *police* operations, not of the women's activity independent of the police presence. If the police weren't there on a Sunday – and they seldom were in this period – then of course no prostitution was registered that Sunday. Therefore the material must always be cross-checked with the police's registration practices and shift system. The other weakness with the material is the objective under which it was collected: naturally the objective of the police was investigation, not research. If we had had the same resources for observation as the task force, we would have, at times, made different choices and used different categorizations.

With the helpful assistance of the police we have analyzed their task force reports resulting from the period April 1982 to December 1984. These task force reports consist of 12,408 observations. Further, the reports include specific background information on 664 women suspected of prostitution and 81 men suspected of pimping. This material is referred to as "task force data."

Observations in the backstreets

In June, 1984, systematic observations were carried out in Oslo's prostitution district. The investigation was part of a preliminary project leading up to a more comprehensive investigation of the customers of prostitutes. Prieur and Taksdal were in charge of carrying out the investigation, and Cecilie Høigård was supervisor of the project. The study is described in detail in Prieur and Taksdal, 1986, where the methodology and its built-in margin of error are also discussed at length. In the course of five days, 8,664 observations, divided amongst 2,834 cars, were registered.

The Oslo Project

Liv Finstad was the director of this project, which ran from August 15, 1979 to October 1, 1981 (see Finstad et al., 1982). The project was in contact with 86 girls or women in prostitution. Of these, 19 became formal clients of the project; particularly for these 19 women the data are extensive and detailed. One source of error for our purposes is that the data are based on a helper–client relationship. This may influence the flow of information from the client to the helper, especially when it concerns the extent of the woman's prostitution and the course her career in prostitution is taking while she is associated with the project. For other types of data, e.g., information on the women's backgrounds, this potential source of error is less important.

Inside information

Not all knowledge can be given a numerical value. We have had the considerable advantage of being known as the Norwegian prostitution researchers. This led to a stream of communications, some of them first-hand, others by phone or letter. Many of these communications were from people who wanted to give us information on aspects of the prostitution market. Others, on the basis of their own experience, wanted to discuss prostitution with us. We have learned a good deal in this way. The information regarding the structure and extent of the prostitution market has been particularly useful.

In-depth interviews

This book is also based on 42 in-depth interviews with participants in the prostitution market. This material is referred to as "the interview data". The interviews were conducted between 1979 and 1985, and the breakdown of those interviewed is as follows: 26 female prostitutes, 7 male prostitutes, 2 transsexual prostitutes, 2 pimps, and 5 customers. Five of the interviews were conducted by Arne-Harald Hanssen, one by Liv Finstad, and the remainder by Cecilie Høigård.

Most of the in-depth interviews resulted from the "snowball" method, a method whereby the person interviewed asks people she knows if they would be willing to be interviewed, they in turn ask others, and so it goes on.

The snowball method will often be the most important scientific method in a field that is closed at the outset, as the field of prostitution is. One inherent, insoluble weakness in the snowball method is the difficulty in obtaining a wide range of subjects. The people interviewed will often come from the same environment and be very similar in certain respects. In our case this is outweighted to some extent by the fact that we have several "original snowballs," i.e., different people each initiating a series of interviews. In addition, eight of those interviewed contacted us directly, independently of each other, when we went to the press and announced that we were seeking such contact. The ages of the women interviewed ranged from 17 to 32. The range of prostitution forms also varied greatly. Those interviewed had experiences in all the forms of prostitution described in chapter 1, the bulk being experiences from the street. The range of the women's experience in relation to that of other prostituted women, on the other hand, is narrower. We primarily interviewed women with a *lot* of prostitution experience. Women on the periphery of prostitution are less well represented. These could be women who have only turned a few tricks, for example; or women who have two or three men concurrently, for whom the line between "nice gifts" and monetary recompense for sex may be fuzzy. These have not been included in our interview data.

The interviews have for the most part been lengthy. A few have been completed in two or three hours. Others have turned into a series of interviews which have extended over a period of months, and in four cases, even years. This type of long-term series of interviews also provides an extremely good opportunity to study the processes these women go through. Many women we interviewed expressed relief over finally being able to speak out about their prostitution experience. This was also the case with women who had been in and out of institutions over a number of years and who were used to having to answer all kinds of questions about their private lives. The fact that they had not previously talked about their prostitution experience is a good indicator of just how how shameful and guilt-ridden prostitution is both for the women involved and for employees in the traditional social services.

Have the women told us what they believe we want to hear? Is our version of what prostitution is like any more reliable or "true" than the versions that appear in male magazines and, less frequently, tabloids? Let's take this step by step. Perhaps the women believed that what we were most interested in hearing about were the atrocities associated with prostitution? Today, we are both known to be opponents of prostitution. Wouldn't this kind of public image of us color the women's expectations of our expectations? Behind this objection there often lies a research ideal in which the researcher is supposed to be the neutral observer of the research object, where one further assumes that the research object is not influenced by the researcher's observations, and where the researcher takes no standpoints on controversies surrounding the area of research. This is not our research ideal. Within the social sciences this research ideal is impossible. The researcher is *in* the society, not outside or above the society. No matter which position she adopts, she will view society from her vantage point. And the research "object" will form a conception of her, based on the researcher's vantage point.

This does not diminish the importance of recognizing the limitations in views and perspectives that one's own vantage point provides. It is the superficial notion of the researcher-outside-society which represents a tremendous source of error in this context. All research-roles are *roles,* and there are specific expectations associated with them originating from the environment and the research "objects." In our case we believe that it was an advantage that we had two different roles. Liv had a job with the Oslo Project, where fighting prostitution was a part of the job. The job involved appearances on radio and television, and in the newspapers. Through this public role she received a lot of information she would not otherwise have acquired. Cecilie worked from another direction. She tried to become acquainted with female prostitutes other than those associated with the Oslo Project. She consciously kept herself out of the public debate on prostitution. Cecilie did 25 of the 26 interviews with prostitutes. These 25 were from milieus not associated with the Oslo Project.

During the interview period Cecilie also interviewed customers and pimps. These interviews were the result of notices in male magazines and newspapers in which men with experience in the prostitution market were encouraged to contact Cecilie. With one exception these men declared themselves to be staunch defenders of prostitution. This can probably be interpreted as a verification of Cecilie's anonymous role in the debate on prostitution. The women who were interviewed could therefore hardly have had any clear-cut opinions about what Cecilie wanted to hear about prostitution. As the book has shown, the interviews taught us things we had never even considered, as well as things that directly contested our pre-conceived ideas.

Even though the interviewed subjects didn't have any definite ideas about Cecilie's views on prostitution, the interviews might still be influenced by the fact that these women are participants in an activity which is hardly considered honorable, and they are relating their experiences to someone who is part of the "straight" society. There is no clear answer as to how this might effect the material. One can imagine that those being interviewed would be intent on making prostitution seem a common, ordinary, even legitimate activity. But one could also imagine that they would want to tell about exotic and terrible things, give the interviewer "juicy details," or engage her sympathy. We believe that Cecilie's place within the "straight" world has had an influence, but we are not quite sure how. Some fortunate circumstances, however, have lessened its significance. The snowball method made it absolutely necessary that people on the inside vouch for Cecilie. This may have diminished the need to resort to facades and games. Over time she also became a well-known figure in parts of the prostitution milieu. In addition, we believe that it was advantageous that some of those interviewed knew that Cecilie is a lesbian. This made her less "straight". In her own way she too was "on the fringe of society." This was of particular advantage in connection with lesbian women in prostitution. The third lucky circumstance is *friendship*. This has been so important that we will describe friendship as its own independent data source. But before we leave the in-depth interviews, a small word of caution.

Originally Cecilie intended to do more in-depth interviews. As time went on it became apparent that after the interviews she was unreasonable, irritable, anti-social, and depressed. To begin with we didn't understand that this was a reaction to the interviews, attributing her mental state to off days, etc. In-depth interviewing demands submersion in the phenomena that the person interviewed is describing. This becomes a considerable mental strain. Even though the snowballs continued to roll, Cecilie had to call a halt to the in-depth interviews. She simply wasn't able to take on any more.

Both of us have extensive interviewing experience with people who are oppressed and expelled from society (Høigård, 1976; and Finstad and Gjetvik, 1980). Interviews with long-term recipients of welfare and prisoners awaiting trial have also weighed heavily on us. Through these interviews we were confronted with human suffering and social injustice, and our only response to this was a hope that our research would ultimately contribute to an improvement of their situation. However, Cecilie's reaction to the prostitution interviews was far more intense. When the field is prostitution, a female interviewer will in some ways also be exposed to persecution and defeat. There will be painful correlations between the experiences of the prostitute and the interviewer's own, albeit less dramatic, experiences as a woman. Welfare recipients and prisoners suffer tremendously. But there are clear limitations to our identification with their suffering. Their situation will never be ours.

Research into related themes such as incest, wife battering, and rape is in a period of intense and major development. Here, too, the interview situation can give rise to painful associations with the interviewer's own life. We mention our experience in the hopes that others might be better prepared than we were.

Friendship

It may appear cynical to list this as a method. But, in fact, this is perhaps the most important source of information, even though the friendships haven't had any goal beyond friendship. We became very close friends with some of the women; these friendships have now lasted many years. Spending time with them, and spending time with them in *their* environment, has taught us a great deal. Subjects that are hard to bring up, even in the best interview atmosphere, can be aired by friends. Friendships that span years provide totally different possibilities for intimate understanding, discussion, and the probing of continually new insights.

Individually, each of these data sources is incomplete and insufficient, but collectively they have produced a comprehensive body of information. We believe the methods supplement each other well. In our judgement, the combination of qualitative and quantitative data is an important strength in our study.

Bibliography

Armstrong, Edward G. 1983: Pondering Pandering. *Deviant Behavior* 4, 2 (Jan.–March), pp. 203–17.

Balvig, Flemming 1982: Ungdomskriminalitet – med særlig henblik på retssystemets udvælgelsesmekanismer. In *Årsberetning 1981 fra Kriminalistisk Institut, Københavns Universitet. Stensilserie*, No. 18, pp. 33–49.

Barker, Pat 1984: *Blow Your House Down*. London: Virago.

Barry, Kathleen 1979: *Female Sexual Slavery*. Englewood Cliffs, NJ: Prentice-Hall, Inc.

Becker, Howard S. 1966: *Outsiders*. Glencoe, NY, The Free Press.

Benward, Jean and Judianne Denssen-Gerber 1975: Incest as a Causative Factor in Antisocial Behaviour: An Exploratory Study. *Contemporary Drug Problems*, 4, 3 (Fall), pp. 323–40.

Bondesson, Ulla 1968: Argot Knowledge as an Indicator of Criminal Socialization. *Scandinavian Studies in Criminology*, 2, Oslo: Universitetsforlaget, pp. 73–105.

Borg, Arne, Folke Elwien, Michael Frühling, Lars Grönwall, Rita Liljeström, Sven-Axel Månsson, Anders Nelin, Hanna Olsson, and Tage Sjöberg 1981: *Prostitution. Beskrivning. Analys. Forslag til åtgärder*. Stockholm; Liber. (Also in a more extended version; Ds S 1980: 9 *Prostitutionen i Sverige*.)

Bowker, Lee H. 1978: *Women, Crime and the Criminal Justice System*. Toronto: Lexington Books.

Bracey, Dorothy 1979: *Baby-Pros*. New York: John Jay Press.

Bødal, Kåre 1982: *350 narkoselgere*. Oslo/Bergen/Stavanger/Tromsø: Universitetsforlaget.

Chodorow, Nancy 1978: *The Reproduction of Mothering*. Berkeley: University of California Press.

Christie, Nils, Johs. Andenæs, and Sigurd Skirbekk 1965: A Study of Self-Reported Crime. *Scandinavian Studies in Criminology*, 1, Oslo: Universitetsforlaget, pp. 86–116.

Christie, Nils and Ketil Bruun 1985: *Den Gode Fiende. Narkotikapolitikk i Norden*. Oslo/Bergen/Stavanger/Tromsø: Universitetsforlaget.

Cohen, Stanley 1985: *Visions of Social Control*. Cambridge: Polity Press.

Davis, Nanette 1978: Prostitution: Identity, Career and Legal-Economic Enterprise. In James M. Henslin and Edward Sagarin (eds), *The Sociology of Sex*, New York: Schocken Books.

Dinnerstein, Dorothy 1976: *The Mermaid and the Minotaur: Sexual Arrangements and Human Malaise*. London/New York: Harper & Row.

Ericsson, Kjersti, Geir Lundby, and Monica Rudberg 1985: *Per + Kari = trøbbel. Ungdom og kjønn*. Oslo/Bergen/Stavanger/Tromsø: Universitetsforlaget.

Fields, Pamela J. 1981: Parent–Child Relationships, Childhood Sexual Abuse and Adult Interpersonal Behavior in Female Prostitutes. *Dissertation Abstracts International*, 42, 5 Nov. 1981, pp. 2053B–2054B.

Finstad, Liv 1984: Anmeldte halliker 1968–82. Del 1, 2 og 3. Mimeo, Oslo: Institutt for kriminologi og strafferett.

Finstad, Liv, Lita Fougner, and Vivi-Lill Holter 1982: *Prostitusjon i Oslo*. Oslo: Pax.

Finstad, Liv and Anne Lise Gjetvik 1980: *Varetektsfanger forteller*. Oslo/Bergen/Tromsø: Universitetsforlaget.

Fredriksson, Torsten and Britt-Inger Lind 1980: *Kärlek för pengar*. Stockholm: Ordfront.

Frigstad, Kirsten 1989: Fra prosjekt til faste tiltak? Oppsummering av hjelpetiltakene. I Prostitusjon i Norge – oppsummering av forskning og tiltak. Hva gjør vi nå? Rapport fra dagsseminar December 9, 1988. *Stensilserien* No. 60, Institutt for kriminologi og strafferett, Universitetet i Oslo.

Gibbens, T. C. N. and M. Silberman 1960: The Clients of Prostitutes. *British Journal of Venereal Diseases*, 36, 2.

Gibbens, T. C. N. 1963: Men and Prostitutes. *New Society*, 43.

Goffman, Erving 1961: *Asylums*. New York: Doubleday.

Guttormsen, Gro and Cecilie Høigård 1976: *Fattigdom i en velstandskommune*. Oslo/Bergen/Tromsø: Universitetsforlaget.

Haavind, Hanne 1985: Endringer i forholdet mellom kvinner og menn. *Materialisten*, 13, 4, pp. 32–50.

Hagemann, Gro 1981: Kapitalismen i dag: Kvinnene inn i samfunnsmessig produksjon. *Materialisten*, 9, 1.

Halvorsen, Ida 1982: Hard Asfalt, Oslo: Pax Forlag. (Norwegian edition)

Halvorsen, Ida 1987: *Harter Asphalt: Autobiographie*. Munich: Verlag Frauenoffensive. (German edition)

Hanke, Erika 1984: Prostitution in the Federal Republic of Germany. In *Prostitution: Survival of Slavery*, Record of the 28th International Congress, International Abolitionist Federation, Vienna 1984, pp. 187–92.

Heyl, Barbara Sherman 1976: The Madam as Teacher: The Training of House Prostitutes. *Social Problems*, 24, pp. 545–55.

Holzman, H. R. and S. Pines 1982: Buying Sex: The Phenomenology of Being a John. *Deviant Behavior*, 4, 1 (Oct.–Dec.).

Høigård, Cecilie 1985a: Halliker – finnes de? *Materialisten*, 13, 1–2, pp. 109–42.

Høigård, Cecilie 1985b: Prostitusjonsdebatten i Nairobi. *Materialisten*, 13, 4, pp. 83–109.

Høigård, Cecilie and Liv Finstad 1986: Bakgater. Oslo: Pax Forlag.
Høigård, Cecilie and Liv Finstad 1988: Der Hurenkunde – ein Spiegelbild. In C. Meyenburg and M. T. Mächler (eds), *Männerhass. Ein Tabu Wird Gebrochen*, Munich: Verlag Frauenoffensive, pp. 109–29.
Høigård, Cecilie, with Guri Eggen, Lillian Høverstad, Elisabeth Jensen, and Randi Aasum 1976: *Arbeidsløs Osloungdom*. Oslo/Bergen/Tromsø: Universitetsforlaget.
Jacobsen, Kirsten, with Alex Frank Larsen and Krass Clement 1982: *Med sød forståelse*. Copenhagen: Borgen.
Jaget, Claude, ed. 1980: *Prostitutes – Our Life*. Bristol: Falling Wall Press.
James, Jennifer 1978a: Prostitutes and Prostitution. In Freda Adler and Rita J. Simon (eds) *The Criminology of Deviant Woman*, Boston: Houghton Mifflin Co.
James, Jennifer 1978b: The Prostitute as Victim. In Robert, Fane and M. Gates (eds), *The Victimization of Women*, Beverly Hills, CA: Sage Publications, pp. 175–201.
Janus, Sam, Barbara Bess, and Carol Saltus 1977: *A Sexual Profile of Men in Power*. New York: Warner Books.
Jessen, L. and K. Frigstad 1988: *Jentene – ut av prostitusjonen*. Oslo: Cappelen.
Kinsey, A. C., W. B. Pomeroy, C. E. Martin, and P. H. Gebhard 1953: *Sexual Behaviour in the Human Female*. Philadelphia/London: W. B. Saunders Co.
Kinsey, A. C., W. B. Pomeroy, and C. E. Martin 1968: *Sexual Behaviour in the Human Male*. Philadelphia/London: W. B. Saunders Co. (1st ed. 1948).
Koch, Ida 1987: *Prostitution – om truede unge og socialt arbejde*. Copenhagen: Munksgaard.
Kongstad, Annalise 1981: Voldtægt, kriser og social kontrol af kvinder. In Gitte Carstensen, Annalise Kongstad, Sidsel Larsen, and Nell Rasmussen (eds), *Voldtægt – på vej mod en helhedsforståelse*, Copenhagen: Delta, pp. 181–215.
La mujer feminista 1984. The Spanish Institute of Women.
Larsson, Stig 1983: *Kønshandeln. Om prostituerades villkor*. Stockholm: Skeab.
Lemert, Edwin, M. 1967: *Human Deviance, Social Problems, and Social Control*. Englewood Cliffs, NJ: Prentice-Hall Inc.
Lo-Johansson, Ivar 1938: *Gaten*. Oslo: Tiden.
Martinussen, Willy 1967: Prostitusjon i Norge. Rapport til Straffelovrådet. Mimeo, Institutt for kriminologi og strafferett, Oslo.
McLeod, Eileen 1982: *Women Working: Prostitution Now*. London/Canberra: Croom Helm.
Milner, Christina and Richard Milner 1973: *Black Players – The Secret World of Black Pimps*. London: Michael Joseph.
Mykle, Agnar 1956: *Sangen om den røde rubin*. Oslo: Gyldendal.
Månsson, Sven-Axel 1981: *Kønshandelns främjare och profitører. Om förholdet mellan hallick og prostituerad*. Karlshamn: Doxa.
Månsson, Sven-Axel and Annulla Linders 1984: *Sexualitet utan ansikte. Könsköparna*. Stockholm: Carlssons.
Network 1983. News from the English Collective of Prostitutes. No. 1 (July).
Odelstingsproposisjon 1914: No. 14: Om forandringer i løsgjænger-loven.

Ohse, Ulla 1984: *Forced Prostitution and Traffic in Women in West Germany*. Edinburgh: Human Rights Group.

Persson, Leif G. W. 1981: *Horor, hallickar ock torskar. En bok om prostitusjonen i Sverige*. Stockholm: P. A. Norstedt & Sönersförlag.

Prieur, Annick and Arnhild Taksdal 1986: Prostitusjon og mannlig seksualitet. In *Institutt for kriminologi og strafferetts småskriftserie*, No. 1. Oslo: Universitetsforlaget.

Prieur, Annick and Arnhild Taksdal 1989: *Å sette pris på kvinner; Mennsom kjøper sex*. Oslo: Pax.

Rasmussen, N. 1987: Hvad ved vi om prositutionen i Danmark? In Cecilie Høigård and Liv Finstad, *Baggader*. Copenhagen: Reitzel.

Schiøtz, Aina 1980: Prostitusjon i Kristiania 1870–1890. *Hovedoppgave* Oslo: Historisk institutt, 1977, reprinted in short version in Anne-Marit Gotaas, *Det kriminelle kjønn*, Oslo: Pax, 1980.

Silbert, Mimi H. and Ayala M. Pines 1981: Occupational Hazards of Street Prostitutes. *Criminal Justice and Behavior*, Vol. 8(4), Dec.

Stein, Martha 1974: *Lovers, Friends, Slaves . . . The 9 Male Sexual Types. Psychic-Sexual Transactions with Call Girls*. Berkeley and New York: Berkeley Publishing Co., and Putnam & Sons.

Sæter, Wera 1988: *Berøring forbudt; To prostituerte forteller*. Oslo: Gyldendal.

Tönnies, Ferdinand 1955: *Gemeinschaft und Gesellchaft*. First published 1887. English translation: *Community and Association*. London: Routledge & Kegan Paul, 1955. Taken from Østerberg, ed., *Handling og Samfunn*, Oslo: Pax, 1984.

Winick, Charles 1962: Prostitutes' Clients' Perception of the Prostitute and of Themselves. *International Journal of Social Psychiatry*, 8, 4.

Index

Note: Page references in italics indicate tables.

abuse, sexual 19, 205
acting out 83–4
acts, unfolding/calculating
    184–8
advertising, as contact location
    10–12, *11*, 126, 130, 162
age,
    of starting prostitution 15,
    76, *16–20*
    see also prostitution, juvenile
alcohol, abuse 24, 157
Armstrong, Edward G. 20n.
availability of prostitutes 96–7

background, social,
    of customer 34–5, 37
    of pimp 155, 157
    of prostitute 15–16, 76, 126
backstreets, as location 9–10,
    17, 124–32, 154
Barker, Pat 67, 106–7
Barry, Kathleen 136, 166, 168
Bødal, Kåre 158
body,
    as asset 18–19, 50, 180,
    185–6
    effects of prostitution on
    107–9, 112–13, 192

body parts, ban on touching
    64, 66–7, 74
bodyguard, pimp as 163–6
Borg, Arne et al. 62–3
boyfriend as pimp 133, 135–7,
    138–9, 158, 181
    non-violent 140, 143–6, 158,
    163–4, 168–9, 193, 202–4
    violent 141, 146–50
Bracey, Dorothy 18
brothels, public 176–8, 181
Bustelo, Carlota 178

cheating customer 71–3, 75
choice, voluntary, prostitution
    as 160, 178–80, 197, 205–6
Christie, Nils, & Bruun, Ketil
    206
clothing 51, 54, 68, 70, 127, 130
Collectives of Prostitutes 181
community as relationship 185
company as relationship 185
condom, use 41, 67, 74, 162
crime 79
    and pimping 157
curiosity, male 94
customer,
    criminalization 199–202, 207

deviant needs 55–7
experience of trick 90–105
needs 51–5
project to 193
research studies 25–6,
  84–90, 211, 214
social status 131–2, 207
violent 57–63, 80
customers,
in-depth interview 28–9
married 28, 29, 32–4, 38, 51,
  95, 97–100
questionnaire 26–8
sailors 27, 29–31, 38
single 28, 29, 31–2, 34, 38–9
women's images 19, 34–9,
  50–2, 106, 132

defense mechanisms 63–75,
  106, 109, 117, 130, 173
Denmark, public services to
  prostitutes 194–5
deviance, and normality 7,
  37–9, 116, 200
distance, maintaining 51, 64–5,
  73, 75, 106, 132, 173
doctors, as customers 35–6
dominance, male 104–5,
  169–70
drugs,
and need for money 17,
  23–5, 40, 44–5, 79, 147,
  179, 205
obtaining 2–5
physical effects 1, 5
and pimping 157
prices 42–3, 43
"dry hustle" 71–3, 75

education, effects 122–3
emotions,

effects on 107, 110–14, 115,
  117, 205
suppressing 64–6, 71, 73–5,
  106–7
employment,
expectations 118–19
possibilities 76–9, 122, 179
enjoyment, sexual 18, 173–5
pretending 68–9, 90–2
excitement, customer need for
  32, 52, 53–4, 88–9, 94

family, women's hopes of 119
fantasy, customer 53–5, 89,
  91–2
Finland, public services to
  prostitutes 194
Finstad, Liv 69, 192, 210, 211,
  212–13
foreplay, length 89, 129–30
Fredriksson, Torsten & Lind,
  Brit-Inger 189
friend, as instigator 17–18, 20,
  22, 80, 163
friendship,
customer need for 52
effects of 122–3
prostitute's need for 79–82,
  127, 166, 215
future, expectations 47–8,
  117–23

Goffman, Erving 70
guilt, women's feelings of 115,
  213

Haavind, Hanne 104, 186
Halvorsen, Ida 18–19, 22, 45,
  68, 78, 112, 171
Hanssen, Arne-Harald 212

Høigård, Cecilie 26, 89, 211,
    212–15
home, use of 7–8, 58, 69
hooker, happy, myth 173–5
hopes, future 47–8, 117–23
hotels, as contact location
    12–13, 40, 126, 128

Iceland, public services to
    prostitutes 194
identity, as prostitute 196
images,
    fantasy 53–5, 89, 91–2
    female 18–19, 40, 61, 207
    male 19
    self-image 18–19, 76, 107–9,
        111–12, 115, 128, 168, 180
impresario, pimp as 161–3
imprisonment, by customer 59
incest,
    effects 19, 205
    male view 175
income,
    disposal 47–50
    estimates 46–7, 131
institutionalization, effects 16,
    63
International Committee for
    Prostitutes' Rights 181
interview,
    with customers 28–9, 37
    in-depth 26, 116, 125, 174,
        212–15
    methods 5

Jacobsen, Kirsten et al. 89–90
Jaget, Claude 50, 55, 57, 63, 64,
    66, 74, 109, 177, 185, 204
James, Jennifer 18

knowledge, previous 17–18

labelling theory 195–6
Larsson, Stig 17n., 40, 124–6,
    190–1, 198
law,
    on pimping 135, 136, 140,
        145–6, 149–50, 156–9, 205
    suggested reforms 199–204
legalization of prostitution
    180–4
lesbians, as prostitutes 73, 75,
    108–9, 137–8, 163–4, 170,
    214
locations 9–14, 17
    choice of 128–30
    overlapping 124–8
lover, pimp as 166–72
luxury, associated with indoor
    prostitution 130–1

McLeod, Eileen 25, 49–50, 65
Malmø Project 188–91, 198
Månson, Sven–Axel 134–5, 168
market,
    and brothels 178
    choices 124–8
    locations 9–14, 17
    overlapping milieus 125–8
    pyramidal model 124–5,
        131–2
massage parlors 13, 95–6, 194
medical checks 176–7
men, prostitutes' attitudes to
    19, 109–10, *see also*
    customers; pimp
methodology,
    research 16n., 25–6, 209–15
    snowball method 73, 212, 214
money,
    need for 21–2, 40, 50, 65, 76,
        79, 185
    see also income; prices

mouth, as forbidden body part
64, 66–7
murder of prostitutes 58, 181
Mykles, Agnar 75
myths, exploded 34, 75–6,
173–5

name, working 69–70
needs,
customer 51–5
deviant 55–7
negotiators 86, 89
Norway, public services to
prostitutes 191–3

object-relation theories 100–1
Olsson, Hanna 58, 62, 64, 74–5
opposition to prostitution
173–88
oppression,
prostitution as 181–4, 192
of women in society 169–70,
183
orgasm,
loss of ability 109–10
pretending 91–2, 110
while working 56, 71
Oslo Project 16, 22, 78, 192–3,
211, 213–14

pairs, working in 7–8, 17–18
partner, as instigator 21–2
peepers 86–8
peer-group, influence 19–20,
22, 40, 79–82
pickpocketing 45, 72, 79
pimp,
advertising 11–12
boyfriend as 133, 135–7
functions 160–72
as instigator 17n., 21, 163

male view 138–9
non-violent boyfriend 140,
143–6, 158, 163–4, 168–9,
193, 202–4
and Norwegian law 135, 136,
140, 145–6, 149–50,
156–9, 205
police charges against 209–10
prostitutes' views 133–8,
159–60
sex 141–2
sex-club 142–3, 159
"stable" 142, 150–6, 158–9
stereotypes 20, 22, 133,
134–5, 155, 160, 206
violent boyfriend 141, 146–50
police,
and charges of violence 158
fear of 1, 2
lack of protection from 61–2,
159, 181
task force 132, 210
victimization by 181, 182
policemen, as customers 36
pornography, and male
expectations 56, 93, 175
power,
of customer 30–1, 59, 88–9,
96–7, 104
over men 82–3, 117
women's lack of 117, 175
prices,
fixed minimum 41–2, 80,
130–1
and price of drugs 42–3, 43
Prieur, Annick & Taksdal,
Arnhild 25n., 26, 28, 30–1,
34, 38, 85, 87, 89, 96–7,
104, 211
procuring via the media 10–11
profession, prostitution as 174

prostitution,
  definition 6
  high-class 124, 126–32
  juvenile 15, 205–6
  legalized 176–8
  organized 13–14
  as voluntary 160, 178–80,
    197, 205–6
protection,
  by pimp 144, 149, 163–6
  by police 61–2
  self-protection 59–61
puritanism, new 175–6

questionnaires 26–7

rape,
  police reaction 61–2
  and power 175
reciprocity, sexual 52
research, sources of
    information 209–15
restaurants, as contact location
    12–13, 17, 22, 126–7,
    129–31
rights of prostitutes 181
role,
  female 117
  sexual 102–5

sailors 27, 29–31, 38
samaritan, prostitute as 34, 53,
    75–6
self, private/public 63–75,
    69–71, 74–5, 80, 106–7,
    110–11, 114, 180, 187
self-disgust 20, 108, 111–15
self-help groups 193
services, public 183, 195–9
  Denmark 194–5
  Finland 194
  Iceland 194

Norway 191–3
  Sweden 188–91
sex,
  anal 67
  oral 32, 67, 68
sex clubs 13, 126, 130, 189
  and pimps 142, 159
sexuality,
  effects of prostitution on
    107–10, 114–15, 117,
    175–6
  female 19, 100–2, 185–7
  male 51–2, 93, 96, 97, 99–103
  as means of exchange 117,
    180, 184–8, 207–8
  as power 83
  seen as dirty 34, 56–7
skill, sexual 53, 94
socialization, effects 63, 100–2
solidarity 20, 41, 80–1
Stein, Martha 29, 96
streets, *see* backstreets
students as prostitutes 122
subordination, female 104–5,
    186
Sweden, public services to
    prostitutes 188–91

talk, customer's need 51–2, 58,
    97–8
Third World, women as
    prostitutes 13–14, 38
Tönnies, Ferdinand 184 n.
tricks 6–9
  first 17–18, 19–20, 22–3
  speed of 68–9, 74, 130–1

variety, customer need for 32,
    53, 93
victim, prostitutes as 182–3,
    201

violence,
  avoiding 59–62
  customer 57–63, 80, 165, 177
  of pimp 141, 142–3, 146–50,
    154, 158–61, 179, 202–3,
    205
  prostitution as   114–17,
    175, 184
  sexual 196, 197–8

visibility of prostitution 17, 130,
  196–7, 198, 200

warmth,
  customer need for 29–30, 34,
    96, 97–9
  women's desire for 118–19,
    166, 168, 170–1
washing, need for 63, 70–1